# Reflections on Contemporary Life

## AN OUTSIDER'S PERSPECTIVE

*In a book, there is wisdom*
*In a thought, a big dream*
*In a heart, a burning desire*
*To find out what is the theme*

Reza Noubary

Archway Publishing books may be ordered through booksellers or by contacting:

Archway Publishing
1663 Liberty Drive
Bloomington, IN 47403
www.archwaypublishing.com
1 (888) 242-5904

ISBN: 978-1-4808-8033-7 (sc)
ISBN: 978-1-4808-8034-4 (e)

Library of Congress Control Number: 2019909450

Print information available on the last page.

Archway Publishing rev. date: 7/19/2019

## My Promise

Look at me one last time
before you say good night, before you fall asleep.
Look at me one last time
before you close your eyes, before you lose me to a dream.
Promise to live.
Promise to love.
Promise to care.
Promise to share.
Promise to think.
Promise to seek.
Then I promise wonderful surprises and pleasant dreams.

### Kindness Is Its Own Reward

Kindness, a simple gift that touches everybody's heart,
Something appreciated by all, never mind how culturally apart.
A present made up of happiness, confidence, and strength.
It gives directions to Happy Land and a point to start.
It brings hope and joy to all and every needy heart.
It gives people a big advantage, a priceless head start.
At the end the giver and receiver appear in the same chart.
Something that is easily realized—no need to be a genius or smart.
People remember you for your kindness, a reward, an exceptional art.
Their hearts become your resting place, they never let the memories depart.

## Love of Child and Grandchild

You came to my life one beautiful sunny day;
You changed everything, it's certainly fair to say.
It was a miracle happening to the family, including me,
A dream I witnessed and could clearly see.
Days passed, watching you play, grow, change, and learn;
First smile, first tooth, first step, and things that are supposed to be.
Now you are stronger, smarter, kinder, a loving individual who cares;
You are all I wished for and everything else you could possibly be.
That beautiful baby did not die, but changed; that is easy to see.
A mature gentleman with knowledge and a wonderful life history.
What the future holds for us, nobody knows, not even you and me;
Let us be grateful for all the joy experienced, not as you and I, but as we.
Now grandfather, all is coming back to me, a beautiful feeling; hope you agree.
Smile, cry, wonder, dream, and all beauty of life beyond self, beyond me.
I now see that life is all about family, kindness, and loving; that is the key.
All these joys can be found and experienced only in a family tree.

## Dedication Poem

I dedicate this book to those who suffer the side-effects of the contemporary life
Exceptional people who function under extreme pressure, fight a daily battle to survive
To those who are resilient with strength to endure their deep wounds and strive
To hard-working people who have positive attitude, motivation, and creative drive.

# Contents

## Chapter 1: Life/Living

## Chapter 2: World/United States

## Chapter 3: Faith/Religion

## Chapter 4: Health/Medicine

# Chapter 5: Math/Mind

## Chapter 6: Sports/Education

## Chapter 7: Global/Social

## Chapter 8: Expository/Miscellaneous

# Preface

*I wish to be granted serenity to accept the things I cannot change, the courage
to change the things I can, and the wisdom to know the difference.*
—*The Serenity Prayer*

I have lived a life of poverty, serious health issues, revolution, war, and the stress of moving from country to country. Today my wife and I live in a beautiful and peaceful college town in Pennsylvania. We are happy and proud to live in a country with amazing institutions, a country that has made significant advances in recent decades, especially in the areas of science and technology.

Though all has been wonderful, I am not yet completely immersed in the US political system and popular culture, especially the changes that have taken place in recent decades. This is partly because I have lived a major part of my life outside the United States and in places with different values and views, and partly because of the changes resulting from globalization. In short, I see the world through multicultural lenses, and this book is an attempt to describe them the best I can.

# About the Book

This collection of short articles and essays was written as opinion pieces for newspapers over the last five years or so, mostly about various aspects of contemporary life and my personal interests. Topics include social and global issues, world affairs, health and medicine, mathematics and mind, and sports and its educational values. The contents also represent lessons I have learned while living in the Middle East, Europe, and North America. I was fortunate to receive useful comments and feedback from people who read these articles, and their responses encouraged me to put them together as a book.

For ease of reading, the articles are presented independently whenever possible, at the expense of occasional repetition. Also, rather than a long list of citations at the end, sources are listed in the end of each article for further readings.

I hope you do not mind my writing, especially my grammar. I started learning English when I was already an adult, and I still have problems with paraphrasing, summarizing, outlining, comparing, contrasting, and properly inferring.

# Acknowledgments

I start with expressing my profound gratitude to my spouse extraordinaire, Zohreh, who does her utmost to help me concentrate on my work, and to Megan Mahle for her invaluable assistance in organizing the book. Hats off to my friends Jim Pomfret, Youmin Lu, and Steven Cohn for their help, support, and encouragement. Also I cannot fail to honor the memory of my brother.

I would also like to acknowledge my colleagues JoAnne Growney, Bill Calhoun, Drue Coles, Steven Kokoska, and John Polhill for their willingness to help whenever I asked. Many thanks to our secretary, Ashley Bilinski, and the writing center staff—director Ted Roggenbuck, Julia Bagnata, and Nancy Zola—and students Dario D'Amato and Joe Carswell for their assistance.

Special thanks to my chairperson and friend, Curt Jones, and Dean Robert Aronstam for providing me with time and opportunity to work on this book. It was always useful to bat ideas about my research around with friends and colleagues.

I should also like to thank and acknowledge the occasional use of well-written definitions and descriptions in the literature. I have greatly benefited from the internet publications, especially for expository articles. Finally, thanks to my students for helping me with some literature surveys.

# About the Author

Reza Noubary was born to an Azari family in 1946, the son of a police officer who was addicted to both drugs and alcohol and an illiterate mother who was forced to marry at a young age. He went through a formal education and received his BSc and MSc in mathematics from Tehran University, followed by an MSc and PhD in probability and geo-statistics from Manchester University in England. He has more than fifty years of experience working in universities in several countries. He has been a visiting professor at Harvard University, Princeton University, the University of Pennsylvania, the University of California at Los Angeles, the University of Maryland, the University of Kaiserslautern, and Catholic University of Leuven. His research interests include risk analysis of natural disasters and applications of mathematics and statistics in sports. He is a fellow of the Alexander von Humboldt Foundation and a fellow or member of numerous professional organizations. He has published several scientific books and more than a hundred research articles in various disciplines.

In addition to academic life, he has experienced life as an insider and outsider, majority and minority, winner and loser, believer and denier, single and married, student and teacher, and son, father, grandfather, uncle, friend, and competitor. He has dealt with a difficult childhood, poverty, physical and mental health issues, revolution, war, shortages, and having to learn and adjust to cultures, visions, rules, and values. He has two sons and a granddaughter and lives with his wife in a small town in rural Pennsylvania.

# Chapter 1
## Life/Living

Life is not measured by our appearance or age,
Nor is measured by our wealth or wage.
It is measured by how often we have felt alive
And what is in our book of life's shiniest page.
It is measured by how often we were admired
And how much love we felt in our heart and head.

Life is the greatest gift; living right is an art.
Our passions and attitude play the main part.
It is about learning to live every day as if it is our last.
It is about learning not to worry about the future, or living in the past.
It is about being grateful for what we are and have,
Realizing that everything will come to an end pretty fast.
It is about considering others' happiness as a part of ours,
Knowing that not having happy people around makes us an outcast.
It is about understanding that choices and possibilities are vast,
Realizing that we play only a small role; we are part of a huge cast.

Life is the greatest gift, living is a reward.
Live the best you can, and be a part of the crowd.
It is not about what you face, but your response.
At the end, your choices should only make you proud.
Love and respect need to be earned; it is not your right.
It is about choices you make, being reasonable and smart.

## MY MOTHER, MY EDUCATION

My mother had no formal education but was articulate and smart
She was a great inspiration for her children's education in mine had a major part
It is not the education that makes someone a wonderful mother, I believe
Mothers give their children many great life lessons formal education cannot achieve

## MOTHERS DAY POEM FOR MOTHERS NOT WITH US ANYMORE

To all the mothers who live in our hearts and minds who are now in heaven
Thank you for your unconditional care and all that love lessons
We miss you more than what you can possibly imagine every single day
Nothing can replace you, you are in our hearts all year round not just one day in May.

# Lessons I Learned

*Raise your words, not your voice. It is rain that grows flowers, not thunder.*

*—Rumi*

*Here are few life lessons I learned the hard way my dear son*
*Though look and think different, we are the same, we are like one*
*Hug the hurt, kiss the broken, befriend the lost, and love the lonely*
*Be someone's sun, let others people shine, be kind, and hate none*

*It is not the size of your house or its location it is the love you feel*
*It is not the material possessions, it is the relationship that is the real deal*
*Conversations, laughter, friendship, respect, things to keep in mind*
*These make your house a home, they heal, and are life's real wheel*

These are lessons I have learned and experiences I have gained through poverty, serious health issues, revolution, war, and the stress of moving from country to country. Some of these may overlap with some famous people's sayings.

- Smart people learn from their mistakes. Wise people learn from other people's mistakes.
- Hope is as important to your mind as oxygen is to your body.
- Life is less about what happens to you and more about how you react to what happens.
- Your age is how many times your breath has been taken away, how often you've felt alive, how many laughs you've shared, how much you've been cared for, and so on.
- Life is like a pyramid: the older you get, the less freedom you have to choose, until finally you get to the single point at the top—and you know what that is.

- I learned not to die in my thirties or forties but not get buried until my seventies or eighties.
- To climb a big mountain, learn to climb a hill first. The mountain is not going anywhere.
- Growing old is a must; growing up is a choice.
- When people bring others down, they're actually trying to promote themselves.
- Most things that bring happiness are free—things such as family, friends, laughter, love, hugs, and kisses.
- When you open your eyes, you open a pair of priceless gifts.
- Never plant the seed of hate in your heart, for it gives birth to a lifetime of suffering.
- Look at both sides. See both bad and good.
- A day or two is not your lifetime.
- Do not assume that your way is the only way.
- Dreams in your head and love in your heart are the requirements for a fruitful life.
- There is no need to win every argument.
- To be loved and respected, give credit when credit is due and take blame for your mistakes.
- Do not compare yourself to others, but only to your own past.
- Pleasing everyone is not your job. Making yourself a priority is not an option.
- Do not assume that you are incapable or undeserving.
- Do not overthink, especially about little things.
- Learn not to live in the past. Learn not to be serious all the time, for we all need to occasionally be silly, wired, funny, careless, and so on.
- To be rewarded in life, you need to work hard. However, understand that working hard is no guarantee of reward.
- Most of us have shortcomings, worries, fears, and so on.
- Other people's happiness promotes your happiness.
- Meaningful life includes passion, compassion, and purpose.
- Find a way to motivate yourself at all ages.
- Look beyond imperfections.
- Memories are made in the best days of life.
- Lessons are learned in the worst days of life.
- Happiness is experienced in good days of life.

- Strength is achieved in bad days of life.
- If you walk alone, you might get to places where others have never been.
- There will always be people who are smarter, stronger, richer, better looking, and funnier than you. So be the person who is kinder, happier, wiser, and cooler.
- Let the past go, appreciate the present, and be positive about the future.
- Learn to dream about things that are available, attainable, and achievable.
- Learn to enjoy little things, for one day you will realize that some little things were actually big things. Also, things that seem little to you might seem big to other people.
- Don't think about things for which you don't have the energy or determination to work. Doing so is a big source of unhappiness.
- Visit a graveyard whenever you are deeply sad or unusually happy.
- Living peacefully is as important as dying peacefully.
- Science cannot provide you with all the answers. Use your intuition as much as you can.
- Life without love is like a land without water in which nothing useful grows.
- Do not die at forty and wait to be buried at eighty.
- Do not make your years carbon copies of each other.
- Do not wait too long. Life has many surprises out of your control.
- Peace and happiness don't mean living without trouble and stress, but living with a calm heart.
- Stay away from jealousy. It is a most effective poison.
- Part of happiness is finding people who are your kind of crazy.
- Do not sacrifice your long-term happiness for a short-term enjoyment.

# Can I Postpone My Deathday?

*We cannot change the beginning, but maybe the end.*

Familiar in countless stories and films is the scenario of a dying person holding on to life until some special event has occurred. Then, as the vital message is delivered, the reunion experienced, or the wrong righted, they succumb swiftly to death. Are such scenes romantic fantasies, or do they reflect patterns of real-life experiences? If some people really do willfully postpone death, how much can the timing be influenced by psychological, social, and other identifiable factors? Of course, we cannot provide conclusive answers to questions of this type, but we can marshal some evidence indicating whether the questions are reasonable.

To take a first step into the territory of the credible, anecdotal evidence indicates that time of death often correlates with important social events. For example, among the first five presidents of the United States, three—Jefferson, Adams, and Monroe—died on July 4, the anniversary of the signing of the Declaration of Independence. Jefferson's last words, as quoted by his physician, suggest that the timing was no coincidence:

> About seven o'clock of the evening of that day … he [Jefferson] awoke, and seeing my staying at his bedside exclaimed, "Oh Doctor, are you still there?" In a voice however, that was husky and indistinct. He then asked, "Is it the Fourth?" to which I replied, "It soon will be." There were the last words I heard him utter.

Eight future US presidents were alive when the Declaration of Independence was signed. The odds that three would die on July 4 would be less than the chance of observing all heads in a series of twenty coin tosses. Obviously, such an event is extremely unlikely, and its occurrence provides strong evidence that the deaths of three presidents on the same day of the year is not coincidental.

Anecdotal records of people resisting death to reach moments personally import-ant to them reflect similar behavior on a larger scale. According to David Phillips,[1] deaths decrease immediately before US presidential elections and—at least in New York City with its large Jewish population—the Jewish Day of Atonement.

## Birthday and Deathday

Phillips has also investigated willfully delayed death days in relation to birthdays, us-ing as his sample 348 famous people listed in Morris, *Four Hundred Notable Americans*. Because of their notability, such people get significant attention on their birthdays. The data shows that more deaths follow birthdays than precede them. In other words, the data strongly indicates that people for whom birthdays are significant events may be able to postpone their deaths to accommodate these events.

Connections between birthdays and deathdays have been noted among several other groups. In "Relationship Between Birthday and Deathday in the Institutionalized Elderly," Margaret Susan Fewkes attempted to identify a facet of death prediction with the subsequent prevention of premature deaths. Previous samples from the general population support the view that people can exercise their will to live until a signifi-cant event occurs. The focus of Fewkes' study was 173 elderly residents who died in either of two long-term care facilities. Findings in one facility showed a dip in deaths in the three months prior to the birthday. Additionally, while only 18 percent of ad-missions to the hospital occurred in the three months before a resident's birthday, 30 percent in both facilities occurred in the three months following the birthday.

The anecdotal and statistical evidence offered here falls well short of conclusive proof, but it does strongly suggest that "romantic" tales of death deferred may indeed hold some truth.

## References

Burgess, Karen E. "The Influence of Will on Life and Death." *Nursing Forum* 15, no. 3 (July 1976): 238–258.

Fewkes, Margaret Susan. "Relationship Between Birthday and Deathday in the Institutionalized Elderly." Master's thesis, University of Utah, 1982. Accessed 2012. http://cdmbuntu.lib.utah.edu/cdm/singleitem/collection/etd2/id/1656/rec/83.

---

[1] David Phillips, *Statistics: A Guide to the Unknown* ([Place]: Holden Day, [date]), p.[number needed].

# Beauty Bias: A Cultural Preoccupation with Attractiveness

*There is more to beauty than just being beautiful in the eye of the beholder.*

Today, most newscasters on major television networks are young and good look-ing. Do good-looking people make better newscasters, or is this another example of so-called *lookism*? Most of us know the answer to this question and the reason behind it. What we may not know is that this kind of bias or discrimination is com-monly allowed and practiced. In a survey by the National Association to Advance Fat Acceptance, more than half of the association's members said that they had been turned down for a job because of their weight and that their concerns have not re-ceived proper attention from the authorities or the media. To put the global dimension of the problem into perspective, we can look at Iran's recent ban of "ugly" teachers: women with facial hair, men with acne, and teachers with scars and/or fewer than twenty teeth are no longer allowed in the classroom.

## Asset or Liability?

Although appearance can be a source of pleasure, it can create pain and suffering too. People who lack conventionally attractive features can experience stigma, dis-crimination, and health problems such as eating disorders and depression. Women often bear a vastly disproportionate share of these costs and pay greater penalties for falling short.

Theoretically, laws protect people from discrimination based on race, sex, and other characteristics that are largely out of their control and not indicative of actual qualifications or skills. Yet the law is not really equipped to deal with lookism. "It hurts to be beautiful" has been a cliché for centuries, but being beautiful is conve-nient. Studies show that good-looking people have a higher chance of being hired, are offered better positions with higher pay, and receive promotions sooner. Teachers, stu-dents, waiters, and even trial juries usually treat them better. Good-looking professors get better course evaluations from students; teachers, in turn, rate good-looking students as more intelligent. Attractive people are assumed to be healthier, nicer, and even more competent. Not even moms are immune, as they favor their more attractive children.

## Is There Any Solution?

Most experts agree that it is hard to come up with any practical solution. In "No One Wants to Admit They're Ugly, Which Makes It Hard to Fight Beauty Bias," Rose Eveleth refers to a proposal designating unattractive people as a protected class. Doing so could create affirmative action programs for the homely or compensate disfigured but otherwise healthy people in personal-injury courts. Another suggestion is using technology to help fight bias through methods such as blind interviews that take attractiveness out of job selection (although in this situation, people with nicer voices may have an advantage).

Eveleth also argues that such laws do not necessarily solve the problem. Some states already have laws that address discrimination against people based on weight and height, but those laws go ignored. The biggest problem, many experts argue, is that unattractive people are not united like many other lobbies are. To enact reform, people need to join the ugly club, which no one wants to do.

## Confirming the Bias

Although it is reasonable to think beauty is in the eye of the beholder, beholders often agree on what is beautiful. Several studies have independently found that peoples' ratings of attractiveness are quite consistent, and this is true across cultural background, sex, race, age, and social class. Facial symmetry and unblemished skin are universally admired. Taller men are rated higher for their height, women are favored if they have hourglass figures, racial minorities get points for lighter skin color, and European facial characteristics and conventionally "white" hairstyles are preferred. The preference even exists in unexpected places such as the justice system. According to "Why Looks Are the Last Bastion of Discrimination," by Deborah L. Rhode, researchers at Cornell University gave students case studies involving real criminal defendants and asked them to arrive at a verdict and punishment for each. The unattractive defendants were given prison sentences that, on average, were twenty-two months longer than those given to attractive defendants.

Beauty may be only skin deep, but the damages associated with its absence go much deeper. Appearance is considered important for self-image by 75 percent of women. As Rhode points out, even if we find a way to tackle this problem, it would trivialize other more serious forms of bias. After all, if the goal is a level playing field, why draw the line at looks?

Finally, if we could prevent discrimination against unattractive people, then as Andrew Sullivan pointed out in his article in London's *Sunday Times* in 1999, "We will be living in a totalitarian state."

## References

Eveleth, Rose. "No One Wants to Admit They're Ugly, Which Makes It Hard to Fight Beauty Bias." https://www.smithsonianmag.com/smart-news/its-really-hard-legally-protect-people-beauty-bias-180950331/?no-ist=.

Rhode, Deborah L. "Why Looks Are the Last Bastion of Discrimination." http://www.washingtonpost.com/wp-dyn/content/article/2010/05/20/AR2010052002298.html?noredirect=on.

# Funniest People Are Often the Saddest

*I see symptoms of a mild depression, I am sorry,*
*I think you need to relax, take your time, and do not hurry,*
*Watch a few episodes of Freddy the clown to laugh and calm down,*
*Eat your favorite food, forget the past and do not worry,*
*Well thanks, these are very good advices Dr. Tory,*
*But I am Freddy the clown that is my problem that is my story.*

Depressed people often try to adopt the so-called "class clown" persona to mask their true inner feelings. In "There's Pain in Laughter: Why the Funniest People Are Often the Saddest," Zara Barriea discusses one notable example: the great Robin Williams. His story made many people wonder how such a bright light could be so heartbreakingly depressed. Other similar examples include Jim Carrey, David Letterman, Conan O'Brien, Ellen DeGeneres, Rodney Dangerfield, Sarah Silverman, Owen Wilson, Larry David, Maria Bamford, and Woody Allen. They are all funny and brilliant, but part of their humor comes from an undesirable place—depression. Watching them can lead us to believe that highly talented comedians, who so often battle with extreme depression and anxiety, use comedy as relief. Why is there such a deep sense of sadness in comedy, which is supposed to be a source of joy and happiness? Why are people who seem full of life so heartbroken inside? Why do these people have the ability and desire to give others laughter and enjoyment?

Of course, comedy does not always come from depression. There is some evidence that the funniest people are often highly intelligent, and as noted by Ernest Hemingway, happiness is rare in intelligent people and there is pain in brilliance. But what does this have to do with comedy? Barriea argues that humor is a natural gift, a highly regarded form of brilliance. A comedian's brain works faster than the average brain. When you're in the presence of a true comedic genius, before you can process what's happening, they will come back with several witty retorts and two spot-on impressions. People who process quickly have a hard time shutting off their creative brain and unwinding. They're hyperaware of everything around them all the time, which can be hopelessly exhausting and deeply unsettling. For them, it's as easy to digest negative energy as positive energy. This is why so many funny people have problems shutting their brains off, so they numb themselves with alcohol or drugs. They need something to stop their never-ending stream of thoughts and ideas, but substance abuse often strips them of their creativity and burns out their brilliance. Witty quips mask insatiable sadness.

## Summary

- Humor can be a defense mechanism, protecting us from intrusion and convincing us that everything is okay.
- Humor can mask the pain underneath.
- Humor makes us feel good, distracting us and offering a few moments of relief from our inner torment.
- Humor provides escape from the outside world.
- Humor is like a shared story, helping both the comedian and the audience feel a sense of belonging.
- Humor can make us feel capable of dealing with things that scare us by helping us look at our fears a different way.

Finally, bipolar disorder has touched a long list of the greatest achievers, including Vincent Van Gogh, Buzz Aldrin, Emily Dickinson, and Ernest Hemingway. Nevertheless, the cognitive-neuroscience community is divided on the existence of a scientific link between creativity and mental illness.

## Heads Up

Humor has real benefits, both physical and psychological. However, we can also use it to avoid facing deep emotional issues. For some people, humor becomes such a strong part of their personality that they find it impossible to reveal their true feelings and seek help. So enjoy a good laugh to help you deal with day-to-day stress and to promote a healthy immune system, but keep an eye on people who make others laugh and pay attention to the deeper feelings behind their comic masks.

# References

Barriea, Zara. "There's Pain in Laughter: Why the Funniest People Are Often the Saddest."

Elite Daily, Elite Daily, 9 June 2015, www.elitedaily.com/life/culture/why-funniest-people-saddest/1057843.

*Learning Mind.* www.learning-mind.com.

# An Hour in the Gym or a Glass of Wine?

*Please do not give me that option.*

Recently there has been some research on the possible association between physical activity and life expectancy for adults. To determine the number of years gained from physical activity, researchers have examined data on more than 650,000 adults. One study that appeared in *PLOS Medicine* in November of 2012 reports that people who engaged in physical activity had life expectancy gains of up to 4.5 years. Based on such studies, physical activity is recommended for anyone who has the time, energy, desire, and money.

Reading this and a few similar studies, I wondered whether there are any drawbacks to regular exercise, and I think there are. While I don't mean to discourage anyone from engaging in physical activity, pointing out a few drawbacks may comfort those who do not or cannot exercise regularly.

Many kinds of physical activity are classified as exercise, but let's consider exercise that requires going to a gym. If someone devotes ten hours per week to exercise, plus travel to and from a gym, for fifty years, they'll spend almost three years of their life on exercise. Moreover, since we cannot exercise while we sleep, exercise actually costs them 4.5 years of their life. So the question is whether exercise extends a person's life sufficiently to offset the time invested in it, and the answer is that we cannot be sure. So we spend a significant portion of our young lives in return for an unsure gain at the end of life, a time when we might not have the energy, desire, or health to enjoy it.

Exercise can improve our quality of life, but for most people, regular exercise provides its own physical, emotional, and mental stress. Just imagine spending three years of your life traveling to a gym or running on a treadmill. Other issues to consider include:

- time taken from other activities,
- cost, especially for people who live in big cities,

- time to shower and wash gym clothes,
- possible injuries during exercise, and
- cost of buying gear, such as shoes.

We could extend this discussion to include other factors. For example, most of us enjoy casual recreation such as walking, biking, or swimming. These are probably the best kinds of physical activity, helpful to both body and mind.

Here's more good news for people cannot exercise regularly. According to a recent study, drinking red wine is better for us than going to the gym. Jason Dyck and his colleagues at the University of Alberta in Canada found that red wine, nuts, and grapes have a complex called resveratrol, which improves heart, muscle, and bone function the same way they are improved when a person exercises. Details of this research can be found in the article by Natalie Roterman.

So to my friends who have busy lives, maybe regular exercise is not always what we need. However, we do need to get up, dress up, and show up, even if we do it as slowly as a turtle. After all, turtles live significantly longer than many creatures who are more physically active.

## References

Roterman, Natalie. "Is Drinking Wine Better Than Going to the Gym? According to Scientists, Yes!" *Latin Times*, September 15, 2014. https://www.latintimes.com/drinking-wine-better-going-gym-according-scientists-yes-261496.

# Is Truth Still a Virtue?

*"Truth" is simply something that has been agreed upon. As such, a "truth"
is not fixed but variable (varies from community to community).*

*The essence of lying is in deception, not in words.*

—*John Ruskin*

We are living in a time when spurious realities are manufactured by the media, politicians, and political groups. Major news agencies present selected news and analyses based on their version of "truth," leaving readers and viewers wondering what to believe and who to trust. Of course, what's happening is not entirely new. Deceptions have been used by many groups, including politicians and the media, since the dawn of Western civilization. The history of humankind is full of well-known lies and crafty, seasoned liars. As Napoleon Bonaparte said, "History itself is nothing but a set of lies agreed upon." Even scientists who are supposed to pursue the truth have been shown to deceive.

## Role of the Lies

According to experts, deceit and falsehoods lie at the heart of our culture. Learning to lie is a natural stage in child development, and some kids become sophisticated liars. Some people believe that lies make the world a better place. As Katherine Dunn has said, "The truth is always an insult or a joke; lies are generally tastier. The nature of lies is to please, whereas truth has no concern for anyone's comfort." Finally, many people find self-deception more comforting than self-knowledge.

## Why Lies?

Deception has played an essential role in the evolution and survival of humankind, and self-deception is an essential element of human relationships, including the relationship with self. Humanity's capacity for dishonesty is as fundamental to us as our need to trust others. According to Y. Bhattacharjee, "Being deceitful is woven into our very fabric, so much so that it would be truthful to say that to lie is human."

## White Lies

A white lie is an unimportant lie, especially one uttered with good intentions in the interest of tact, politeness, or to spare someone's feelings. White lies concern trivialities and risk few consequences if caught, and they're often told to prevent an argument or bad feelings about something generally meaningless. In "The 15 Most Common White Lies and Why," Marc Chernoff notes that some white lies ease unpleasant situations, some save relationships, and others give people opportunities to make up for mistakes by buying time. Human instinct looks for the easy way out by stretching the truth. We all do it, so there's no reason to deny it.

## What Is the Limit?

As long as we're not harming anyone or doing something illegal or immoral, "innocent" white lies can make life a little more pleasant by eliminating friction as we deal with other people in our daily routines. Sometimes white lies can also cushion us from ourselves. We just need to be careful not to destroy other people's trust in us. As noted by Al David, "Most lies have the power to tarnish a thousand truths." Finally, lying has shown signs of being detrimental to health, as it takes so much energy out of the liars. After all, as pointed out by Abraham Lincoln, "No man has a good enough memory to be a successful liar."

At the community level, lies can have severe consequences. Societies work on the premise that we speak with truth and integrity, which are considered prerequisite for certain responsibilities and privileges. Leaders and the media reporting lies need the trust and loyalty of their followers, readers, or listeners. Consistent and intentional utterance of untruths removes all integrity from what should be the bastion of truth and justice. Lies tear the very fabric that holds people and communities together and threatens the health of democracies.

## References

"Al David Quotes (Author of Tarantulas)." *Goodreads*, Goodreads, www.goodreads.com/author/quotes/1196316.Al_David.

Bhattacharjee, Yudhijit. "Why We Lie: The Science Behind Our Deceptive Ways."

*National Geographic*, 5 June 2017, www.nationalgeographic.com/magazine/2017/06/lying-hoax-false-fibs-science/.

Chernoff, Marc. "The 15 Most Common White Lies and Why." *Marc and Angel Hack Life* (blog). http://www.marcandangel.com/category/humor/.

Dunn, Katherine. *Geek Love*. Vintage Contemporaries, 2002.

# Treasure What Really Matters

*Family is a smooth circle with no sharp edge,*
*Equally far from its center, regardless of their age.*
*Circle may turn to an ellipse under life's pressures,*
*Family's care brings it back; that is the love's gauge.*
*Family is the best source of support you can have.*
*In your book of life, it is certainly the shiniest page.*
*The family defines who you are and could be;*
*Appreciate it and play your part in their stage.*

In June of 2013, I faced a major health issue that had a significant impact on my life. Suddenly everything looked and felt different. My normal life, which I had always taken for granted, became a sweet memory. I felt born again, but this time as an adult with less energy, curiosity, and desire. Doctors, nurses, and hospital staff members became my colleagues and teammates. More than ever, I felt the need for the love and care of my family and friends. Life around me, especially nature, became my main focus. Unlike in the past, I could now sit and watch the birds for hours.

After settling into my new routine, I began to review my past, hoping to figure out how I had gotten to that point and whether I could have avoided it. I had always been aware that eventually we all face the day when the curtain comes down. As a typical self-centered human, however, I had hoped to be an exception. I had always treasured the love of my family and friends, and I believed their love was superior to the illusions created by the materialistic world. I believed that the key to happiness was to enjoy simple things and to have dreams in my head and love in my heart.

## Steve Jobs

I thought of what the great Steve Jobs said from his sick bed: "We may reach the pinnacle of success. In other's eyes, our lives may be an epitome of success. At the end, recalling our whole life, we realize that all the recognition, wealth, etc. that we took so much pride in, have paled and become meaningless in the face of the impending end of life issues."

## Something to Ponder

I also thought of George Carlin—a comedian of the '70s and '80s—who, after losing his wife, wrote these eloquent words:

> We have learned how to make a living, but not a life. We have added years to life, not life to years. We have been all the way to the moon and back, but have trouble crossing the street to meet a new neighbor. We have done larger things, but not better things. We have cleaned up the air, but polluted the soul. We have conquered the atom, but not our prejudice. We have planned more, but have accomplished less. We have learned to rush, but not to wait. We have been unable to realize that life is not measured by the number of breaths we take, but by the moments that our breath was taken away. We have not noticed that heaven is not the place we go when we die, but that moment in life when we actually feel alive.

## Who Will Remember Me?

According to Lori Gard,

> In our life what really matters the most is so simple, so ordinary that its intense impact can be disregarded. That is the thing about kindness: it seems basic. Yet its impact is astronomical. Others will remember us for our genuine concern about their welfare. They will remember us for our care, for a time when our connection with them mattered. They will recall that we reached out to them in their time of need. They will remember that we offered them hope when they were desolate. That we extended them a warm welcome when they felt estranged. They will remember that we placed them first above their own needs.

So my dear friends, someday, someone will remember you. More often than not, that someone is a family member or friend. That person's heart and mind will be your final resting place. Treasure them and give them your time. After all, giving your time is the same as giving part of your life that you cannot get back.

## References

"A Wonderful Message by George Carlin." *The Paradox of Our Time In History - The Complete Version!*, www.jodyhatton.com/files/paradox.htm.

Gard, Lori. "How Will People Remember You After You Die?" *Huff Post*, June 8, 2016. https://www.huffingtonpost.ca/lori-gard/legacy-after-death_b_7531758.html?utm_hp_ref=ca-tribute.

# Legacy of Kindness

*Kindness: hard to comprehend, easy to realize. Kind people look good regardless.*

*Kindness, a simple gift that touches everybody's heart,*
*Something appreciated by all never mind how culturally apart,*
*A present made up of happiness, confidence, and strength*
*It gives direction to happy land and a point to start,*
*It brings hope and joy to all and every needy heart,*
*It gives a big advantage, a valuable head start,*
*At the end the giver and receiver appear in the same chart,*
*It is easily realized no need to be genius or even smart.*
*People remember you for your kindness, it is an exceptional art.*
*Their hearts become a resting place, never let your memories depart.*
*—Reza Noubary*

*Kindness speaks the words,*
*Your heart could never speak.*
*Your wings hold me up,*
*And give me strength when I am weak.*
*The warmth of your protection,*
*Brings music to my heart.*
*You open up the doors,*
*You show me where to start.*
*—Anne Marie Cline*

I clearly remember the day my sweet high school friend passed away after a massive heart attack. He was an incredibly warm man, brilliant and vibrant. At his funeral, his close friends shared their heartwarming memories of him, all about the kindness he had displayed throughout his life. Loved by many, he was remembered as a helpful, gentle, and affectionate man who always had kind words to say—an eternal optimist and life enthusiast.

Watching his funeral, I felt great appreciation for the beautiful traditions we use to honor a life. I was moved by the heartfelt words of comfort, concern, and joy at the ways in which he had touched many lives. Every story—sad, happy, or funny—brought a torrent of tears. I realized how much we have in common and are bound together, especially in moments when we feel like parts of the same body, so that pain in one results in unrest in others. My friend had been a humble, hardworking family man, a man of faith, and yet an ordinary man. His story revealed a life of extraordinary love, patience, kindness, and caring—no ordinary feat.

It took me some time to absorb the impact of all those heart-warming words. Within our human connectedness, what matters the most are the simple, ordinary things and the ways our interactions are affected by them. Among our relationships, intimate and otherwise, what matters beyond all else is that we are authentically kind to one another. It does not matter what successes we've enjoyed, what failures we've suffered, what kind of work we did, how high we climbed the ladder, or how much we acquired. If we haven't been kind and helpful, nothing else has any value. What matters is whether we live our lives with compassion and kindness.

> What could be greater than to realize this?
> That kindness is the way to all gain and all knowing
> That kindness is the only thing that ever matters
> What else is there to be which takes us further
> Than being kind to someone for no reason?
> Other than to be kind!
> —Gordon Rosenberg

## Kindness

We all can be kind. We all have the choice to show kindness. We can be caring, extend our hearts, and radiate love to the people we meet. At the end of the day, this choice will linger long in hearts and minds. Kindness is hard to comprehend but easy to realize. It's the basic driving force of nature, taught by every religion and even emphasized by scientists. According to the Bible, kindness is one of the seven virtues and a reason for salvation and eternal life, for it sets in motion our compassion, humility, dignity, and respect.

## The Lesson

So let us choose to leave a legacy of kindness and perform random acts of kindness for strangers. Remember, if kindness, humility, generosity, sympathy, humanity, and compassion penetrate young minds today, the world can be a better place tomorrow. Also don't forget that being kind to ourselves is just as important as being kind to other people.

> Kindness planted in the soil,
> of another with a need …
> Will one day blossom back to you,
> a product of this spirit seed."
> —Kate Buxbaum-Prado

## References

Gard, Lori. "How Will People Remember You After You Die?" *Huff Post*, June 8, 2016. https://www.huffingtonpost.ca/lori-gard/legacy-after-death_b_7531758.html?utm_hp_ref=ca-tribute.

Rosenberg, Gordon. "Kindness." https://www.scrapbook.com/poems/doc/23301/251.html.

# Is It My Anniversary? Should I Buy Flowers?

*Is there any need for two people to remember the same date?*

Let's start with the concept of expected value or return. Suppose you flip a fair coin, winning a dollar for heads and losing a dollar for tails. If you play this game for a few hours, theoretically you expect to break even—that is, neither win nor lose. You expect to win half the time and lose half the time. Mathematically, this is calculated as $1/2 (+1) + 1/2 (-1) = 0$. These types of games are called fair games.

Now suppose that John, not sure if today is his anniversary, is wondering whether he should buy flowers on the way home or do nothing. Remembering what he learned in statistics class, John decides to treat the situation as an expected value problem. He formulates the problem as follows: Let A be the event that it is his anniversary and B be the event of buying flowers. Suppose that the probability of A (today is his anniversary) is some unknown and value p between 0 and 1. The four possibilities are (a) it is their anniversary, buy flowers; (b) it is their anniversary, do not buy flowers; (c) it is not their anniversary, buy flowers; and (d) it is not their anniversary, do not buy flowers. Knowing his wife and based on his experience and knowledge, John comes up with the following monetary payoffs for each choice.

|  | Anniversary(A) | No Anniversary(A') |
|---|---|---|
| Flowers(B) | 10 | $-1$ |
| No Flowers(B') | $-10,000$ | 10 |

If he buys flowers, the expected return or payoff will be $10p + (-1) (1 - p)$. This is because the possible values are 10 and -1 with respective probabilities p and $1 - p$. If he does not buy flowers, the expected return or payoff will be $-10,000p + 10 (1- p)$. To see which values of p buying flowers result in a greater payoff, we should solve the following inequality:

$10p - (1 - p) > -10,000p + 10 (1 - p)$ or $10,021p > 11$ or $p > 1/911$

So the expected payoff for buying flowers is larger if $p > 1/911$.

Let's analyze this further. First, there are 365 days in a year, so the probability that any given day is his anniversary is $1/365 > 1/911$. A man who has been married for several years should know this without any calculation. Also, 911 is a well-known number because of its association with a sad and unexpected event that changed America.

# Risk, Lottery, and Big Dreams

*Would you like to buy a sweet dream for only a few dollars,*
*a dream that could come true?*

Most things we do involve some degree of uncertainty. Our return on an investment—whether money, time, love, etc.—may or may not meet our expectations, so making life decisions is like gambling. Some decisions, such as investing in education, usually have a positive expected return, but gambling more often has a negative expected return. Decisions with a negative expected return are usually made based on other types of utility or gain, such as peace of mind, fun, excitement, joy, or even a short-term dream such as winning a lottery.

## Risk and Intuition

Making individual decisions in the face of uncertainty reflects our response to loss and reveals a great deal about our personality and our intuition about the risk. Consider a study in which a company, as a bonus, is inviting employees to choose between two options:

1. Option A: 100 percent chance of receiving $250.
   Option B: 25 percent (1 out of 4) chance of receiving $1,000; 75 percent (3 out of 4) chance of receiving nothing.

The expected gain is 250 x 1 = $250 for option A and 1,000 x 0.25 + 0 x 0.75 = $250 for option B. That is, the expected gain is the same for both options. However, 84 percent of employees chose option A, preferring a sure gain, a bird in the hand ...

A year later, the company lost business to its competition and asked employees to share the loss by offering two options:

2.  Option A: 100 percent chance of paying $250.
    Option B: 25 percent chance of paying $1,000; 75 percent chance of paying nothing.

Here again the expected loss is $250 for both options. However, this time 80 percent of employees chose option B, hoping to avoid any loss.

## A Related Study

A related study puts these results in a different light through increasing the possible gains/ losses and decreasing their probabilities:

3.  Option A: 100 percent chance of winning $5.
    Option B: 1 in 1,000 chance of winning $5,000.

The expected gain is $5 for both options. However, 75 percent of respondents chose option B, and the percentage increased to 85 percent when $5 and $5,000 were replaced by $1 and $1,000 respectively. This explains why people buy lottery tickets.
    Also comparable to paying back, the following options were considered:

4.  Option A: 100 percent chance of losing $5.
    Option B: 1 in 1,000 chance of losing $5,000.

Expected loss is $5 for both options, but 80 percent of respondents chose option A.
    So with small probability (1 in 1,000), we see different patterns. In example 3, respondents believed the 1 in 1,000 chance of a gain was large enough and worth taking. In example 4, however, they believed that the 1 in 1,000 chance of a loss was large enough to be avoided. Combining this finding with the previous examples, we have a general rule: At least in a gambling context, people tend to be risk seeking to avoid a loss and risk-averse to protect a gain. These examples demonstrate that our intuition about risk could be remarkably unreliable.

## Lottery

In a similar study, participants were offered an option of paying $1 for a one-in-one-million chance of winning a million dollars. Nearly half of the respondents accepted the offer, including a large number of risk-averse people. The study also showed that a more extreme case (one in ten million chance of winning ten million dollars) led to a significant increase in the number of participants in general and risk-averse participants in particular. This explains why lotteries attract so many people whose real reward is, in fact, a short time during which to dream about a life with that much money. The bigger the prize, the bigger the dream—never mind how small the likelihood.

# Old and Slow, But Smart and Happy

*A win-win situation, young and foolish or old and ugly. Sixty is the new forty if you make sure that 9 p.m. is the new midnight, one beer is three, and ten fries is thirty.*

As we grow older, we usually pay more attention to our physical, emotional, and mental changes. While we often consider physical and emotional changes a normal part of growing old, most of us have a harder time dealing with mental changes and wonder if these are signs of degeneration. Who was that woman? Why do not I remember the name of that restaurant? Why did I come to this room? Are my memory and intellectual skills declining? Am I losing my ability to think and reason? We also think of the possible reasons for these lapses. Are they happening because my brain doesn't function as efficiently as it used to, or is it because I now have more on my mind? Could my problems—forgetfulness, for example—be due to emotional issues I'm facing, or is something really happening in my brain?

Like other people, I've asked myself these questions many times. When we hit our late twenties, we begin losing neurons, the cells that make up the brain and nervous system. In our sixties, our brains have literally begun to shrink, but is it downhill from there? Seeking a credible answer, I have done some experiments on myself, and I've concluded that the answer to this question is definitely *no*. I have noticed that as my cognitive speed slows, my brain makes up for some of the deficit by, for example, relying on experience to anticipate and predict upcoming tasks and by employing mental shortcuts. It does this by eliminating extraneous information and paring down incoming information to essential core nuggets of relevant material.

In my view, while we may get slower, we also get smarter. After all, most great scientists, business leaders, politicians, and so on are relatively old, and more often than not, great thinkers don't peak until they get older. We don't mentally decline with age; we just deal with our problems differently. It takes us longer to retrieve information from all we have stored in our brains for years. In fact, a team at Tubingen

University in Germany demonstrated that even computers get slower when a large amount of information is stored in them.

This idea could have far-reaching implications for measuring cognitive performance. For example, tests that inadvertently favor young people should not be administered to older people, and tests to measure the cognitive performance of older people should account for their problem-solving methods. In fact, ignoring these factors could lead older people to have a negative and sometimes incorrect perception about themselves and old age, which could actually contribute to their forgetfulness by undermining their confidence and brain relaxation.

By the time a person reaches their sixties, they've had many experiences, learned many names, visited many places, and memorized lots of things. Most of what they've learned or experienced is now just a collection of memories that are of little significance. So when older people are introduced to new ideas, people, or places, they aren't excited because they see no value in storing even more information in their already "crowded" brains.

When we're young, we're eager to learn because everything is relatively new. As we get older, most of us no longer have a strong reason or incentive, because life has already taught us a lot about what is real and significant. We often don't concern ourselves with long-term issues and their possible consequences. Also, the responsibility of running our own and sometimes other people's lives makes us less receptive to new, less important matters. Our brains become a bit more relaxed, as we understand that what was cogently important to us when we were young no longer concerns us as intensely. This could also be a reason for older people to feel happier.

## References

Park, Alice. "Our Brains Begin to Slow Down at Age 24." *Time*, April 15, 2014. http://time.com/63500/brain-/?cv=1.

# The Second Half, the Better Half

*Life starts after fifty, but only if you get there.*

It can be hard to accept, but many people believe that life really starts after fifty or sixty. We get older and slower, but wiser and happier. We learn to see the big picture and prevent little things from taking us hostage. Our problem-solving strategies become more insightful, and we approach problems with more ease. We become more compromising and less confrontational, realizing that hate leads only to bitterness and suffering. As we learn to listen, be patient, and avoid arguments, our relationships become more respectful and harmonious. We develop senses to deal with our aging, recognizing that to some extent, we can control our biological and psychological age by staying active, socializing, eating healthier, and being cheerful and optimistic. We learn to live in the moment and stop worrying about the future or past. We accept changes and try to adapt to them. In sum, we accept who we are and try to be wiser, happier, kinder, and more considerate. More importantly, we stop criticizing ourselves and try to be kind instead.

There are also other supporting facts. Most of us agree that life is really worth living—or at least, it's more enjoyable—when we have more choices and fewer constraints and restrictions. We learn to accept and believe in ourselves, stop dictating or taking orders, and don't worry about what other people think of us. We stop worrying about losing our jobs and become free of the need to impress. Most of us become free from having to work except for fun and enjoyment, and free of intense physical needs and sexual desires except for emotional fulfillment. We gain the freedom to sleep long hours, spend our money on what we like, and enjoy more time with like-minded people. We have time and freedom to travel, walk along a river, listen to music we love, and reflect on past loves—and we know that nobody can take these freedoms away from us.

As we grow older, we realize that life is about family and love, not wealth and luxury. We give up jealousy, having realized that it's not healthy. We no longer care about buying more stuff; in fact, we even want to get rid of what we have and give it to people in need. We realize that simplicity and honesty are the best; life is short, and tomorrow is not promised. We try to enjoy our time by paying attention to nature and enjoy its beauty. We appreciate the complexity of the world. We laugh at our mistakes and shortcomings. We dress for comfort, not fashion. We see goodness in other people and find ourselves in the same boat as them, regardless of our past differences, successes, or failures.

Finally, we enjoy our grandchildren even more than we enjoyed our own children, free of the responsibility for their welfare and well-being. We feel free to spoil them and do what we did not do with our own children.

# Make Aging a Smooth Ride

*Aging is much more than living long. It is how many sunsets you have
seen, laughs you have shared, people you have loved and helped.*

As we age, living well requires taking care of several dimensions of wellness: physical, emotional, mental, social, intellectual, occupational, spiritual, environmental, and financial. It requires understanding age-related issues and following a plan to stay active, healthy, happy, and useful.

## What Is Aging?

According to "Aging: What to Expect," aging is the progressive accumulation of changes associated with increasing susceptibility to health issues. In addition to wrinkles, turkey necks, and gray hair, aging can lead to many other changes. Although we cannot stop the aging process, we can minimize its effects through making appropriate choices. It is well established that maintaining physical and social activities, avoiding loneliness, securing family love and support, having a positive attitude, staying curious, finding ways to motivate oneself, welcoming opportunities to learn new things, laughing as much as possible, and having a four-legged friend can all help to slow down the process. However, there are several additional things that we can do.

**Cardiovascular System**—As we age, our hearts need to work harder because of the increased stiffness of our blood vessels and arteries, which often causes hypertension and cardiovascular problems. To avoid, eat healthy, do not smoke, manage stress, and get enough sleep.

**Muscles, Bones, and Joints**—As we age, our bones tend to shrink in size and density. As a result, they weaken and become more susceptible to fracture. Things that help include adequate amounts of calcium and vitamin D. Things that hurt include substance abuse and extensive use of painkillers.

**Digestive System**—Many factors, such as a low-fiber diet, dehydration, and a lack of exercise can contribute to digestive problems. To avoid, eat healthy, don't ignore the urge for a bowel movement, drink whole milk and lots of water, and eat veggies and nuts. In short, eat like the Greeks and live like the Amish.

**Urinary Tract and Bladder**—A loss of bladder control is common with aging. To avoid, go to the toilet regularly, maintain a healthy weight, do not smoke, do Kegel exercises, avoid bladder irritants, and avoid constipation.

**Senior Moments**—Unlike the rest of our body, brain and nerve cells cannot regenerate. So when brain cells are damaged, our memory might become less efficient, making it difficult to remember familiar words or names or learn new things. To avoid, eat healthy, stay mentally active, be social, lower your blood pressure, and quit smoking. Find your purpose, embrace your faith, take a vacation, consider mountain life, watch your grandkids, read, make peace with your family, and drive less.

**Eyes and Ears**—With age, we become more sensitive to glare and have trouble adapting to different levels of light. Our hearing might also diminish. To avoid, schedule regular checkups, wear sunglasses and a hat when you're outdoors, and use earplugs when around loud machinery or other loud noises.

**Teeth**—Our gums might pull back (recede) from our teeth and, as a result, our teeth and gums might become slightly more vulnerable to decay and infection. To avoid, brush, floss, and schedule regular checkups.

**Skin**—According to "Aging: What to Expect," our skin thins and becomes less elastic and more fragile, with a simultaneous decrease of fatty tissue just below the skin. To avoid, bathe in warm (not hot) water, use mild soap and moisturizer, use sunscreen, wear protective clothing, and do not smoke.

**Weight**—Maintaining a healthy weight is more difficult as you get older, so eat healthy and watch the portion sizes.

**Sexuality**—With age, sexual needs and performance might change. To avoid, share your needs and concerns with your partner, get (or stay) hitched, and talk to your doctor.

## Final Words

For centuries, people have dreamed of defying old age with tales of a mythical fountain of youth. Today, scientists are a bit closer to unlocking the secrets of longevity. Aging could be an investment or an expense, depending on the choices we make. Rather than a burden, old people could become a source of wisdom and love for their own grandchildren and society at large. According to the United Nations, by 2050, 20 percent of the world's population will be over sixty years old, and in regions such as North America and Europe, the proportion will be even higher—almost a third. The fastest-growing subgroup are people who live alone, who, not surprisingly, also age faster than other people. In sum, other than problems for the families, in future aging could pose a greater challenge to society unless older people take on responsibility for their own healthy aging.

## References

"Aging: What to Expect." Mayo Clinic. https://www.mayoclinic.org/healthy-lifestyle/
   healthy-aging/in-depth/aging/art-20046070.
News Channel 21. KTVZ. https://www.ktvz.com.

# You Are More Than a Parent to Your Children

*Parents are often children's first love, first hero, and sometimes both. However, there are periods when they express their love in some strange ways.*

Children seek real or imaginary role models to look up to and imitate. In today's information-driven world, role models are part of everybody's lives. Our role models are often educators, civic leaders, celebrities, athletes, family members, clergy, peers, and even ordinary people encountered in everyday life. Role models can have positive or negative impacts. Some role models put forth the effort to make a positive difference and inspire other people to live meaningful lives, encouraging integrity, optimism, hope, determination, and compassion. They practice what they preach and are often active in their communities, using their knowledge, time, and talents to benefit others, including people they do not know. Some even become heroes through sacrifice or overcoming huge life obstacles.

In our media-driven society, it is not surprising for actors, athletes, singers, and national and international leaders to be chosen as role models, especially by youth. According to "Motivation by Positive or Negative Role Models," young people choose role models based on the mind-sets they develop toward accomplishing their goals. Combined with other factors, this can lead them to choose negative role models, such as certain popular celebrities. As a result, the impact of Hollywood culture on society, especially on young people, has come under scrutiny. For example, the glorification of "super-skinny" celebrities on popular social media sites has been cited as an influence in the rise of eating disorders in young people. It is logical to assume that long-term exposure to Hollywood culture can have a negative impact on young people's sense of identity and their health and well-being. Of course, how this happens and to what degree is complex. Fortunately, most youngsters choose to connect with people whom they feel best represent them. Indeed, it is fair to suggest that many young people have no interest in celebrity culture at all.

So who are the main role models for today's youth? "Role Models: Who They See

When They Look Up" refers to a State of Our Nation's Youth survey by the Horatio Alger Association, which states that more than 75 percent of America's children consider family members, friends, teachers, coaches, and community leaders as their real role models. Of the 75 percent of children who consider a family member their role model, 36 percent chose their mother, 28 percent chose their father, and 36 percent chose another family member. The article also says that one survey looked at women business owners involved in the 1,000 Stories Project and found the following: "24 percent of our project participants choose their mothers, mothers-in-laws or grand-mothers … Fathers, parents in general and other relatives are named as key influences by one-fifth of our participant pool." This article goes on to say, "Some 28 percent of participants aged 30 and younger, and 26 percent of those in the 31-to-40 range, name a woman family member or matriarch as their role model. Compare that to the mere 11 percent of women business owners aged 61 and older who did so."

These two studies, which look at people of different ages, suggest that mothers are the most popular role model. Since we spend most of our time with family members, these results may not be surprising. Overall, the data shows that role models tend to be a parent or a family member. While this may be, it just goes to show how important family relationships are. From the statistics, you can infer that people look up to those with whom they spend the most time and from whom they receive the most love, care, and advice.

Role models play an important role in inspiring young people. Parents, grandparents, aunts, uncles, teachers, civic leaders, clergy, coaches, athletes, artists, or people who just happens to enter a child's life—they all have the ability to inspire young people to learn and overcome obstacles.

## References

"1,000 Stories of Women Business Owners." *The Story Exchange.* https://thestoryex-change.org/1000-stories-women-business/.

Erwin, Caitlin. "Why Are Positive Role Models Important for Children?" Livestrong.com, Lead Group, June 13, 2017. www.livestrong.com/article/240340-why-a-positive-role-model-is-important-for-children/.

Lockwood, Penelope, Christian H. Jordan, and Ziva Kunda. "Motivation by Positive or Negative Role Models: Regulatory Focus Determines Who Will Best Inspire Us." *Journal of Personality and Social Psychology* 83, no. 4 (November 2002): 854–864.

http://www.psych.utoronto.ca/users/lockwood/PDF/Lockwood%202002%20
Motivation.pdf.

"State of Our Nation's Youth." Horatio Alger Association. https://horatioalger.org/
news-events/state-of-our-nations-youth/.

"Role Models: Who They See When They Look Up." *The Story Exchange*, June 9, 2016.
www.thestoryexchange.org/1000-role-models/.

Roots of Action. www.rootsofaction.com.

# Napping Is More Than a Luxury

*I would like to die when napping like my grandpa, not screaming like his passengers.*

In many parts of world, including Europe, businesses shut down in the afternoon to allow employees to nap and refresh. In the United States, not only are midday naps considered a luxury, but many people perceive them as indications of downright laziness.

According to the experts, people who appreciate the occasional midday snooze should continue the habit, as it is normal and beneficial. Short naps can improve awareness and productivity, and for many people they can make a world of difference. In "Napping Can Dramatically Increase Learning, Memory, Awareness, and More," David Vanallen refers to a study at the University of California, Berkeley, detailed in "An Afternoon Nap Markedly Boosts the Brain's Learning Capacity," that found that adults who nap regularly have improved memory function and ability to learn. Naps benefit children and young adults too. The article "Nap-deprived tots may be missing out on more than sleep" explains how University of Colorado–Boulder researchers discovered that children who take an afternoon nap display more joy and interest, less anxiety, and higher problem-solving skills than children who do not nap regularly.

## Nap Length

Vanallen also refers to studies that have shown that a ten-to-twenty-minute nap is quite enough to refresh the mind and increase energy and alertness. Naps are not the same as deep sleep, and people are able to get back to work immediately after waking up from naps. A thirty-minute nap may require dealing with a thirty-minute post-nap grogginess period, because the body has started to enter a deeper stage of sleep. Vanallen also points out that the same can be said about one-hour naps, even though long naps provide an excellent memory boost. The longest naps—lasting about ninety minutes—are recommended for people who do not get enough sleep at night, because ninety minutes is sufficient for a complete sleep cycle and can improve emotional memory and creativity.

All things considered, afternoon naps are good for our physical and mental well-being and should be taken as often as possible. However, an afternoon nap should not be used to replace a good night's sleep, only to supplement it.

## When to Nap

In "13 Tips for the Best Nap Ever," Kelly Fitzpatrick points out that the right time and place to catch up on sleep varies depending on a person's lifestyle, although some strategies are universal. According to the book "*Take a Nap!*" by Sara Mednick, the best time to nap depends on when we wake up in the morning. Early risers who are up around 5:00 a.m. should nap around 1:00 p.m., whereas those who sleep until around 9:00 a.m. should not nap until 3:00 p.m. Regardless of the time we wake up, napping after 4:00 p.m. is not recommended.

It is important to remember that sleeping fewer than eight hours a night increases the risk of falling asleep at the wheel. Fitzpatrick says a thirty-minute nap has been shown to improve alertness and prevent unsafe driving nearly as well as coffee. Young adults in particular benefit the most from a quick snooze. Finally, for people who have insomnia, walking after lunch instead of taking a nap is especially helpful. In fact, napping is not always the best bet for people with sleeping disorders.

## Nap Smart

To make the most of your nap, consider the following tips, including some recommended by Fitzpatrick.

1. Set an alarm to avoid worrying about not waking up on time.
2. Use a quiet, dark place. If necessary, use a mask, earplugs, or white noise to help tune out disruptions.
3. Drink coffee or a quick cup of something caffeinated before a short nap. This is helpful because caffeine takes about twenty minutes to kick in just as you wake up.
4. Before napping, calm yourself with meditation techniques such as breathing and visualizations.
5. Avoid long naps; they can throw off your internal clock, which keeps track of days and nights.

# References

Anwar, Yasmin. "An Afternoon Nap Markedly Boosts the Brain's Learning Capacity." *Berkeley News*, February 22, 2010. https://news.berkeley.edu/2010/02/22/naps_boost_learning_capacity/.

"Expert-Approved Tips for a Perfect Midday Snooze?" *BeWellBuzz*. https://www.bewellbuzz.com/news/expert-approved-tips-perfect-midday-snooze/.

Fitzpatrick, Kelly. "13 Tips for the Best Nap Ever." http://dailyburn.com/life/lifestyle/nap-tips-sleep-better/?mtype=5&partner=huff&sub_id=09092014_insomnia&utm_campaign=09092014_insomnia&utm_content=09092014_insomnia&utm_medium=huff&utm_source=huff.

"Nap-Deprived Tots May Be Missing Out on More than Sleep, Says New CU-Led Study." *CU Boulder Today,* January 3, 2012. https://www.colorado.edu/today/2012/01/03/nap-deprived-tots-may-be-missing-out-more-sleep-says-new-cu-led-study.

Reflectionofmind.org.

Vanallen, David. "Napping Can Dramatically Increase Learning, Memory, Awareness, and More." http://reflectionofmind.org/napping-can-dramatically-increase-learning-memory-awareness/.

# Fairness: Equality or Equity

*The winner takes all, the loser has to fall. The limits of fairness are always set by the strong.*

Equality versus equity is often illustrated by pictures of three people of different heights watching a baseball game over the top of a fence. In one picture, all three have the same number of crates to stand on, representing equality. Although this is helpful for the average person, it is not enough for the short person and superfluous for the tall person. In contrast, the second picture represents equity, as each person has the number of crates they need to enable them to watch the game.

In another example, advocating for equality in school funding would mean ensuring that all schools receive the same amount of resources. Advocating for equity, however, would mean that each school receives the resources they really need to achieve the required levels.

In both examples, the problem has to do with where the initial inequity presents itself. In the first example, some people need more help to see over the fence because they are shorter, a characteristic that is inherent to the people themselves. In the second example, students in low-income or marginalized communities are "shorter" and therefore need more resources in their schools.

Cutting a hole in the fence that allows the shorter person to see the game symbolizes the creative and often subversive ways that people can work around systems to get what they need.

## Fairness

So which is more fair, equality or equity? It seems that the appropriate answer is culture dependent. For example, Americans in general have greater tolerance than Europeans for income inequality and less tolerance for inequality of opportunity. In "Imagining Fairness," Jorge Reina Schement points out that certain policies tend to succeed with Americans because they appear to include everyone and reinforce their dominant construction of fairness as equality. Also, policies aiming to achieve equity often face the challenge of being viewed as unfair. As is well known, Affirmative Action, an attempt by Lyndon Johnson to overcome generations of injustice and discrimination against women and minorities, became the law of the land without the approval of the American people. Some people saw it as unfair because it appeared to favor some people over others, which differs from the more commonly understood American concept of fairness as equality.

Like a few other countries, the United States has attempted to apply the concept of equality to situations based on gender differences. Some people consider this application of equality inappropriate, arguing that equity is more meaningful here. They believe that dismissing equality does not imply that one gender is superior to the other, but instead recognizes and celebrates gender differences. They point out that difference, not equality, is a source of strength. For example, our fingers are various sizes and shapes and have different roles. It would be unwise to force our ten fingers into equal lengths or identical functions as a way of creating equality.

In the United States, the concept of equality is twisted through the promotion of Hollywood culture. Although entertainment is not critical for the survival of a society, the price tag for singers and actors is high, and items with their name or trademark are priced much higher than their real value.

## Final Words

As Schement points out, if public policy concentrates solely on the objective of equality without reference to equity, its achievements will be flawed because people struggling to catch up will fall even farther behind. On the other hand, if policy concentrates on equity by targeting groups who need special programs to improve their opportunities for access, it will reap backlash from the many people who resent that as being unfair. We need to find middle ground and gradually position our social programs within the range of what Americans consider to be fair. This may require, through education, a gradual change in society's understanding of fairness.

## References

Schement, Jorge Reina. "Imagining Fairness: Equality and Equity of Access in Search of Democracy." American Library Association, June 2002. http://www.ala.org/aboutala/offices/oitp/publications/infocommons0204/schement

# Pets and Family

*Pets are often a part of their owners' lives, but their owners are their whole lives.*

Many people believe that it is not genetics that determines one's family, but love, attention, loyalty, trust, support, honesty, acceptance, gratitude, and compromise. Pets, especially dogs, often give you all that at a low cost. Most pet owners consider their pets as members of the family and treat them as such, for their mutual benefit. According to the US Pet Ownership Statistics presented in "A Guide to Worldwide Pet Ownership," 36.5 percent (43,346,000) of American households own dogs and 30.4 percent (36,117,000) own cats. The average number of dogs and cats owned per household is 1.6 and 2.1 respectively. The total number of dogs in the United States is 69,926,000, and the total number of cats is 74,059,000. The mean number of veterinary visits annually per household is 2.6 for dogs and 1.6 for cats. The mean veterinary expenditure annually per household is $378 for dogs and $191 for cats.

It is typical for most American families to own a pet; 68 percent of households, or about eighty-five million families, own a pet according to the Joybird blog, 2017–2018 National Pet Owners Survey conducted by the American Pet Products Association (APPA). In addition to dogs and cats, 12.5 million households own a freshwater fish, and 7.9 million own a bird. However, households typically own more freshwater fish than cats or dogs. According to the APPA, US families own 139.3 million freshwater fish, followed by 94.2 million cats, 89.7 million dogs, and 20.3 million birds.

According to many surveys, pets positively impact their families' lives, especially the children's lives. Pets can offer a variety of benefits for children including increasing their sense of responsibility; reducing loneliness, stress, and feelings of negativity; lowering the risk of developing allergies; and stabilizing blood pressure. Having a pet in the household definitely affects the dynamic of the family. According to Tara Parker-Pope, "Pets alter not only a family's routines, but also its hierarchy, social rhythm, and its traditional relationships." They may also cause tensions between family members and stress as a result of misbehavior.

"12 Fascinating Stats about Pet Ownership in the US" presents statistics showing that women are slightly more likely than men to own a pet, and 51 percent of the men surveyed reported that they did not own any pets compared with only 42 percent of women. More than 50 percent of pet owners in the United States admit to talking to their pets. According to "A Guide to Worldwide Pet Ownership," pet ownership in the United States has more than tripled since the 1970s. Nine in ten Americans say they consider their pet to be a part of their family. Thirty-six percent give their dogs birthday presents, and 27 percent have professional photographs taken of their pets. Americans spend more than $50 billion per year on their pets.

"A Guide to Worldwide Pet Ownership" also reports some interesting facts about how pet ownership statistics differ around the world. According to "12 Fascinating Stats," Romania has the world's most balanced pet population, with 45 percent of households owning dogs and 45 percent owning cats. Switzerland's dog population is shrinking, and India has the fastest growing dog population in the world. Fish are the most popular pet in the United Kingdom.

Over half of families own more than one pet. The benefits of owning a pet obviously outweigh the disadvantages. The positive feelings of companionship are accompanied by health benefits too. A study of these benefits published in the journal *Gerontology* found positive correlation between pet ownership and mental health. After eight weeks, elderly people who were given five crickets in a cage were less depressed than a control group. The act of caring for a living creature seems to make the difference. There also may be circumstances that require people to own pets, such as the need for a service dog. These pet owners may not necessarily want a pet, but they may require it if their health problems are too overbearing for their family to deal with alone. The act of caring for a living creature seems to make the difference. In Australia, non–pet owners visit their doctors more often than pet owners and recover from illnesses slower.

Essentially, domesticated animals are a staple in the typical American family that offer much more than simple companionship; some are now trained in aiding people with disabilities, police, or local farmers. The number of pets in the United States is increasing, and ideally people can continue to treat their furry friends with the respect and love they deserve.

## Animal Laws

Under US law, animals are considered property with no inherent rights, protected only by anticruelty laws. According to "Animal Cruelty Laws State By State," published by Stray Pet Advocacy, this is how animals are protected by law in Pennsylvania:

> Cruelty to animals is defined as: "wantonly or cruelly illtreats, overloads, beats, otherwise abuses any animal, or neglects any animal as to which he has a duty of care, whether belonging to himself or otherwise, or abandons any animal, or deprives any animal of necessary sustenance, drink, shelter or veterinary care, or access to clean and sanitary shelter which will protect the animal against inclement weather and preserve the animal's body heat and keep it dry." …
>
> It is a Misdemeanor in the second degree if a person: "kills, maims or disfigures any domestic animal of another person or any domestic fowl of another person; administers poison to or exposes any poisonous substance with the intent to administer such poison to any domestic animal of another person or domestic fowl of another person; harasses, annoys, injures, attempts to injure, molests or interferes with a dog guide, hearing dog or service dog." …
>
> It is a Felony in the third degree if a person: "kills, maims or disfigures any zoo animal in captivity; or administers poison to or exposes any poisonous substance with the intent to administer such poison to any zoo animal in captivity." …
>
> It is a Misdemeanor in the first degree if a person: "kills, maims, mutilates, tortures or disfigures any dog or cat, whether belonging to himself or otherwise; or administers poison to or exposes any poisonous substance with the intent to administer such poison to any dog or cat, whether belonging to himself or otherwise." …
>
> Exemptions to these clauses are veterinary care, protecting other domestic animals or fowl, game laws, pest control, and farming.

# References

"12 Fascinating Stats about Pet Ownership in the U.S." Joybird. https://blog.joybird.com/pet-ownership-statistics/.

Stray Pet Advocacy. "Animal Cruelty Laws State by State," 2003. straypetadvocacy.org/PDF/AnimalCrueltyLaws.pdf.

Oaklander, Mandy. "Pet Therapy: Science Proves Owning a Pet Is Good for You." *Time*, April 6, 2017. http://time.com/4728315/science-says-pet-good-for-mental-health/.

Parker-Pope, Tara. "When Pets Change the Family Dynamic." *New York Times*, March 15, 2011. http://well.blogs.nytimes.com/2011/03/15/when-pets-change-the-family-dynamic/.

Parslow R, A, Jorm A, F, Christensen H, Rodgers B, Jacomb P: Pet Ownership and Health in Older Adults: Findings from a Survey of 2,551 Community-Based Australians Aged 60–64. *Gerontology*. 2005;51:40-47. doi: 10.1159/000081433.

Pet Secure: Protecting Your Pets. www.petsecure.com.au.

Walden, Liz. "A Guide to Worldwide Pet Ownership." Pet Secure. https://www.petsecure.com.au/pet-care/a-guide-to-worldwide-pet-ownership/.

# Living in the Binary World

*There are two types of people in the world you know*
*Those who think that there are two types and those who think no*
*What is surprising opposites often attracting each other*
*They end up marrying, many stay married for a long time I don't know how*

*When I work with binary numbers*
*I feel at home, somewhere I have been*
*When I do mathematical manipulations*
*I feel comfortable, something I have seen*

## Irish Philosophy of Life

In life, there are only two things to worry about: you are either well or sick. If you are well, there is nothing to worry about, but if you are sick, you have two things to worry about: you will either live or die. If you live, there is nothing to worry about, but if you die, you have two things to worry about: you will go either to heaven or to hell. If you go to heaven, there is nothing to worry about, but if you go to hell, you'll be so busy shaking hands with your friends that you won't have time to worry! So why worry?

Many aspects of life are binary: things are either present or absent. Some are classified as binary to make life simpler or more practical, and some are presumed to be binary due to a lack of understanding or knowledge. For a long time, for example, gender was assumed to be binary: male and female. Depending on the situation, either of the binary options could be good/desirable or bad/undesirable. Learning how to deal with binary situations is therefore beneficial or even necessary. Understanding the presence or absence of something requires facing or experiencing its presence or absence. In other words, things cannot be appreciated or even realized without awareness of their opposite. For example, without experiencing pain, we would not realize or appreciate the absence of pain.

To analyze binary situations, mathematicians have developed Boolean logic, a binary system with only two states—yes or no, true or false, on or off—sometimes represented by 1 and 0. Sometimes other states could be simply a combination of these two states or a fraction of each. A single digit 1 or 0 is a called a bit, which is a contraction of the words *binary* and *digit*. The binary system has proved quite useful, especially in the era of computers.

## Life in a Binary World

Imagine that you are living in a binary world where everything is either true or false, similar to a black and white world where no other color is recognizable. This is the case in pure mathematics. How will this affect our reasoning? Consider a village where people are binary and always either lie (0) or tell the truth (1). Suppose you hear the following exchange:

"This is impossible!" says Jim.
"Jim and I are different types!" says John.

Question: Is Jim telling the truth?
Answer: If John is telling the truth and they *are* different types, Jim must be lying. But if John is lying, which means that he and Jim are the same type, then Jim is lying too.
The point is that our logic worked because of two possibilities/binary assumptions. Here are two similar problems to try:

Jim says, "John is a liar."
John says, "We both tell the truth."

"We both tell the truth," says Jim.
"We are both liars," says John.

## Binary System Operations and Implications

For most of us, the commonly used decimal number system feels so natural and useful that it is hard to think of any other system, especially a binary system. The binary system is a positional number system similar to the decimal system. It uses 2 as a base rather than the base 10. Unlike the decimal system with ten symbols 0, 1, 2, 3, 4, 5, 6, 7, 8, 9 for representation, a binary system uses only the two symbols/digits 0 and 1, so it's a more efficient system. The system works with powers of 2, just as the decimal system works with powers of 10. For example, the binary representation of the numbers 0 to 10, using only two digits, are respectively 0, 1, 10, 11, 100, 101, 110, 111, 1000, 1001, and 1010.

Example: What does 10011 represent in decimal and binary systems?

$$\text{Binary } 10011 = 1^\star(2)^4 + 0^\star(2)^3 + 0^\star(2)^2 + 1^\star(2)^1 + 1^\star(2)^0$$
$$\text{Decimal } 10011 = 1^\star(10)^4 + 0^\star(10)^3 + 0^\star(10)^2 + 1^\star(10)^1 + 1^\star(10)^0$$

Also:

Binary representation Decimal value

$$1 = 1 = 1 * (2)^0$$
$$10 = 2 = 1 * (2)^1 + 0 * (2)^0$$
$$100 = 4 = 1 * (2)^2 + 0 * (2)^1 + 0 * (2)^0$$
$$1000 = 8 = 1 * (2)^3 + 0 * (2)^2 + 0 * (2)^1 + 0 * (2)^0$$
$$10000 = 16 = 1 * (2)^4 + 0 * (2)^3 + 0 * (2)^2 + 0 * (2)^1 + 0 * (2)^0$$

For example, if in the decimal world a person is 4 years old and has $64, in the binary world he is 100 years old and has $1,000,000.

Operations in a binary system are no different from operations in a decimal system. For addition, stack the numbers first and remember that here $0 + 0 = 0$, $0 + 1 = 1$, but $1 + 1$ equals 10 instead of 2. Record the 0 and carry the 1 to the next column. If you have $1 + 1$ with a carried 1, that equals 11, so record one 1 and carry the other 1. For example:

```
1111111              (carry)
110111110
+111001100
1110001010
```

Subtraction is done in the same manner except for borrowing. Just like decimal $0 - 0 = 0$, $1 - 1 = 0$, and $1 - 0 = 1$. When borrowing, it is always when you have to subtract a 1 from a 0. To do this, you go left until you find a 1 and then borrow 1 from it, making it a 0. Then add that 1 to the number on its right (a zero) making it 10 in binary (2 in decimal). Then subtract 1 from 10, giving you an answer of 1. For example:

```
  111111                    (borrow)
 ⁰1¹⁰1¹⁰1¹00⁰1¹0110
  - 1 1 10 0 1 010
   1 1 00 0 0 100
```

Multiplication in the binary system is also the same as multiplication in the decimal system. However, we need to remember that $0 * 0 = 0$, $1 * 1 = 1$, $1 * 0 = 0$, or $0 * 1 = 0$. This makes it actually easier to do binary multiplication because we do not have to remember a multiplication table. For example:

```
    10110
    x 101
    10110
   000000
 + 1011000
   1101110
```

Division is simpler because the divisor can only go into the dividend 0 or 1 times, so no multiplication is required. For example:

```
         10011 r 1
   11)111010
      -11
       01010
       -11
        100
        -11
          1
```

Here are a few other rules. For example, if the last digit of a binary number is 1, the number is odd; if it is 0, the number is even. Also in a binary system, a negative number x is the same as the positive number 2n−1 + x, except that the leading (left-most) bit is 1 instead of 0. Here n is the number of bits.

Finally, some people are curious about the binary representations of well-known irrational numbers such as *pi*. As expected, like other irrational numbers, they are mathematically infinite strings of 0s and 1s with no discernible pattern. Pi's first 22 bits are

11.0010 0100 0011 1001 0101 1000

Here's an interesting observation: In a decimal system, March 14 (3/14) is designated as pi day, but that doesn't work in a binary world.

And lastly, in order to convert texts into binary, codes are assigned to letters and characters used in writing. For example, a = 01100001, b= 01100010, c= 01100011, …, z= 01111010.

## What If the World Started with Binary Instead of Decimal?

The binary system is used in almost all computers today as the most basic way to represent data. Computers are basically a series of transistors that can have only two states: *on* or *off*. Most digital file formats—such as mp3, jpeg, and mpeg—also use binary to store data.

Binary calculations take more time and space, but they're easier because we use only two digits, 0 and 1. In a world without advanced technology, of course, it is faster to perform calculations in the decimal system. After all, most of us learn counting using our ten fingers, although we can learn the binary system using only our thumbs. Also, for most of us it is easier to recognize the significance of the decimal number 2,435 than the binary representation 1111 0110 01111101. In general, operations in binary system are easier and can be done almost instantly using computers, and it's cheap to build circuits that only take on two values. Still, the decimal system is much more practical. By the way, if you use your fingers as binary digits—extended means 1, folded means 0—then you can count to 1023 on your fingers. (Four—or 00100—looks like a rude gesture, however.)

Someday the binary system might become obsolete due to the introduction of quantum technology. Presently this system is powering computer systems and enables us to deal with complex tasks.

And finally, you might like to know that there are two types of people: those who think that there are two types of people, and those who don't.

## References

Binary Subtraction Examples. http://sandbox.mc.edu/~bennet/cs110/pm/sub.html.

The Binary System. http://www.math.grin.edu/~rebelsky/Courses/152/97F/Readings/student-binary.

The Math Forum: Ask Dr. Math. http://mathforum.org/library/drmath/view/55969.html.

Why Computers Use Binary. https://chortle.ccsu.edu/java5/Notes/chap02/ch02_3.html.

# How Did We Get Here?

*Sometimes it is less about where we are and more about how we got here.*

The day we began to think and reason was the day we began to look for answers to many questions regarding the world around us. Where did I come from? What am I doing here? What is this all about? What is that bright thing up there and where does it go at night? What are those shiny little spots in the sky, and why are they not there during the day?

Our primary focus was taking care of our basic needs—food, water, and shelter, but we frequently returned to wondering about those larger questions. Gradually finding ourselves confronted by ever more complicated questions about life and survival, we learned about the fascinating concept of cause and effect, which gave us a framework for thinking and reasoning. Those with more insight took the lead and came up with convincing answers for our fundamental questions. What we now think of as classical ideologies began to take shape, and in a generation or two, we became followers of our predecessors' ideologies and beliefs.

Some people tried to force their beliefs on others—a practice that still happens today in certain parts of the world, and a practice for which the human race has paid dearly. Some even went further and classified people outside their circles as outsiders, nonbelievers, and thus subject to isolation and punishment. Rather than improving their belief systems over time, some decided to accept only changes that fit their ideology, and they opposed or ignored other people's ideas.

Of course, it is only fair to point out that at the time, people did not have many choices. They needed to believe in something to comfort themselves, confront risk, and give meaning and purpose to life. They realized how fragile life is and how much we need to hold on to something bigger than ourselves. The dominant idea was to believe in and rely on a higher power, life after death, and personal accountability for one's actions. This motivated people to be accountable and police themselves, since it wasn't possible to police everybody all the time.

Today this powerful way of thinking is still followed by a significant percentage of the world's population. The only thing new is that we are more focused on living better, longer, more comfortable, and more enjoyable lives. This addition has led to a variety of lifestyles, each with their own pros and cons. The major challenge has been to find meaningful replacements for traditional values. Partially successful replacements have included money, art, music, sports, sex, and so on, while other replacements include some form of community membership or partnership. Compared to going to church on Sunday, activities such as concerts or football games make us feel like part of something bigger than ourselves or like we belong to a group.

These thoughts, as we know, have led to a great deal of positive change, but they've also resulted in new social problems by changing our focus, role models, values, and so on. Today, as is evident from recent social movements and election results, some communities are going back to the old ideas and values, hoping to counter the social problems they face.

Also, now more than ever, material things have become a major part of our lives. Most people know the price of everything and the value of almost nothing. A large percentage of the young generation live a fast-paced, risky life with no direction and lots of fantasy. The popular media has changed our focus, and most of us prefer to follow whatever is popular and make assumptions about everything. Self-centeredness is at an all-time high. Americans care less about world affairs than people in other countries. Individualism has taken over and minimized human interaction. Emptiness and loneliness have led to a significant increase in drug and alcohol use and abuse. Suicide, depression, crime, addiction, and teenage pregnancy have become almost normal, daily occurrences. Young people seem confused as they face many distractions, and parents are often too busy to take proper care of children and their education. Schools face their own problems. Young people are less patient, more fun loving, more demanding, face more distractions, and have less desire and excitement about learning and working hard.

Globalization has led to tensions and nervousness in some societies. Technology has taken over certain aspects of life. Women have distanced themselves from their uniqueness and capabilities, needlessly trying to do what men do. Unlike in the past, what divides people today is not ideology but political views. Islam has become the fastest growing religion in the world, including in the United States. According to "The Future of World Religions," by the year 2050, Muslims and Christians will be nearly equal in numbers around the world. Interestingly, by that year almost 20 percent of the world's population will be over sixty years old. Both of these changes have great potential to create problems that will require us to plan carefully as we address them.

## References

Pew Research Center. "The Future of World Religions: Population Growth Projections, 2010–2050." http://www.pewforum.org/2015/04/02/religious-projections-2010-2050/.

# Probability and Genetics

*It is a great insult and disrespectful to think that probability theory is about gambling.*

Merriam-Webster's Online Dictionary defines genetics as "a branch of biology that deals with heredity and variation of organisms." According to the Cold Springs Harbor Laboratory, Gregor Johann Mendel, a German Augustinian priest, is viewed as the father of genetics for his work with pea plants in the mid-1800s. Between 1856 and 1863, Mendel bred two types of pea plants: green-smooth (green with smooth pea pods), and yellow-wrinkly (yellow with wrinkled pea pods). He observed and tested some 2,900 pea plants through many generations, cross breeding the purebred plants (green-smooth with yellow-wrinkled) and then once more cross breeding the new generation of plants. After each generation, Mendel observed and recorded the presence or absence of the aforementioned characteristics. The first generation of these plants always yielded all green-smooth plants; however, the second generation yielded mostly green-smooth but also some yellow, wrinkled, or both. He repeated this experiment many times and noted that the traits of green and smooth had approximately a 3:1 ratio to green and wrinkled.

The results of this and similar experiments can be explained through the application of probability models. A simple application of the probabilistic models yields the same results as Mendel's extensive empirical data. In this sense, probability is used in the field of genetics, though typically in a more complicated capacity. Gene transferal are not necessarily equally likely (equal probable), but generally models are created in a similar fashion to determine the probability of offspring possessing or lacking certain traits, given the knowledge of the genes of the parents.

## Illustration

Consider the problem of the distribution of chromosomes when two parents produce a child. An individual has twenty-three pairs of chromosomes, which are made up by receiving a set from each parent. The number of possible pairs or combinations is then 2 (number of options) times itself 23 times, a huge number. Traits can be dominant and recessive. Certain traits can only be passed down to offspring if they receive the recessive trait from both parents. The probability of receiving these traits can actually be determined. For example, consider the determination of the hair color of a child when the mother has red hair, a recessive trait hh, and the father has brown hair, a dominant trait Hh. When crossed, the possible outcomes are Hh, Hh, hh, hh. Since each outcome is equally likely, we can say that there is a fifty-fifty chance that the child will have either red or brown hair. This method can be applied to situations where there are many traits. Remembering that recessive traits can only be expressed if no trace of the dominant trait is passed on, it is easy to determine the probability that certain traits will show in the offspring.

## Color Blindness

An important application of probability in genetics involves calculation of the probability of color blindness in offspring, using the well-known Bayes' theorem. Since the gene for color blindness is recessive, it occurs only when the dominant trait is not present. The gene for color blindness appears on the X chromosome, so the odds differ significantly, depending on whether the child is female with two X chromosomes or male with only one.

Red-green color blindness is passed from mother to son on the twenty-third chromosome, which is known as the sex chromosome because it also determines sex. The twenty-third chromosome is made up of two parts, either two X chromosomes for a girl or an X and a Y for a boy. The faulty gene for color blindness is found only on the X chromosome. So, for a male to be color blind, the faulty color blindness gene has to appear only on his X chromosome. For a female to be color blind, it must be present on both of her X chromosomes.

A color-blind boy cannot receive a color-blind gene from his father, even if his father is color blind, because his father can pass an X chromosome only to his daughters. A color-blind daughter therefore must have a father who is color blind and a mother who is a carrier (who has also passed the faulty gene to her daughter). If her father were not color blind, a carrier daughter would not be color blind. A daughter can become a carrier only by acquiring the gene from a carrier mother or a color-blind father. This is why red-green color blindness is far more common in men than in women. Blue color blindness affects both men and women equally, because it is carried on a nonsex chromosome. It is estimated that more than 250 million people worldwide are color blind.

## References

"Concept 2 Genes Come in Pairs." *Johann Gregor Mendel - the Man, the Monk :: DNA from the Beginning*, www.dnaftb.org/2/bio.html.

# The History of Social Security Numbers

*A Social Security number is not a number, but an identification tool.*

Social Security numbers as a form of identification were originally introduced as a result of the limited number of available names. Clearly there are not enough names to uniquely identify the population, whereas numbers, being different and unlimited, do not have that problem.

The Social Security program began as a type of insurance policy for America's elderly after the Great Depression. The United States Census Bureau provides a variety of statistics related to poverty. During the 1930s, poverty among senior citizens escalated to nearly 50 percent. According to "Income and Poverty in the United States: 2017," only 12.3 percent of all people living in the United States were below the poverty level threshold in 2017. By simple virtue of this comparison, it is clear why President Franklin Roosevelt felt the Social Security program was necessary for the economic survival of the nation.

In "The Story of the Social Security Number," Carolyn Puckett explains that Social Security was enacted into law in 1935 as part of Roosevelt's New Deal. The law was primarily designed to allow retirees and unemployed people to begin receiving benefits within two years. The program was, and still is, funded by the collection of payroll taxes based on a worker's wages. The exact financial ratios have been amended over the years, but the basics of the program have remained the same. Changes over the years have included the addition of survivor's benefits and benefits for the retiree's spouse and children. The way that benefits are paid also has changed. Initially the program allowed for a one-time, lump sum payment, but now benefits are paid monthly. These benefits are paid out according to the universal adaptation of the Social Security number.

According to the Social Security Office's website, a treasury regulation was issued in 1936 that required an account number for each employee covered by the Social Security program. A Social Security number is a nine-digit number assigned to people at birth (and subsequent application to the Social Security Administration) in the United States. The nine digits of the number are broken into three sections, each separated by a hyphen. The first three numbers are area numbers, based on the zip code of the city where the application for a Social Security number was first made. The second two numbers (ranging from 01 to 99) are group numbers that serve to break Social Security numbers with the same area numbers into more manageable groups. The final four digits are serial numbers that range from 0001 to 9999. These numbers run consecutively within the group number designation.

The Social Security Administration states on its "Social Security Number Chronology" webpage that between 1936 and 1937, approximately thirty million applications for Social Security numbers were processed. Since that time, the Social Security number has come to be used as an identifying factor by countless groups. In 1961, the Civil Service Commission adopted the Social Security number as an official Federal employee identifier. The Internal Revenue Service requires use of the Social Security number as the taxpayer identification number. The Department of Defense adopted the Social Security number in lieu of the military service number for purposes of identifying Armed Forces personnel. These government agencies are not the only ones to embrace use of the Social Security number. Private agencies such as banks, creditors, health insurance companies, and employers now use the Social Security number as a form of identification.

Concerns have been raised about duplication of Social Security numbers and the ill effects that would follow such duplication, but since there are nearly one billion different Social Security numbers available, this is not an immediate problem. A more timely concern would be worrying about running out of Social Security funds before running out of numbers.

The Social Security program is truly genius, functioning not only as an identifier for the delivery of retirement checks, but also as an avenue that creates choices. It is much more than a simple paycheck or number. The Social Security program allows for vocational rehabilitation, disability pay, Medicare health insurance, and supplemental security income. The number that each American is assigned provides for a financially stable future that previous generations could only dream about.

## References

Puckett, Carolyn. "The Story of the Social Security Number." https://www.ssa.gov/policy/docs/ssb/v69n2/v69n2p55.html.

Social Security Administration. "Social Security Number Chronology." https://www.ssa.gov/history/ssn/ssnchron.html.

United States Census Bureau. "Income and Poverty in the United States: 2017." https://www.census.gov/library/publications/2018/demo/p60-263.html.

# Happiness, Family, and Country

*Happy people look beyond imperfections. There are only*
*a few places where happiness may be found.*

Happiness is often defined as a mental state of well-being characterized by positive emotions ranging from contentment to intense joy. Its pursuit is enshrined as a fundamental right in many countries including the United States and occupies most of our time. But what is happiness? Is it something that we can study? Is it in our genes? Do we have power or skills to make ourselves happier? What type of people are happy, and why? And more importantly, what makes one happy?

Although defined above, some people think that defining happiness can be as elusive as achieving it. Several aspects of life—biological, psychological, religious, and philosophical—are used to define happiness and identify its sources. Beyond the problems with trying to define an elusive feeling, its source is also important, since happiness is a fundamental emotion that human beings strive to achieve. Various factors correlate with happiness, but no validated method has been found to improve happiness in a meaningful way for most people. According to the psychologist Martin Seligman, "Humans seem happiest when they have pleasure, engagement, relationships, meaningfulness, and accomplishments."

In which countries are people the happiest? In terms of the average feeling of happiness, Danes top the list, followed by Swiss and Austrians, in a survey by the Humboldt Foundation that included approximately 80,000 respondents. The people who are most satisfied with their personal circumstances are those who have access to good health care, education, and good paid jobs. Other European countries—Austria, Iceland, Finland, and Sweden—made the top ten. A *Humboldt Kosmos* article titled "World Map of Happiness" says that "This is because they are all prosperous, have functioning healthcare and education systems, relatively low levels of unemployment and little social inequality. Despite their increasing prosperity, Asian countries such as China, Japan, and India achieve relatively low ratings. The great sense of community and the strong collective identity characteristic of the people of these countries do not seem to promote happiness. According to the happiness researchers, freedom, democracy and the possibility of determining one's own life and even having an interesting, responsible job are far more conducive to increasing people's happiness quotient."

On a personal level, social ties are shown to be an extremely reliable indicator of happiness. Many social scientists believe that nothing creates as much happiness as being sociable and interacting with like-minded people. According to the *Humboldt Kosmos* article, "People are most often and most intensely happy when they are with friends and family. Even in this age of individualism, love, friendship, sociability and companionship are the best means to happiness. Happy people invest in their social relationships, receive support from friends and family, and feel valued and liked. Even happier are those who share their own happiness and help others."

A perceived quest or feeling that you belong to something bigger is another reliable indicator. For some this could be achieved by joining a fan club. The article also points out the following:

> Believers are happier people because beliefs mean hope, and people who have hope think positively. Surveys show that those who are confident in their beliefs are more resilient to life's adversities. In addition, many ideologies have always been strongly linked to intoxication-like states of happiness. Mystics, for example, describe the divine encounters attained through contemplation and meditation as an intense moment of happiness or ecstasy. The body's own "happiness hormone," serotonin, also contributes to this feeling, as its production is increased through meditation. Considering the latter, some life scientists believe happiness is no more than the right mixture of oxytocin and serotonin in our blood. People in love, for example, produce increased amounts of the "happiness chemicals" oxytocin and phenyl ethylamine, as well as endogenous endorphins.

It is interesting to note that several other studies have discussed the way religion relates to happiness. In "Correlates of Avowed Happiness," Wilson shows that religion is more prevalent in happier people and suggests that this correlation may be the result of community membership and not necessarily belief in religion itself. Another component may have to do with ritual, according to a 2009 article in *Frontiers in Evolutionary Neuroscience*.

According to the *Humboldt Kosmos* article,

> Non-religious people may take comfort in the knowledge that is it
> not intoxication or ecstasy that is important for lasting happiness
> but meaning and purpose. Anyone who recognizes what is most
> important to him or her in life and concentrates on it can experience
> this "value-based happiness" that gives life meaning. There are many
> ways in which one can increase his or her likelihood of happiness. One
> has only to know what to do and what not to do. There is, indeed, a
> link between happiness and knowledge: the knowledge of what we
> can do to be happy. Consequently, answers to the question of hap-
> piness may be found precisely where you would least expect them:
> in science. That may surprise many, because to most people, science
> and happiness are not compatible. Science is objective, cold, cerebral,
> and calculating; happiness, on the other hand, is subjective, warm,
> and a gut feeling. For example, science helps us to better understand
> why desiring something is not the same as owning or consuming it.
> Positive psychology helps to scientifically study the strengths and
> virtues that enable individuals and communities to thrive.

Who is happy? "A Comparison of Contemporary American Notions of Happiness
to the Epicurean View" points out the following:

> People who are viewed as happy in our culture today are also seen
> as being rich, having a big house, and holding a great occupation.
> Our society is attracted to material things rather than spiritual ones.
> Can a person who does not have these items still live a happy life?
> Epicurus believed that each one of us could achieve true happiness,
> and our only problem is that we stubbornly search for it in all the
> wrong places. Epicurus states that we only need three things to be
> happy besides the essentials needed for survival: family and friends,
> freedom, and an analytical life.

For the latter, science and art both help.

# References

"A Comparison of Contemporary American Notions of Happiness to the Epicurean View." https://www.123helpme.com/a-comparison-of-contemporary-american-notions-of-happiness-to-the-epicurean-view-preview.asp?id=178416.

"Nr. 97 / Humboldt kosmos. Das Magazin der Alexander von Humboldt-Stiftung. Glück Happiness." http://docplayer.org/30723126-Nr-97-humboldt-kosmos-das-magazin-der-alexander-von-humboldt-stiftung-glueck-happiness.html.

Schueller, Stephen & E.P. Seligman, Martin. (2010). Pursuit of pleasure, engagement, and meaning: Relationships to subjective and objective measures of well-being. The Journal of Positive Psychology. 5. 253-263. 10.1080/17439761003794130.

Tahiliani, Devidas. *Live and Let Live Under One G-O-D*. Pittsburgh, PA: Rosedog Books, 2016.

Wilson, W. "Correlates of Avowed Happiness." *Psychological Bulletin* 67, no. 4 (April 1967): 294–306. https://www.ncbi.nlm.nih.gov/pubmed/6042458.

"World Map of Happiness." *Humboldt kosmos*. http://www.humboldt-foundation.de/web/kosmos-cover-story-97-2.html www.123helpme.com.

# Get Richer, Live Longer

*Money does not bring happiness, but it is nice to reach that conclusion through experiment.*

According to "Unequal America," by Elizabeth Gudrais, income inequality has risen steadily in the United States in recent decades. After World War II, the top 1 percent of earners took home less than 10 percent of all income, and this continued through the 1960s and 1970s. Since then, their share of income has risen—to 15 percent in 1996, 20.3 percent in 2006, and 23 percent in 2012. This increase reflects the upward move of money, as salaries have grown significantly at the top. According to Gudrais, in 1965 the average salary for a CEO of a major US company was 25 times the salary of the average worker. Today, the average CEO's pay is more than 250 times that of the average worker. Further detail may be found in "An Epidemic of Extinctions," by Emily Dugan.

Why may this be considered a problem? Gudrais refers to some published studies showing that, for example, the life expectancy for Americans at the upper 5 percent of income is nine years longer than those at the lower 10 percent. According to data published by the United Nations, Japan comes second only to Denmark in terms of equal-income distribution among its inhabitants. The life expectancy at birth for the Japanese is 82.3 years, compared with 77.9 for Americans, even though per-capita GDP in the United States is about $10,000 more than in Japan.

Between 1983 and 1999 in the United States, men's life expectancy decreased in more than fifty counties according to a recent study by Ezzati, an associate professor of international health at the Harvard School of Public Health, and his colleagues. For women, the news is even worse: life expectancy decreased in more than nine hundred counties. As a result, the United States no longer boasts anywhere near the world's longest life expectancy. It doesn't even make the top forty. It also ranks twenty-first among the thirty nations in the Organization for Economic Cooperation and Development in terms of life expectancy.

Considering the present income distribution, it seems that Americans would elect leaders whose policies favor the poor and middle class. In 2004, the mean household income in the United States was $60,528, but the median (50-50 point) was only $43,389. This means that more than half of American households earned less than $60,528. Gudrais says that we might conclude that more than half of voters should favor policies that redistribute income from the top down. Instead, nations—and individual states—with high inequality levels tend to favor policies that allow the affluent to hang on to their money. In my view, this is mainly because Americans look at countries who have adopted such approaches and assess the outcome. For example, Canada the second largest country in the world, with a large volume of natural resources and population comparable to that of California, has an economy almost 30 percent below California's. Furthermore, a large number of talented Canadians choose to live in the United States. I spent more than a year in Canada, and it's clear to me that the breadth of services available in the United States is hard to find in countries such as Canada. The number and quality of academic institutions in the United States is admirable, and in my opinion, no free education or university can achieve the level of top private institutions that exist here.

Also, it is known that Americans, on average, have a higher tolerance for income inequality than their European counterparts. In fact, American attitudes focus on equality of opportunity rather than on equality of income. Many Americans believe that inequality serves to motivate and acts on the human psyche to elicit hard work and high achievements, even though it makes people more individualistic. Gudrais and Dugan point out that Americans, perhaps motivated by inequality and the prospect of getting ahead, work longer hours than their European counterparts—about two hundred more hours per year, on average, than the British and four hundred more hours per year than the Swedes.

## References

Dugan, Emily. "An Epidemic of Extinctions: Decimation of Life on Earth." *Independent*, May 16, 2008. https://www.independent.co.uk/environment/nature/an-epidemic-of-extinctions-decimation-of-life-on-earth-829325.html.

Ezzati, Majid, et al. "The Reversal of Fortunes: Trends in County Mortality and Cross-Country Mortality Disparities in the United States." *PLoS Medicine*, Public Library of Science, Apr. 2008, www.ncbi.nlm.nih.gov/pubmed/18433290.

Gudrais, Elizabeth. "Unequal America." *Harvard Magazine*, July 1, 2008. http://www.precaution.org/lib/08/prn_unequal_america.080701.htm.

Organic Consumers Association. https://www. organicconsumers.com.

"UNdata | Record View | Life Expectancy at Birth for Both Sexes Combined (Years)." *United Nations*, United Nations, data.un.org/Data.aspx?q=life expectancy&d= PopDiv&f=variableID:68.

# Wildfires

*An increasingly destructive and costly disaster*

Among all disasters, natural or man-made, wildfires often appear at the top of the most destructive list We all remember the 2017 and 2018 California wildfires and the extent of their destruction.

Though a natural and beneficial part of many forest ecosystems, fires are often a big challenge for communities on the west coast. Some believe that the frequency of large wildfires and the total area they burn have steadily increased as a result of more fuel for forest fires, longer fire seasons, drier conditions, and increased frequency of lightning. It is projected that the overall area burned across eleven western states area will double by the late century if the average summer temperature increases by 2.9 degrees Fahrenheit. The states hit particularly hard will include Montana, Wyoming, New Mexico, and Utah.

Since 1970, according to "Wildfires and Climate Change," the area consumed by large wildfires has more than doubled, and the season on average is 78 days longer.

> Wildfire risk depends on a number of factors, including temperature, soil moisture, and the presence of trees, shrubs, and other potential fuel. All these factors have strong ties to climate variability and climate change. Warmer temperatures and drier conditions increase the chances of a fire starting and help a burning fire spread. Such conditions also contribute to the spread of the mountain pine beetle and other insects that can weaken or kill trees, building up the fuels in a forest. Although our choices regarding land use and firefighting tactics can also play a role in lowering or raising risks, observed and anticipated changes in climate have and are expected to increase the area affected by wildfires in the United States.

See also www.c2es.org.

According to "Wildfires and Climate Change,"

> Since the year 2000, 10 forest fires in the United States have caused at least $1 billion in damages each, mainly from the loss of homes and infrastructure along with firefighting costs. In 2015, wildfires burned more than 10.1 million acres across the country—the highest annual total acreage burned since record keeping began in 1960. The costliest fires occurred in California, where more than 2,500 structures were destroyed in the Valley and Butte wildfires. In 2011, the Las Concha's Fire in New Mexico became the state's largest in history by a factor of three. In 2012, that record was broken as the Whitewater-Baldy Complex fire burned nearly twice as many acres as the Las Concha's Fire. Wildfires burned more than 9 million acres in 2012. Colorado's two most destructive fires ever—the Waldo Canyon and High Park fires—happened during this particularly destructive season.

"Wildfires and Climate Change" also mentions that the estimates of the percentage increase in the area burned in regions across the West for a 1.8 degrees Fahrenheit, 1 degree Celsius warming. The different regions correspond to different "eco provinces," which distinguish areas with distinctive vegetation types and climate conditions. Values are drawn from median burn estimates from a fire model. According to the National Research Council, all areas exhibit increases; many show a double increase (i.e., value shown is more than 100 percent) and some areas show a fivefold increase (i.e., value shown is more than 400 percent). Damage to homes and other buildings can be substantial, in part from the recent and rapid development of areas near fire-prone forests. The number of homes near forests and at risk of wildfire has increased over the past two decades. As a result, according to "The Rising Cost of Fire Operations," US Forest Service fire suppression expenditures have risen from 16 percent of their appropriated budget to more than 50 percent. State wildfire expenditures also increased substantially. While more buildings add to the risk of damage from natural fires, the presence of people in wildlands increases the risk of fires starting. In fact, as many as 90 percent of wildfires in the United States are caused by people.

Finally, beyond direct damage to the landscape, several public health risks are related to wildfires. Smoke reduces air quality and can cause eye and respiratory illness, especially among children and the elderly. Wildfires can also hasten ecosystem changes and release large amounts of $CO_2$ into the atmosphere—contributing to further climate change.

## How Wildfires Affect Climate

As pointed out by Jennifer Judge Hensel in "How Wildfires Affect Climate," "Forest fires can affect the Earth's climate in several ways. They release greenhouse gases. They send soot and other aerosol particles into the atmosphere. And they change how the Earth's surface reflects sunlight, especially in areas where snow falls. Mark Flanner, assistant professor of atmospheric science, says that whether the ultimate effect is warming or cooling varies, as does how long these impacts last. The greenhouse gases are very long-lived, on the order of a century, while the smoke effects are short-lived, lasting roughly a week."

Chris Mooney writes the following in "The Really Scary Thing About Wildfires Is How They Can Worsen Climate Change":

> "In California, two-thirds of the carbon loss came from the six percent of the land that had burned in our nine-year period," says Patrick Gonzalez, a researcher with the National Park Service and lead author of the study. Since the study period ended (in 2010), the state has seen several more mega fires, including the gigantic 2013 Rim Fire, the third biggest ever in California's history, consuming over 257,000 acres. It is not just California. Many forest scientists today are signaling a disturbing idea: That forests across the world could, like California's, start to burn more, or burn in more devastating fires—ultimately contributing a volume of greenhouse gases that could be large enough to further stoke climate change. Which would be sadly ironic, in that these same scientists think climate change is making fires worse to begin with.

## References

Hensel, Jennifer Judge. "How Wildfires Affect Climate." *Michigan Engineering*, August 30, 2013. https://news.engin.umich.edu/2013/08/how-wildfires-affect-climate/.

Mooney, Chris. "The Really Scary Thing About Wildfires Is How They Can Worsen Climate Change." *Washington Post*, May 14, 2015. https://www.washingtonpost.

com/news/energyenvironment/wp/2015/05/14/how-massive-wildfires-can-actually-warm-the-planet/?utm_term=.28b3cfba16d6.

National Research Council. 2011. Climate Stabilization Targets: Emissions, Concentrations, and Impacts over Decades to Millennia. Washington, DC: The National Academies Press. https://doi.org/10.17226/12877.

US Forest Service. "The Rising Cost of Fire Operations: Effects on the Forest Service's Non-Fire Work." http://www.fs.fed.us/sites/default/files/2015-Fire-Budget-Report.pdf.

"Wildfires and Climate Change." http://www.c2es.org/content/wildfires-and-climate-change/.

# Road Rage and Aggressive Driving

*A good reason to embrace driverless cars*

Recent statistics reveal that road rage is far more dangerous than we may think. According to Wikipedia, "Road rage is aggressive or angry behavior exhibited by a driver ... including rude and offensive gestures, verbal insults, physical threats or dangerous driving methods targeted toward another driver or a pedestrian in an effort to intimidate or release frustration." Based on this description, most people who drive regularly encounter "road rage" in one form or another. The National Highway Traffic Safety Administration (NHTSA) defines road rage as when a driver commits moving traffic offenses so as to endanger other people or property; an assault with a motor vehicle or other dangerous weapon by the operator or passenger of one motor vehicle on the operator or passengers of another motor vehicle. Road rage can lead to altercations, assaults, and collisions that result in serious physical injuries or even death. The NHTSA makes a clear distinction between road rage and aggressive driving, where the former is a criminal charge and the latter a traffic offense. This definition of road rage places the blame on the driver.

According to an annual study by the American Automobile Association (AAA), on average there are more than 1,200 incidents of road rage in the United States each year, some of which end in serious injuries or even fatalities. These rates have risen yearly throughout the six years of the study. Also studies have shown that individuals with road rage are predominantly young (thirty-three years old on average) and 96.6 percent of them are male. There are many shocking examples of road rage. In Germany, for example, a gun-wielding truck driver who was arrested in 2013 was accused of firing at more than 762 vehicles, an exceptional case of road rage. According to authorities, the autobahn sniper was motivated by "annoyance and frustration with traffic."

The AAA has reported that learner drivers and driving instructors are becoming targets of road rage at an increasing rate. According to one study presented in en-wikipedia.org, people who customize their cars with stickers and other adornments are more prone to road rage. Road rage is not an official mental disorder recognized in the *Diagnostic and Statistical Manual of Mental Disorders*, although according to an article published by the Associated Press on June 2006, the behaviors typically associated with road rage can be the result of a disorder known as intermittent Explosive Disorder. This conclusion was drawn from surveys of some 9,200 adults in the United States between 2001 and 2003 and was funded by the National Institute of Mental Health.

## Road Rage Questionnaire

Road rage could happen to anybody. If you wonder if it could happen to you, ask yourself the following questions from www.melhimesinsurance.com:

- Do I regularly drive over the speed limit?
- Do I try to "beat" red lights because I am in a hurry?
- Do I tailgate or flash my headlights at a driver in front of me that I believe is driving too slowly?
- Do I honk the horn frequently?
- Do I ever use obscene gestures or otherwise communicate angrily at another drivers?

If you answered yes to any of these questions, it is possible that you are susceptible to road rage. If you answered no to the questions, you could be causing others to lash out with road rage.

Ask yourself the following questions as well (www.safemotorist.com):

- Do I frequently use my phone while driving, or otherwise drive while distracted?
- Do I keep my high beams on, regardless of oncoming traffic?
- Do I switch lanes or make turns without using my turn signal?
- Do I fail to check my blind spot before switching lanes to make sure I am not cutting someone off?

If you answered yes to any of these questions, you may be contributing to causing road rage in others.

## Some Statistics

The following statistics compiled from the NHTSA and the Auto Vantage auto club show that aggressive driving and road rage are causing serious problems on our roads.

- Sixty-six percent of traffic fatalities are caused by aggressive driving.
- Thirty-seven percent of aggressive driving incidents involve a firearm.
- Males under the age of nineteen are the most likely to exhibit road rage.
- Half of drivers who are on the receiving end of an aggressive behavior, such as horn honking, a rude gesture, or tailgating, admit to responding with aggressive behavior themselves.
- Over a seven-year period, 218 murders and 12,610 injuries are attributed to road rage.
- Two percent of drivers admit to trying to run an aggressor off the road!

## Final Word

What has been presented above may be added to the list of reasons in favor of driverless cars.

## References

AAA Foundation for Traffic Safety. http://aaafoundation.org/.

"Aggressive Driving and Road Rage." SafeMotorist.com.
https://www.safemotorist.com/articles/road_rage.aspx.

Cardone Law Firm. "Consequence of Road Rage."
https://www.louisianainjurylawyersblog.com/consequences-of-road-rage/.

"Road Rage." https://en.wikipedia.org/wiki/Road_rage.

Wellskopf, Jill Erin. "4 Signs You're an Aggressive Driver." Hupy and Abraham, S. C.
https://www.hupy.com/library/4-signs-you-re-an-aggressive-driver.cfm.

# Educational Systems: United States Versus Japan

*Diversity or homogeneity? We can learn a lot by comparing educational systems.*

When it comes to education, Japan is one of the countries ranked much higher than the United States in science, technology, engineering, and mathematics (STEM) programs. This is simply because of their elementary and high school educational systems.

Japan's national curriculum exposes students to a "balanced and basic education" known for its equal treatment of students. The United States does not have a national curriculum. Individual state boards of education set statewide curriculums and students do not specialize in any specific field of study until, at the earliest, their second year of college. However, some schools offer elective courses that are in specific areas of study that students may take. In most cases, students are taking broad courses without any specialization. Also, Japanese schools are more focused on "narrow and deep" learning, whereas the United States has a more "wide and shallow" approach. Some states consider a 70 as a passing grade, but several others require only a 60. According to Craig Wieczorek, Japan has a universal scoring code, which allows all students to be compared with each other. Wieczorek points out the differences between Japanese and American teachers and administrators:

> Japanese schools enforce a shared system of "high-quality" teaching and learning. Students are required to wear school uniforms from elementary to high school and are never sent to the principal for bad behavior. Instead, teachers communicate with the parents. Japanese schools employ one principal and one assistant principal or "headmaster" teacher who is active in the classroom as well. Also, homeroom teachers are required to visit homes after school to meet with parents, build good relations, and communicate students' strengths and weaknesses. They believe that parental involvement is strongly

associated with the students' success. It seems that the whole-class instruction and a comprehensive approach play a large role in the Japanese students' academic success. In contrast, American schools have a split in their approach to student success. A strict structure with a large staff of specialists raises student isolation and a negative climate is created through standardized testing. American schools lack a comprehensive and nurturing approach to education.

Clearly, all these factors lead to a difference in students' attitudes toward learning. Japanese students are highly motivated and continually strive to reach the top in anything they participate in. This difference can be created by teachers, society, and the media. In Japan, teaching is highly respected and remains an honored profession. Teachers' high social status comes from the Japanese culture and public recognition of their important social responsibilities. In contrast, teaching in the United States is not seen as an honored profession. Some secondary education teachers apply for the job because the schooling itself is easier and they get "time off" after their 180-day school year. Also, because of the low pay, most American students try to get into professions other than teaching. Americans need to realize that we are falling behind in our educational systems. We should examine systems in other countries, such as Japan, and focus more on the future of our education system in the changing world.

## References

Wieczorek, Craig C. "Comparative Analysis of Educational Systems of American and Japanese Schools: Views and Visions." *Educational Horizons* 86, no. 2 (Winter 2008): 99–111. https://files.eric.ed.gov/fulltext/EJ781668.pdf.

# Chapter 2
## World/United States

*The world is now like an ocean; a storm in any part will affect other parts.*

*When I look at the world, guess what I see.*
*Lots of hate and grief; I do not want it to be.*
*See what some put others through for their own gain,*
*Things that could bring the world to its knees.*
*Even though the world is huge and we are small,*
*Our collective act could be harmful and make it fall.*

# Appreciate America

*America, a unique country*

I teach at a state university with an enrollment of around ten thousand students. Our students have several dining options on campus, but the Commons is the largest and most popular. The Commons is an all-you-can-eat cafeteria with an unbelievable variety of food organized in several separate sections. In addition to all types of sweets, such as cakes and ice cream, the dessert section even offers fresh-baked cookies just out of the oven. The cost of eating at the Commons is surprisingly low, and yet some students complain.

I often remind them that what they have here is simply a dream to people in most other countries. To emphasize my point, I add that I know this because I have lived and worked in several other countries. How many students believe me and actually think about it for more than a few seconds, however, I'm not sure.

## The Other Extreme

The report titled *2018 World Hunger and Poverty Facts and Statistics* addresses the other extreme. The Food and Agriculture Organization of the United Nations produces reports on the state of food security and nutrition across the world. They estimate that worldwide, about 800 million people, or one in nine, were suffering from chronic undernourishment from 2014 to 2016. Of these, 780 million lived in developing countries, representing 12.9 percent, or one in eight, of the population of these countries. Asia is home to two out of three of the world's undernourished people. There are also eleven million undernourished people in developed countries.

The *2018 World Hunger* report also references a study by the World Bank Group. According to their estimates, as of 2016 there were 900 million poor people in developing countries who lived on $1.90 a day or less. As expected, children were the most visible victims of undernutrition. According to estimates, undernutrition in aggregate was a cause of 3.1 million child deaths—or 45 percent of all child deaths—in 2011. It is well known that undernutrition also magnifies the effect of every disease, including measles and malaria.

Unfortunately, all of this happens while the world produces enough food to feed everyone. For the world as a whole, per capita food availability was about 2790 kcal/person/day from 2006 to 2008. For developing countries, availability is over 2640 kcal/person/day. The principal problem is that many people in the world still do not have sufficient income to purchase—or land to grow—enough food.

## Poverty in America

The Office of the Assistant Secretary for Planning and Evaluation publishes information regarding poverty guidelines. Recently, the US Department of Health and Human Services set the poverty threshold for a single person as $12,140. The United States Census Bureau also publishes statistics related to income and poverty. During 2017, the official national poverty rate was 12.3 percent, or 39.7 million people. According to the US Department of Agriculture Economic Research Service in 2017, households that had higher rates of food insecurity than the national average included households with children (15.7 percent), households with children headed by single women (30.3 percent) or single men (19.7 percent), Black non-Hispanic households (21.8 percent), and Hispanic households (18 percent). An article titled "Hunger in America: Hunger and Poverty Facts and Statistics" lists the twelve states with statistically significantly higher poverty rates than the US national average (13.7 percent.) as Mississippi (20.8 percent), Arkansas (19.2 percent), Louisiana (18.4 percent), Alabama (17.6 percent), Kentucky (17.6 percent), Ohio (16.1 percent), Oregon (16.1 percent), North Carolina (15.9 percent), Maine (15.8 percent), Oklahoma (15.5 percent), Texas (15.4 percent), and Tennessee (15.1 percent).

## Poverty in Numbers

There is an array of publications estimating the poverty, hunger, income, and malnutrition across the world. See, for example, "Hunger Statistics," published by the Food Aid Foundation. To put into perspective the scope of what half of the world's population faces, here is what poverty looks like in numbers: Over eight hundred million people worldwide do not have enough food to eat. Every day 8,500 children die from malnutrition. Three billion people live on less than $2.50 a day. More than

1.2 billion live in extreme poverty on less than $1.25 a day. In comparison, the poverty threshold for a single person in the United States is $33 a day. In addition, poor people in developing countries spend around 60 to 80 percent of their income on food, while Americans spend less than 10 percent of their income on food.

## Concluding Remarks

As Americans, let us be more appreciative of our country and what it offers. We have a variety of food available to us, as well as kind, generous, and caring people; innovative and productive institutions; some of the best universities in the world; freedom of speech and lifestyle; and the opportunity to grow and succeed. These and so many other aspects of American life are things that people in other countries can only dream about.

## References

England, Gary. "Hunger in America: Hunger and Poverty Facts and Statistics." Marion County Community Ministries. May 1, 2017. http://mccmfbgn.org/Results/?p=1817.

Food and Agriculture Organization of the United Nations. "2018: The State of Food Security and Nutrition in the World." http://www.fao.org/state-of-food-security-nutrition/en/.

Food Aid Foundation. "Hunger Statistics." http://www.foodaidfoundation.org/world-hunger-statistics.html.

Office of the Assistant Secretary for Planning and Evaluation, US Department of Health and Human Services. "Poverty Guidelines." https://aspe.hhs.gov/poverty-guidelines.

US Department of Agriculture, Economic Research Service. "Food Security in the U.S." https://www.ers.usda.gov/topics/food-nutrition-assistance/food-security-in-the-us/key-statistics-graphics.aspx.

US Census Bureau. "Income and Poverty in the United States: 2017," September 12, 2018. Report #P60-263. https://www.census.gov/library/publications/2018/demo/p60-263.html.

US Census Bureau. "Income, Poverty and Health Insurance Coverage in the United States: 2014," September 16, 2015. Release #CB15-157. https://www.census.gov/newsroom/press-releases/2015/cb15-157.html.

World Bank. "Poverty: Overview." https://www.worldbank.org/en/topic/poverty/overview.

World Hunger Education Service. "2018 World Hunger and Poverty Facts and Statistics." *Hunger Notes.* https://www.worldhunger.org/world-hunger-and-poverty-facts-and-statistics/.

# Presidential Coincidence

*Once upon a time, Americans cared more about the Fourth of July than the Super Bowl. Now such an event is an example of coincidences.*

There are many stories about the presidents of the United States, some so unlikely and surprising that they are classified as coincidences. One of the most famous and well-studied coincidences is the connection between Abraham Lincoln and John F. Kennedy, which spans a full century. Here are a few examples:

- Abraham Lincoln was elected to Congress in 1846, and John F. Kennedy in 1946.
- Lincoln was elected President in 1860, and Kennedy in 1960.
- Andrew Johnson, who succeeded Lincoln, was born in 1808. Lyndon Johnson, who succeeded Kennedy, was born in 1908.
- John Wilkes Booth, who assassinated Lincoln, was born in 1839. Lee Harvey Oswald, who assassinated Kennedy, was born in 1939.

## Coincidences

A coincidence is a surprising concurrence of events perceived as meaningfully related, but with no apparent causal connection. Because coincidences are puzzling, we sometimes overreact to them. Perhaps it's our biology that makes coincidences seem more meaningful than they really are, tempting us to search for reason, explanation, or pattern. Some people consider them insignificant, arguing that the world is so large that anything could happen and so small that weird things happen all the time. People who look for patterns do so because we are pattern-seeking animals; we quickly forget uninteresting patterns, but we pay attention and remember the interesting ones. For instance, basketball fans notice sequences of successful shots, but they ignore other equally unlikely but uninteresting occurrences. People who win the lottery often attribute their winning to having chosen a special number pattern, but they ignore the fact that all numbers are equally unlikely and thus the role of luck in their success. In short, many events or incidences classified as coincidences are bound to happen, even though the particular form of, a coincidence is unpredictable.

Some coincidences are not as unlikely as we think. A classic example is the birthday match, which surprises some people so much that they refer to it as a coincidence. With only twenty-three people in one place, the chance of two or more people having the same birthday is more than 50 percent. With forty, it is almost 90 percent. The number of people needed to have a 50 percent chance of three, four, five, and six people with the same birthday are just 88, 187, 313, and 460 respectively. Rather than being a coincidence, two family members or friends sharing a birthday is actually a commonplace event.

## A Presidential Coincidence

One strange historical coincidence concerns the early presidents of the United States. Among the first five presidents—Washington, Adams, Jefferson, Madison, and Monroe—three of them (Adams, Jefferson, and Monroe) died on the same day of the year. That date was none other than the Fourth of July. Of all the dates to die on, that must surely be the most significant to any American. The probability that three people out of five die in the same day of the year is about one in five million. That three of our earliest presidents died on July 4 make this coincidence even more surprising. To the early presidents, the anniversary of independence meant so much that they were keen to hang on until they had reached it.

## Likelihood

Assuming that all days are equally likely, the chance that a randomly selected individual might die on July 4 is $1/365$. The chance that three randomly selected individuals all die on July 4 is therefore $(1/365) * (1/365) * (1/365)$. The chance that out of five people, three specific individuals die on July 4, while the other two die on other days, is

$$(1/365) * (1/365) * (1/365) * (364/365) * (364/365) = (1/365)^3 * (364/365)^2.$$

Rather than three specific individuals, if we require only that any three people out of five die on July 4, then we must consider the number of ways we can divide those five people into a group of three and a group of two. There are ten ways to divide five people into more than two groups. Putting everything together, the chance that three of five people would die on July 4 is $10 \, (1/365)^3 (364/365)^2$. This is equal to 0.0000002045, which is less than 0.0000002384 or $(1/2)^{22}$. Put in different terms, the chance that three people out of five would die on Independence Day is less likely than flipping a coin twenty-two times and getting all heads. Obviously, such an event is extremely unlikely, which provides evidence that the deaths of Presidents Jefferson, Adams, and Monroe on the same day cannot be attributed to chance alone.

## Statistical Test

We can also analyze this event by testing the following hypotheses:

H1: Coincidence (null hypothesis) and H2: Not a coincidence (alternative hypothesis). Clearly all we can do is to provide evidence for or against each hypothesis and draw a conclusion. We already showed that the probability of this event is very low. This probability, known as the P-value, plays a key role in decision making. In this case, *low* means less than the chosen level of significance. Low probability provides evidence that what occurred was not a commonplace event. In other words, an event like this cannot occur as a result of chance alone. The event with low probability is not expected to occur, so its occurrence indicates that our assumption (null hypothesis) is not valid.

## References

American Patriot Friends Network. www.apfn.org.

# The United States, an Amazing Country

*Everything considered, the United States has made the world a better place for all. Regardless of where we live, we are all, to some degree, American.*

The United States is an amazing country. Globally, it tops the list when it comes to productivity, economy, science, technology, and military. This country has more Nobel prizes winners than the next five countries combined and many unique institutions. It is home to a wide range of people with various physical appearances, skin colors, nationalities, ethnicities, religion, and political views. Open to liberal ideas, Americans also hold conservative values and views concerning some critical issues.

Unfortunately the same cannot be said about social issues, despite the fact that Americans are among the most generous, caring people on earth. In fact, despite all the initiatives and efforts, the gap between poor and rich continues to grow, spawning problems and unrest. Some reasons contributing to this situation are discussed below.

First, the United States is home to a great deal of unreal expectations. This is especially true among American youth, partly because popular media, their 24-7-365 school, promotes so much fantasy and fiction. Popular media tells us that most Americans are wealthy, healthy, and enjoy a comfortable life. But we all know this not true, and being forced to face reality is disappointing and often leads to negativity and anger.

Second, American role models tend to be actors, singers, and athletes, rather than people such as inventors, scientists, writers, and community leaders. School children look up to football players and cheerleaders. Kids who are good in math and science are called names, bullied, and make fun of. Young people who aren't athletic or lack social charm are often left out and become disappointed, depressed, and occasionally see themselves as losers.

Third, it seems that one cause of crime and unrest in the United States relates to men's obsession with sex and the lack of legalized prostitution. Studies such as "Comparing Sex Buyers with Men Who Do Not Buy Sex" have confirmed this. Many social scientists believe that for people who do not have charm, time, or skill, prostitution provides a form of release. It decreases tension in the society and reduces the level of crime against women, especially in open societies such as the United States. Some people find it puzzling that in a country considered the global leader of capitalism, the only thing that can't be bought is sex, despite the fact that most women believe they have the right to use their bodies however they please.

The negative effects of the absence of legal prostitution are exacerbated by the media's obsession with sex. Why should television newscasters be young and good-looking? Why do competitive sports need cheerleaders, and why should they be young and sexy? Why is everything somehow related to sex? What is the effect of this on guys watching sports? Does it encourage addiction to sexual fantasies, and is it healthy? Middle Eastern countries have tried to ease this problem by asking women to dress conservatively and not showing sexy images on television. Most European countries, on the other hand, have legalized prostitution.

Next, most news media in the United States earn money through advertising that depends upon viewership and ratings. To attract viewers, they often look for sensational news and stories. News media consider individuals and groups as important, or not important, based on their news value. This is especially true for identifiable individuals and groups. Athletes, actors, singers, and population segments such as women and African-Americans have high news value. People serving in the military or Peace Corps, scientists, nerds, community leaders, and population segments such as Native Americans and Latinos have much less news value.

Although there is noticeable discrimination against old, ugly, and fat people, such people are rarely discussed in the media. At the same time, discrimination against certain minorities is magnified and presented unfairly for its news value. News related to the White House and controversial politicians, especially their sex lives, has high news value, while political issues, such as elections, in the rest of the world do not.

Sometimes the news media even attempt to keep a newsmaker conflict ongoing and fresh, no matter the price, or they create so-called heroes and role models while ignoring real heroes. Major television networks have devoted significant air time to the lives and deaths of entertainers such as Aretha Franklin, Prince, and Whitney Houston, but almost none to the lives and accomplishments of major scientists or Nobel Prize recipients whose effects on our lives are obvious and priceless. I often ask my students to name any American scientist, but of course they cannot. However, they all know the names of popular rappers, football players, and so on. Finally, the news media spends significantly more time on negative news than on positive news.

## Effects

In a media-driven society, people feed off the media and the media feeds off people's interests and focus. We often fall into traps created by politicians and the media who coerce us into buying their news and views. Some people become addicted to certain types of news, including fake news, which plants hatred and can lead to anxiety and anger, sometimes for life. To escape this, some people try to look at different aspects of the issues and use multiple sources. This, of course, requires having easy access to international media, knowing other languages, and learning to be open to outside views.

Finally, the United States has basically a two-party political system. People often choose a party for personal reasons and then accept that party's views as truth, blaming the other party for not caring about our country and its problems. Some people experience chronic anger and even hatred for opposition leaders, which creates an unhealthy environment. A related issue is the limited choices that exist in a two-party system. When people disagree with the policies of one party, their only choice is the other party, which explains why political power swings back and forth between the two parties.

## References

Farley, Melissa, Emily Schuckman, Jacqueline M. Golding, Kristen Houser, Laura Jarrett, Peter Qualliotine, and Michele Decker. "Comparing Sex Buyers with Men Who Don't Buy Sex." Paper presented at Psychologists for Social Responsibility Annual Meeting, July 15, 2011, Boston, MA. http://www.prostitutionresearch.com/pdfs/Farleyetal2011ComparingSexBuyers.pdf.

# Are Americans Healthy?

*Americans are not the gold standard of health, but I'm not sure whether they really want to be, as they are not ready to give up life's little pleasures.*

Most Americans believe that they are indeed healthy. However, according to Paul Loprinzi et al., only 3 percent of Americans meet the basic requirements for a healthy lifestyle. This study defined a healthy lifestyle as moderate or vigorous exercise for at least 150 minutes a week, a diet score in the top 40 percent on the Healthy Eating Index, a body fat percentage under 20 percent (for men) and under 30 percent (for women), and lastly, not smoking. Loprinzi et al. looked at a sample of 4,745 people who participated in the 2003–2006 National Health and Nutrition Examination Survey. In this survey, physical activity was measured with an accelerometer, which each participant wore for a week, and their diet was scored based on a 24-hour food diary. Some requirements were easier to meet than others. The results showed that 71.5 percent of adults were nonsmokers, 46.5 percent did enough exercise, 37.9 percent had a healthy diet, but only 9.6 percent had what the study defines as a normal body-fat percentage. Lastly, only 2.7 percent of people met all four requirements.

"Americans Far Less Healthy, Die Younger than Global Peers" includes information related to life span and health care. According to "U.S. Health in International Perspective: Shorter Lives, Poorer Health," even though the United States spends significantly more on health care than most other countries combined, Americans live shorter, unhealthier lives compared with other high-income countries. This report by the National Institutes of Health compares the health statistics in sixteen high-income democracies in western Europe, Australia, Canada, and Japan. The United States was ranked last in most categories. Dr. Steven H. Woolf, chairman of the committee that wrote the report, said on *PBS NewsHour*, "The U.S. is doing worse than these other countries both in terms of life expectancy and health throughout their entire lives. This is a pervasive problem from birth to old age; it affects everyone and has been a long-standing problem."

A large number of studies agree that Americans in general are not healthy. Of course, there are Americans who have healthy lifestyles, but that number is slim. Americans are choosing easy options rather than healthy options, more likely to visit a drive through at a fast-food restaurant than stay at home and cook. Many Americans prefer staying in and playing video games or watching TV, instead of going out and taking a walk on a nice day.

## Summary Statistics

Most Americans are not healthy. Many people assume that just eating fruit or salad makes them healthy, but they're not getting the necessary nutrients and exercising. According to the US Department of Health & Human Services, fewer than 5 percent of adults get thirty minutes of physical activity per day. Most middle-aged adults focus on what they call a "good life." Children spend their time watching television or playing on their phones and computers, rather than actually taking time to go outside and play. Statistics show that children spend a minimum of eight hours a day on some type of electronic device. Nationwide, about 25 percent of people with a disability are reported as being physically inactive, compared with the 15 percent who are not disabled but are physically inactive.

Surprisingly, less than 5 percent of adults participate in at least thirty minutes of exercise a day, in spite of the fact that adults often make plans to exercise more, especially around the new year. They join gyms, but more than 60 percent give up within the first month or two. That leaves 40 percent who manage to go to the gym, but not regularly. A lot of Americans think that if they exercise, they can treat themselves to things such as ice cream and fast food, and some have dessert after even a short exercise session.

## References

"Americans Far Less Healthy, Die Younger Than Global Peers, Study Finds." *PBS NewsHour*, January 9, 2013. https://www.pbs.org/newshour/health/report-americans-less-healthy-die-younger-than-global-peers.

Beck, Julie. "Less Than 3 Percent of Americans Live a 'Healthy Lifestyle.'" *The Atlantic*, March 23, 2016. https://www.theatlantic.com/health/archive/2016/03/less-than-3-percent-of-americans-live-a-healthy-lifestyle/475065/.

Loprinzi, Paul D., Adam Branscum, June Hanks, and Ellen Smit. "Healthy Lifestyle Characteristics and Their Joint Association with Cardiovascular Disease Biomarkers in US Adults." *Mayo Clinic Proceedings* 91, no. 4 (April 2016): 432–442. https://www.mayoclinicproceedings.org/article/S0025-6196(16)00043-4/abstract.

US Department of Health and Human Services. "Facts & Statistics: Physical Activity." https://www.hhs.gov/fitness/resource-center/facts-and-statistics/index.html.

"U.S. Health in International Perspective: Shorter Lives, Poorer Health." Panel on Understanding Cross-National Health Differences Among High-Income Countries; National Institutes of Health. http://sites.nationalacademies.org/DBASSE/CPOP/US_Health_in_International_Perspective/index.htm#.UO2oiaw71vd.

# Election Drama

*Would Americans ever forget the drama of the 2016 election?*

I wrote this note in response to the 2016 election drama and the anger expressed by some of my family members and friends. It isn't my goal to insult anybody or to claim that my views are right or even relevant. I respect other people's opinions and believe that communication is the best approach for conflict resolution. I think that the current climate of disrespecting others is completely counterproductive because (1) regardless of their political views, almost all people love their country, and (2) others people's happiness is part of our happiness. With this in mind, let us ask the following question: how and why did America reach this point, and whose fault was it?

Looking back at the last thirty to forty years, it's apparent that we all contributed to what has happened, some more than others. This was not caused by one party, one race, or one religion, but by everybody. Some people contributed by doing nothing, and others by doing the wrong things. We pushed our country to the limit in several directions and let our divide grow bigger and bigger. We stopped communicating, believing in unity, and learning from history. We stopped interacting with each other and focused on interacting with smart devices.

We restricted ourselves to certain media—American news sources that aligned with our own political views—and followed their logic and reasoning. Occasionally we even allowed them to brainwash us. We fell into the trap of believing that everything bad is the fault of certain groups or a specific political party. With the help of the media, we gradually separated ourselves from the rest of the world, believing that we knew better and had nothing to learn from them. We practically isolated ourselves from the rest of the world.

We let Hollywood define our values, and we chose entertainers and athletes as our heroes and role models. We watched reality shows and pushed learning channels, the History Channel, the Discovery Channel, and the National Geographic channel aside. We created an environment in which our children look up to athletes and entertainers rather than scientists, inventors, and public servants. We didn't educate ourselves and our children about the differences between the political parties and their ideologies. Instead, we used the false logic of taking the behavior of a few as representative of those ideologies. We didn't realize that the media's top goal is ratings and that what really matters to the media is not the person but the person's news value. They made us think that the world is black and white, and that if you're not a follower of one party, you have to follow the other party. We got used to a two-party system so that every time a third party started growing, we joined forces and destroyed them.

We saw globalization as a useful idea and joined the rest of the world in promoting it, without realizing that globalization makes some communities feel they are gradually losing their livelihood, identity, and freedom of action while trying to reshape, recreate, or readjust to the rapid changes occurring around the world. Moreover, the massive shift of people, capital, and production systems has made many individuals and groups vulnerable and anxious, and as a result, it has created an environment of frustration, conflict, and social unrest.

Now rather than getting angry, torturing ourselves, fighting, making fun of each other, and breaking up with our family members and friends, let us think a little deeper. The system needs to be changed and repaired. The blame game is not a solution, but another problem. Politicians are by definition politicians, mostly tricky and mostly wealthy. Few politicians are trustworthy and really care about the middle class and poor, simply because the poor and the middle class cannot give them what the rich can. Most of them just want our vote, nothing more.

We need to go back to basics and carefully look at the teachings of the founders of our democracy. We need to learn to appreciate the contributions of some amazing people and institutions who quietly push this country and the world forward. We need a media that values such individuals more than athletes, singers and actors. We need to demand access to media from other countries, rejoin the rest of the world, and compare our system to others. We need to demand to know what our country is doing in various parts of the world and what could be the consequences of those actions. We need to ask more questions and respect people who practice what they preach.

# Unhappiness and Unrest

*People hardly ask if you are happy. Maybe somebody knows*
*how to be happy or where happy people live.*

In recent years, the world has witnessed many riots and other forms of social violence, causing fear and raising many questions. What are the reasons behind the recent unrest? Does it result from factors such as immigration, discrimination, or income inequality? Is it caused by the internet and social media such as Facebook and Instagram? Finally, is this a phenomenon only in certain poor countries, or is it universal?

Clearly, most contributing factors manifest themselves in what we may refer to as unhappiness. Unlike the energy spent to create opportunity and reduce income equality, factors affecting citizens' happiness have been neglected in both literature and government policy. Much research, such as what we read about in "The Drivers of Happiness Inequality," has been done on happiness and inequality. Research on happiness has shown, for example, that income inequality is not the main driver of happiness inequality. Governments can adopt simple, inexpensive policies to enhance happiness and reduce happiness inequality, which can reduce both political and social tensions. Not even the world's superpower, the United States, which has made significant economic and technological progress, has achieved a significant gain in the self-reported happiness of its citizenry. In fact, recent political and social unrest indicates a high level of unhappiness, anxiety, social distrust, and lack of confidence in government. Even the richest Americans are only marginally happier than the average American, and life satisfaction has remained nearly constant during decades of rising Gross National Product (GNP) per capita.

Would higher levels of community happiness and lower levels of happiness inequality reduce these tensions? Why are people happier in some countries than in others? Why do some countries experience more crime and social unrest than others, and what factors contribute to this? The happiness map produced by the United Nations indicates that the happiest countries in the world are mostly in northern Europe, while the least happy countries are in Sub-Saharan Africa. Research tells us that at an individual level, it is not wealth but personal freedom, good mental and physical health, job security, and stable families that make people happy. We also know that other contributing factors include the type of government, political freedom, scarcity of corruption, and presence of strong social services.

We need to determine whether there is any connection between happiness at individual and community levels. Most people with whom I've talked see a strong connection. One simple reason is that we often compare ourselves to others and become unhappy when we see or feel inequality. Scientific examinations of happiness by psychiatrists such as Manfred Spitzer have revealed that happy people are less egoistic, aggressive, abusive, and prone to illness. They are also more sociable, understanding, tolerant, and successful with learning and work. Happy people are less likely to commit crimes and develop addictions. In fact, happy people are better citizens.

So what conclusions can we draw from this? I think, as is recognized in the World Happiness Report, there is a worldwide demand for attention to happiness, both individually and within communities. This means including community happiness as a major criterion for government policies. Countries that have paid attention to such issues have created better living conditions, resulting in healthier citizens and communities.

According to a *New York Daily News* article from 2015, Switzerland is the happiest country in the world, closely followed by Iceland. Denmark, Norway, Canada, Finland, the Netherlands, Sweden, New Zealand, and Australia all rank high. The top ten includes seven Western European countries, but the United States trails in fifteenth place, behind Israel and Mexico.

## References

Becchetti, Leonardo, Riccardo Massari, and Paolo Naticchioni. "The Drivers of Happiness Inequality: Suggestions for Promoting Social Cohesion." https://pdfs. semanticscholar.org/4a6b/4727fc35721647408e6eaa3d5d96bc6862ab.pdf.

"Switzerland Is the Happiest Country in the World; U.S. Is 15th: Study." *New York Daily News*, April 24, 2015. http://www.nydailynews.com/life-style/health/switzerland-happiest-country-world-u-s-15-article-1.2197221.

Helliwell, J., Layard, R., & Sachs, J. (2018). World Happiness Report 2018, New York: Sustainable Development Solutions Network.

# Korea: A Beautiful, Torn Country

*Could one day Koreans unite and start over?*

Recently, I became father-in-law to a beautiful South Korean lady and grandfather to a cute little girl. While attending the wedding in Seoul, I used the opportunity to tour South Korea, including the demilitarized zone and a border tunnel used by North Koreans for spying. While there, I wished I could cross the border to see how North Koreans live and how different it is from South Korea.

After separating at the end of World War II, these two countries walked quite different paths, adopting the political ideas of their occupiers. South Korea favored a democratic approach that led them to become one of the world's G-20 major economies. North Korea, led by a family dynasty, followed Russia and adopted a Communist system based on the Juche philosophy of self-sufficiency. Based on what we hear, we believe this decision turned the country into a bitterly poor and unpredictable nation, and not much else is known about North Korea. Information provided by the United Nations and other organizations deviates a great deal from reports by visitors, which makes it hard to do a thorough comparison.

Talking to a few locals, I learned that after living in South Korea for some time, a surprising number of North Korean refugees return to North Korea. What this indicates is hard to judge. I was also surprised to learn that South Korea often allocates local detectives to keep an eye on newly arrived North Korean defectors. Sometimes they even warn outspoken defectors that their names are on a target list of people whom the North Korean regime might try to eliminate.

## Media Effects

*Dangerous*, *isolated*, and *repressive* are words we usually associate with North Korea. Based on what we learn from news coverage, we also believe North Korea to be vastly different from South Korea. During my visit to the demilitarized zone, two people on the tour pointed out that trees on the North Korean side seemed a little mystical to them, and I personally had the same feeling. Also, as we got closer to North Korea, I experienced a faster heart rate for no apparent reason.

## A Major Question

Judging by what we know, it is clear that South Korea is in much better shape than North Korea, at least economically. Nevertheless, I still wonder how these nations compare themselves to each other. Do they still have similar views and values, follow the same traditions, and have the same focus? Has years of living under different governments changed their outlooks? Unfortunately, we may never find satisfactory answers to these questions. Remaining aloof from outside influence, North Korea has made sure that its people are well regulated and live in a controlled environment. According to the metrics of the free world, this is a recipe for poverty and unhappiness. South Korea, on the other hand, is westernized with an economy and social life similar to most democratic countries. This, as expected, has led to the usual advantages and disadvantages of a fast-paced life.

## Concluding Remarks

In Seoul, the capital city of South Korea, I witnessed a few unity demonstrations by South Koreans. As in other countries with comparable political situations, it was clear that the major problem is the leadership, not the people themselves. Leaders who have no checks or balances to their power tend to become corrupt, greedy, and thirsty for more power and dominance. As pointed out by Lord Acton, "Power tends to corrupt, and absolute power corrupts absolutely." This is surprisingly evident in the case of President Park Geun-hye, who was impeached by the South Korean National Assembly over a corruption scandal. If Koreans wish to reunite, the North should give its people more freedom to choose and perhaps an honest election. If this were to happen, the border would disappear just as the wall did in Berlin.

## References

Edward, J. & Acton, B. (1906). Letter 1, Macmillan and Co. Limited New York: The Macmillan Company.

# Vietnam

*An old enemy and yet a new friend.*

The history of Vietnam is full of affiliating with dominant civilizations and adapting their ideas, institutions, and technology to Vietnamese purposes and taste. As we read in Encyclopedia Britannica, this pattern is evident in Vietnam's historical relations with China and their combat and response, as descendants of Mandarins, to Western colonialism by becoming communists. After adopting this approach, Vietnam experienced a period of prolonged warfare in the mid-twentieth century that led to partitioning (1954–75), first militarily and later politically, into the Democratic Republic of Vietnam, better known as North Vietnam, and the Republic of Vietnam, usually called South Vietnam. Following reunification in April 1975, the Socialist Republic of Vietnam was established in July 1976.

## Geography and Society

From north to south, Vietnam extends about 1,025 miles and in the narrowest part is about thirty miles wide. It is bordered by Cambodia and Laos to the west, China to the north, the South China Sea to the east and south, and the Gulf of Thailand (Gulf of Siam) to the southwest. The estimated population of Vietnam is about 96,160,200 with a life expectancy of 73.7 years. The country is made up fifty-four officially recognized ethnicities and has only two major religions: 7.9 percent Buddhist and 6.65 percent Catholic. Almost 82 percent of Vietnamese profess no religion, and in 2015 the literacy rate was 94.5 percent.

## Economy

Like most countries in the area, Vietnam is densely populated. It is a developing country trying to move away from the rigidities of a centrally planned, highly agrarian economy to a more industrial and market-based economy. Since 1986 the country has raised its income substantially, exceeding its 2017 GDP growth target of 6.7 percent (currently 647.4 billion) with growth of 6.8 percent and inflation of 3.5 percent. Their success is primarily attributed to unexpected increases in domestic demand and strong manufacturing exports. Several factors make Vietnam an attractive country for investors—a stable political system, commitment to sustainable growth, relatively low inflation, stable currency, strong FDI inflows, strong manufacturing sector, commitment to continuing global economic integration, and a young and vibrant population.

## Views toward Americans

Most Americans who have traveled to Vietnam report that they were warmly welcomed. Some attribute this to the fact that most Vietnamese are under forty years old and thus have no first-hand memories of the war. According to the 2014 Global Attitudes Survey, it is fair to say that most Vietnamese have a positive mix of admiration and fascination for Americans and the United States. Possible reasons for this include:

1. the fact that seventy-five percent of Vietnamese were born after the war;
2. the economic hardships that people experienced under Communism;
3. an overwhelmingly positive view of capitalism;
4. the popularity of American culture, movies, music, and so on;
5. fascination with American lifestyle and innovations;
6. the success of countries, such as Japan and South Korea, who have close alliances with the United States; and
7. greater exposure to the United States and close encounters with American tourists.

Much of the credit for the relatively positive view of Vietnamese toward Americans should be given to Hanoi. Throughout the Vietnam War, the leadership in Hanoi generally maintained that their real enemy was the US government and military, rather than the people of the United States or even individual soldiers.

Finally, some tension might still exist among a small part of the older population in places that suffered during the war. However, most Vietnamese have forgiven the United States and now view Americans as their friends and partners.

## War Remnants Museum

The War Remnants Museum in Ho Chi Minh City, a popular tourist attraction, presents a one-sided view of war atrocities and defeats of the French and American military. One museum display, which floor many visitors, displays a quote from a speech made by Ho Chi Minh: "All men are endowed by their Creator with certain unalienable Rights; among these are Life, Liberty, and the pursuit of Happiness." Ho Chi Minh admired and studied another well-known revolutionary, Thomas Jefferson. According to "The War Remnants Museum" on quora.com, "It is oddly ironic that the Communist victors of the American war are capitalizing period. They set up the museum to show Vietnam as a victim."

## Love Affairs and Amerasian

No one knows how many children, known as Amerasians, were born and ultimately left behind in Vietnam during the decade-long war that ended in 1975. According to government statistics, the number of Vietnamese–American marriages was around 1,400 in 1970. Many of the wives were Vietnamese "bar girls" who had migrated to Saigon from rural areas solely to meet wealthy Westerners. Others were from middle-class families, and parents often disapproved of their daughters' marriages to American soldiers. Most of the couples returned to the United States, where they were harassed much less than in Vietnam, where mixed marriages generally were not popular. In Vietnam, when mixed couples went out together, it wasn't uncommon for people to yell crude insults at them, or even bump or kick them. Vietnamese women coming from such a diverse culture often experienced culture shock in New York.

According to David Lamb, Amerasians kids were commonly dismissed by the Vietnamese as "children of the dust." "The care and welfare of these unfortunate children ... has never been and is not now considered an area of government responsibility," said the US Defense Department in a 1970 statement. "Our society does not need these bad elements."

According to a BBC news magazine article, more than forty years after the end of the Vietnam War, dozens of aging former American soldiers have gone back to Vietnam to live. Some had difficulty adapting to civilian life in the United States after their term of enlistment ended, and others have returned to Vietnam hoping to atone for wrongs they believe were committed during the war.

## Views of a Vietnamese Friend (To Yen)

Traffic: Vietnam has one of the highest rates of motorcycle ownership in the world, second only to Taiwan. The street dust and loud whistles will make you tired after spending some time in road traffic in Vietnam. People drive fast and sometimes run red lights. The irony is that children are being taught to obey traffic laws, but adults are breaking those same laws. Visitors will have some exciting experiences when entering traffic, and they will feel like simply crossing the road is a game of adventure.

Welcoming: Vietnamese are quite friendly and welcoming. Even not speaking the language won't prevent you from having a great time with Vietnamese friends, and being a bad singer won't prevent you from enjoying karaoke with them either. Vietnamese people love to have foreigners visit Vietnam, because it's an opportunity for the country to show that it has grown. Because of what they see in movies, American people still think of Vietnam as it was during the war, or they believe that Vietnam is still poor. The Vietnamese people want to change Americans' perspective about their country.

How Vietnamese See America: For older generations, the war surely left a huge, permanent scar in their memories. However, for younger Vietnamese born since the war, the horror of war is something they can only learn about from books, documentaries, and personal stories. The number of Vietnamese students in the United States has increased consistently for the past sixteen years. America's education system offers a rich field of choices to international students, and Vietnamese view America as a beautiful, developed country with a lot of opportunities and freedoms.

Personal Experience: I came to the United States when I was twenty. For seven years, I've been learning and adapting to this new environment. I've been working hard, and I've made great achievements in my career of which I'm proud. I still remember the difficulties that I faced when I first came to this country—culture shock, different food, American lifestyles, and so on. I've grown through my mistakes, and I've learned to explore myself as well as my abilities. I believe that life doesn't require us to *be* the best, but only that we *try* our best. In general, Vietnamese people see America as a great place to work and live. So live as healthfully as you can, no matter what.

Vietnamese in America: Most Vietnamese in the United States have settled in California and Texas, mainly in Orange County, San Jose, and Houston. The warm climate in these states is similar to the weather in their homeland, so they can plant various types of Asian fruit trees. Living in these places, where they can find all types of Vietnamese food within only a short drive, is the best they can ask for—short of actually being in Vietnam.

Also, the feeling of being surrounded by people from their homeland—enjoying the same activities, experiencing the same culture—makes them feel like they're living in their own country.

## References

Turley, William S., Milton Edgeworth Osborne, Gerald C. Hickey, Neil L. Jamieson, Joseph Buttinger, and William J. Kuiker. "Vietnam." *Encyclopaedia Britannica.* https://www.britannica.com/place/Vietnam.

Lamb, David. "Children of the Vietnam War." *Smithsonian*, June 2009. https://www.smithsonianmag.com/travel/children-of-the-vietnam-war.

Lubin, Lisa. "War Is Hell." LL World Tour. https://www.llworldtour.com/war-is-hell/.

Hubbard, Charlie. "What do the Vietnamese People Think of Americans?." Quora. August 2018. https://www.quora.com/What-do-the-Vietnamese-people-think-of-Americans.

"How Asians View Each Other." Pew Research Center's Global Attitudes Project. June 01, 2015. https://www.pewresearch.org/global/2014/07/14/chapter-4-how-asians-view-each-other/.

Hoekstra, Ate. "The US Veterans Going Back to Live in Vietnam." BBC News. May 23, 2016. https://www.bbc.com/news/magazine-36363537.

# Media in America

*Media, a school bigger than all the other schools combined and with students of all ages.*

*Every time I watch TV, talking about the current issues,*
*I end up with wet eyes, using a large number of tissues.*
*Every time I try to look for some meaningful clues,*
*I end up finding myself needing a glass and a bottle of booze.*
*The booze often changes my focus; that is a good excuse.*
*I promise to stop and never again watch TV, especially the news.*

As in most other countries, media in the United States consists of television, radio, film, newspapers, magazines and internet-based websites. The US Federal Communications Commission regularly releases broadcast station totals. As of September 30, 2018, there were 15,493 radio stations and 33,243 total licensed broadcast outlets (AM/FM/TV) in this country. To appreciate this number and the variety, compare it with the 80 television and 594 radio stations in Canada.

Media outlets in the United States broadcast a great variety of programs. Broadcast networks take advantage of the freedom of expression that is guaranteed by the constitution. Public broadcasting is partly government funded, but they also receive support from private grants. The government sponsors television, radio, and online outlets aimed not only at American audiences, but also at people in such places as the Soviet bloc, the Middle East, and Asia in English and other languages. Media is usually used for good, but some people use it to promote violence and hate among various groups and people with opposing political views. Media in the hands of the wrong people can cause a great deal of problems, between individuals or groups of people.

Media plays a big role in people's lives, especially since it is our main source of information. The media is like a huge university where people attend classes, learn good and bad, become followers, stop caring about critical thinking, and sometimes get brainwashed. Statistics from the Nielsen Corporation and other sources tell us that Americans spend approximately four hours a day watching television. Popular media has become a huge influence, especially during critical times such as elections. In recent years, more and more people have gotten their hands on technology and spend more time following the media.

The second highest number of minutes spent on technology is on mobile devices such as cell phones and tablets. Many Americans believe that they cannot live without their cell phones, and they won't leave home without them. They spend a lot of time playing video games, texting, scrolling through social media, and so on. Social media has sparked such an uprising in mobile device technology that most people now carry a device of some sort.

Social media usage is another topic that has generated research interest. According to "Social Media Use in 2018," 78 percent of people 18 to 24 years old use Snapchat and Instagram. Roughly two-thirds of American adults report that they use Facebook, and three-fourths of those users access it daily. The largest number of people using social media apps are young adults 18 to 22 years old. Media shows everything we need to know about anything going on in the world, and it trickles down into our daily lives. This powerful tool gets viewers addicted to certain types of products or changes their focus to issues that concern them, thus generating more viewers and higher ratings.

In the last couple of years, many American media providers have declined in popularity because of their biased political views. Most Americans do not have easy access to media from other countries, making it easy for American networks to control people's opinions about critical issues, both internal and external. This is unfortunate. As a result, most Americans have little knowledge about the rest of the world and—perhaps more importantly—are unaware of other countries' approaches to problem solving. In short, the media isolates viewers so that they consume only internal news and products that generate more income for the networks.

## Media-Driven Society

Most news media in the United States operate based on advertising income that depends upon viewership and ratings. To attract viewers, they often look for sensational news and stories. The extent to which news media considers individuals and groups important is based on their news value, and this is especially true for identifiable people. Athletes, entertainers, and population segments such as women and African-Americans have high news values. People serving in the military, the Peace Corps, scientists, nerds, community leaders, and groups such as Native Americans and Latinos have less news value.

Although there is notable discrimination against old, ugly, and fat people, that subject is hardly discussed in the media. At the same time, lower levels of discrimination against certain minorities are magnified and presented with bias for their news value. News related to the White House and controversial politicians, especially regarding their sex lives, has high news value. Political issues such as elections in the rest of the world do not have high news value.

Sometimes the media even attempts to keep an internal newsmaker conflict ongoing and fresh, regardless of the price. They may go so far as to create non-deserving heroes and role models, ignoring the real ones. For example, notice how much time the major television networks have devoted to the lives and deaths of entertainers such as Aretha Franklin, Prince, and Whitney Houston, while spending almost no time on the life and accomplishments of a major scientist whose impact on our lives has been obvious and priceless. I often ask my students to name any American scientist, but they can't. However, they know the names of many rappers, athletes, entertainers, and so on. Finally, media spends significantly more time on negative news, for its sensational effects, than on positive news.

## A Social Effect

In a media-driven society, people feed off the media and the media feeds off the people's interests. Viewers often fall into traps created by political institutions or parties and the media representing them, whose goal is to find followers who will buy their news and views. Some people become addicted to certain types of news, including fake news, which leads to hate, anxiety, and anger, sometimes for life. To escape this, some people try to look at different aspects of the issues and use multiple sources. This, of course, requires having easy access to international media, knowing other languages, and learning to be open to views outside the local or cultural ones.

## References

Federal Communications Commission. "Broadcast Station Totals as of September 30, 2018." https://docs.fcc.gov/public/attachments/DOC-354386A1.pdf.

Nielsen Corporation. "Time Flies: U.S. Adults Now Spend Nearly Half a Day Interacting with Media." July 31, 2018. https://www.nielsen.com/us/en/insights/news/2018/time-flies-us-adults-now-spend-nearly-half-a-day-interacting-with-media.html.

Smith, Aaron, and Monica Anderson. "Social Media Use in 2018." Pew Research Center: Internet and Technology, March 1, 2018. http://www.pewinternet.org/2018/03/01/social-media-use-in-2018/.

# Accidental Inventions

*Surprisingly, at least one-third of scientific discoveries were in some way accidental.*

Surprisingly, some of the most lucrative products of all time were discovered by chance or mistake. Searching for one thing occasionally leads people to find something entirely different, sometimes simply because they forget to wash their hands or clean their tools. According to Katie Serena in "21 Accidental Inventions That Changed Our World," "Some of the products and procedures used in medicine were discovered in this way. The scientists who discovered X-ray imaging, for instance, were not even looking to advance medical technology, but their discovery ended up changing the world. Alexander Fleming, the discoverer of penicillin, almost threw away the petri dish upon which it first grew, thinking that it was simply covered in mold. Had he discarded it instead of taking a closer look, there is no telling where medicine would be today." Other examples includes snacks such as potato chips, popsicles, and chocolate chip cookies.

The stories surrounding these discoveries are interesting too. According to "10 Accidental Inventions That Changed the World," by Melissa Breyer,

> Not all chance discoveries came at the hands of scientists fiddling in labs. Sometimes they happened to cooks twiddling in kitchens and sometimes in the kitchens of restored tollhouses. Case in point is the beloved Toll House Cookie. Ruth Wakefield and her husband owned and operated the Toll House Inn in Massachusetts where Ruth cooked for the guests. According to legend, one day in 1937 while making cookie dough, she realized she was out of melting baker's chocolate and instead used a chocolate bar that she chopped into bits, hoping it would melt as well. It did not and thus was born America's favorite cookie. Did the chocolate chip cookie change the world? Probably not, unless you calculate the combined moments of pleasure derived

from biting into one fresh from the oven. They have certainly been responsible for changing many moods.

Experts such as Dunbar and Fugelsang estimate that as much as 30 to 50 percent of all scientific discoveries are in some way accidental. This reveals another human ability, namely recognizing the usefulness or potential of unexpected outcomes. In "24 Unintended Scientific Discoveries," Alvin Ward lists several accidental inventions. Here are some from Ward's and a few other sources.

- The pacemaker was accidentally invented by Wilson Greatbatch.
- In 1827, English pharmacist John Walker was stirring a pot of chemicals that included antimony sulfide and potassium chlorate. Noticing a dried lump at the end of his mixing stick, he tried to scratch it off. But it burst into flames, and the world had its first prototype of the strikable match.
- The microwave oven was accidentally invented in 1945.
- In the early 1990s, Pfizer test a drug called UK92480, intended to treat patients with angina. That drug ended up being marketed as Viagra, a side effect of which is—wait for it—heart attacks.
- In 1907, Belgian chemist Leo Baekeland, looking for a replacement for shellac, produced the world's first plastic instead. He named the plastic "Bakelite" in honor of himself.
- In 1879, after a day spent reacting coal tar with phosphorous, ammonia, and other chemicals, Russian chemist Constantin Fahlburg forgot to wash his hands. He later realized that his hands tasted sweet—Sweet'n Low, that is.
- Robert Chesebrough was looking to strike it rich in the oil fields, but in 1859, he noticed workers complaining about rod was, an annoying, waxy substance that gummed up their drilling equipment. Chesebrough called it Vaseline.
- DuPont chemist Roy Plunkett was at work on a new chlorofluorocarbon refrigerant in 1938 when he accidentally invented Teflon.
- Ninth-century Chinese alchemists searching for an elixir for eternal life accidentally invented gunpowder.
- Alfred Nobel's invention of dynamite was partially inspired by an accident while transporting nitroglycerin.
- In 1856, a teenage chemistry student named William Perkins, attempting to create an artificial quinine to treat malaria, invented the world's first synthetic dye.

- Safety Glass was accidentally discovered by French chemist Edouard Benedictus in the early 20th century.
- While experimenting with cereal recipes in 1895, Will Keith Kellogg forgot about some boiled wheat he left sitting out. The wheat became flaky, but Kellogg and his brother cooked it anyway. The resulting crunchy and flaky material became Corn Flakes.
- Proctor & Gamble scientists, working on a nutritional supplement for premature infants in the 1960s, instead discovered Olestra, a fat substitute with zero calories.
- Kodak engineer Harry Coover was working with chemicals known as cyanoacrylates during World War II in an attempt to make clear plastic for gun sights, when his team instead discovered what today is known as super glue.

## References

Breyer, Melissa. "10 Accidental Inventions That Changed the World." *Mother Nature Network*, March 28, 2013. https://www.mnn.com/leaderboard/stories/10-accidental-inventions-that-changed-the-world.

Dunbar, Kevin N., and Jonathan A. Fugelsang. "Causal Thinking in Science: How Scientists and Students Interpret the Unexpected." In *Scientific and Technological Thinking*, edited by M. E. Gorman, R. D. Tweney, D. C. Gooding, and A. P. Kincannon, 57–79. Mahwah, NJ: Lawrence Erlbaum, 2005.

Serena, Katie. "21 Accidental Inventions That Changed Our World." *All That's Interesting*, December 4, 2017. https://allthatsinteresting.com/accidental-inventions.

Ward, Alvin. "24 Unintended Scientific Discoveries." *Mental Floss*, May 2, 2015. http://mentalfloss.com/article/53646/24-important-scientific-discoveries-happened-accident.

# Are Diamonds Really Rare?

*Are diamonds rare, or have we made them so?*

Diamonds, though difficult to find and extract, are quite common compared with other gemstones. According to Seth Rosen, many people believe that diamonds have captured public attention as a result of one of the most successful advertising campaigns in history. Advertising by De Beers has made consumers believe that impressive engagement rings should always have a diamond. De Beers cleverly struck deals with movie stars, who wore their diamonds in movies that placed the gems in the public eye. Rosen says, "As a result, diamonds became a top status symbol for the rich and famous. This peaked perhaps with Marilyn Monroe's performance of the song 'Diamonds Are a Girl's Best Friend' in the 1953 film *Gentlemen Prefer Blondes*." The site www.gemsociety.org includes more detailed information about the history and properties of diamonds.

According to Rosen, "Diamonds are the hardest material found on earth. They resist scratching better than anything else. Other than that, they hold no unique distinctions. All gem-quality materials are rare. While we have much to learn about the Earth's interior, our current knowledge of gem formation indicates that diamonds are probably the most common gem found in nature." In fact, diamonds are made of carbon—one of the most common elements in the universe, only after hydrogen, helium, and oxygen. Of all diamonds mined on Earth, less than 20 percent are gemstone quality. Of that 20 percent, most yield only smaller sizes with low quality and color.

Although presently diamonds are the most popular gemstone, this is a new phenomenon. According to Rosen, only in the last century did diamonds become readily available. Prior to that, rubies and sapphires were the most popular gems, especially for engagement rings.

## Are Diamonds the Most Brilliant Gemstone?

According to Rosen, "The faceting and the refractive index (RI) of a gem determines its brilliance, or how much light it reflects back to the viewer. Diamonds do have a very high RI of 2.41. If properly cut, they have the potential for exceptional brilliance. However, that pales in comparison to rutile's RI of 2.90. Not counting synthetic gems, at least fifteen minerals have a higher RI than diamonds."

Rosen adds that "Diamonds are also known for their 'fire' or dispersion. This refers to their ability to separate white light into the colors of the rainbow. In fact, diamond does have quite a high dispersion value of 0.044. However, that is very different from rutile, again, with a dispersion of 0.280. In fact, synthetic rutile stones, known as 'Titania,' used to be sold as imitation diamonds. However, they showed too much dispersion to make passable diamonds!"

Hardness is another measure of a material's durability. Diamonds have a hardness rating of 10, the highest of all natural materials. Of course, it is possible to create harder substances, but those created by scientists so far have no practical use because they are extremely brittle.

## Conclusion

Ehud Arye Laniado says this in "Rethinking Rarity":

> There is clearly no doubt that gem-quality diamonds are rare objects. There is also no doubt that finding, mining, and extracting diamonds is a major scientific and economic challenge. Compared to the number of mines currently active, many are past their prime, which means they are producing less diamonds. Even 1-carat top color and clarity diamonds are counted among the exceptionally rare natural white diamonds. They are intrinsically luxury items, but their value is not limited to their luxury. Given their rarity, they can also serve as an asset that preserves value. Because they are luxury items, they should be promoted and sold as such.

Fast-forward to today, when gem diamonds are easily synthesized. Although diamond cutting is still a difficult, precise, and expensive process, the price of diamonds is heading south. Technology will continue to put downward pressure on pricing, and five-hundred-dollar "D Flawless" stones are on the way out.

Although diamonds are not rare, high-quality diamonds that are perfect for jewelry *are* rare. Layers of the earth's crust are dismantled to extract diamonds, and this dismantling process requires hard work and modern equipment. Most diamonds found during mining are too small or don't meet acceptable standards, so they're used for industrial purposes.

## References

Laniado, Ehud Arye. "Rethinking Rarity." April 11, 2016. https://www.ehudlaniado.com/home/index.php/news/entry/rethinking-rarity.

Rosen, Seth I. "Are Diamonds Really Rare? Diamond Myths and Misconceptions." International Gem Society. https://www.gemsociety.org/article/are-diamonds-really-rare/.

# Geography of Peacefulness

*A wish to live in a peaceful place can, in fact, come true.*

Everyone wishes for a peaceful world, but not everyone has the same idea of peace and peacefulness. Could we measure the degree of peacefulness to determine how peaceful the world is today? When quantifying peacefulness, researchers consider many factors—the number of casualties from terrorism, conflicts, and murders per capita, together with the ratio of military spending to gross domestic product. Indicators are scored on a 5-point scale.

According to Megan Trimble in "The 10 Most Peaceful Countries in the World," "Iceland topped the list with the lowest score, or peace index, making it the most peaceful country—a title it has held since 2008." Iceland is joined at the top of the list by New Zealand, Portugal, Austria, and Denmark, all of which were ranked highly in previous evaluations. Europe remains the most peaceful geographic region despite recent terrorist attacks, claiming eight of the top ten countries ranked on a number of peace factors.

Trimble's article, based on the eleventh annual study published by the Institute for Economics and Peace, presents the scores of 163 independent states and territories for their levels of peacefulness. The report shows that the world has become 0.28 percent more peaceful compared with the previous year, with 93 countries improving in peacefulness and 68 deteriorating. "Six of the world's nine regions have become more peaceful, with the largest overall improvement being recorded in South America…. Peace trends over the last decade, however, are a bit grimmer."

Trimble also reports the following:

> The global peace level has deteriorated by 2.14 percent since the organization released its 2008 index, with an increase in both battle deaths and deaths from terrorism during that time. According to a study, only eighty countries improved during the last decade, while

83 countries deteriorated. North America's regional peace score fell in large part because of the United States. While Canada saw an improvement, its score was offset by a much larger drop in America's peace ranking. The U.S. ranked 114th out of 163 in the global assessment, falling from 103rd and 94th in the 2016 and 2015 Global Peace Indexes, respectively.

According to the study, the years around the last election have been deeply worrying for the United States, highlighting the deep divisions within American society. "Data highlighted a declining level of trust in the US government, as well as growing social problems such as income inequality, heightened racial tensions and rising homicide rates in several major American cities…. The Middle East and North Africa were the least peaceful region in the world," a title they've held since 2015.

According to *Global Peace Index 2017*, a report from the Institute for Economics and Peace (IEP), "There was also very little change at the bottom of the list. Syria remains the least peaceful country in the world, preceded by Afghanistan, Iraq, South Sudan, and Yemen. Six of the nine regions in the world improved. South America registered the largest improvement, overtaking Central America and the Caribbean as the fourth most peaceful region."

The IEP report points out that "South America's score benefited from improvements across all three domains, with particularly strong gains in Societal Safety and Security":

> The largest regional deteriorations in score occurred in North America, followed by sub-Saharan Africa and the Middle East and North Africa (MENA).… The United States also has experienced the fourth largest drop in Positive Peace globally, after Syria, Greece, and Hungary in the ten years leading up to 2015. Europe remains the most peaceful region in the world…. However, while 23 of the 36 countries improved, the average peace score did not change notably due to the substantial deterioration in Turkey; the impact of the terrorist attacks in Brussels, Nice, and Paris; and deteriorating relations between Russia and its Nordic neighbors.

The IEP report also says the following:

MENA is the least peaceful region in the world for the fifth successive year. Saudi Arabia, followed by Libya, recorded the largest deteriorations in the region. Saudi Arabia fell because of its involvement in the Syrian and Yemen conflicts and increased terrorist activity, mainly conducted by ISIL and its affiliates, while the fall for Libya was due to its increased level of internal conflict.

The indicator with the largest improvement was *number, duration and role in external conflicts.* This was mainly due to many countries winding down their involvement in Iraq and Afghanistan. While in most cases the withdrawal of troops occurred some years ago, the indicator is lagging in order to capture the lingering effect of conflict. The indicator measuring *political terror* also significantly improved in all regions except sub-Saharan Africa and the MENA. There were also general reductions in the *number of homicides per 100,000 people* and the *level of violent crime.*

Of the three GPI domains, both Militarization and Safety and Security improved. However, there was a deterioration in the Ongoing Conflict domain, due to an increase in the intensity of conflicts in the MENA region.

## References

Institute for Economics and Peace. "Global Peace Index 2017." *Relief Web*, June 1, 2017. https://reliefweb.int/report/world/global-peace-index-2017.

Trimble, Megan. "The 10 Most Peaceful Countries in the World." *U.S. News & World Report*, June 1, 2017. https://www.usnews.com/news/best-countries/articles/2017-06-01/the-10-most-peaceful-countries?offset=10.

# Costa Rica

*Home to beautiful butterflies and amazing hummingbirds.*

According to the article "20 Things You Should Not Do in Costa Rica" by Catherine Forth, exotic Costa Rica is known for its jungles, cool creatures such as butterflies and hummingbirds, and some of the finest beaches in the world. Visitors to this prosperous Central American country enjoy the friendly locals, pristine coastline, endemic wildlife, and, of course, food. Here are a few amazing facts about Costa Rica (see e.g. en.wikipedia.org):

- The sun rises and sets at the same time in Costa Rica—365 days a year!
- It is Central America's longest-standing democracy.
- It is smaller than Lake Michigan in the USA.
- It is surrounded by eight hundred miles of coastline and bordered by both the Atlantic and Pacific Oceans.
- It has had no standing army since 1949.
- It is one of the most eco-minded countries in the world; 25 percent of the land is protected.
- Approximately 10 percent of the world's butterflies live in Costa Rica.
- Approximately fifty-two species of hummingbirds are native to Costa Rica, making it a hummingbird capital.
- Approximately twenty thousand species of spiders live in Costa Rica.
- Costa Rica is a common retirement choice for American expatriates, many of whom own bars and restaurants here.

Forth also says, "Costa Rica grows some of the richest, boldest, and most coveted coffee beans in the world. However, most of the crop is for export, so the local cups of joe are not necessarily homegrown. To drink Costa Rica grown coffee, you can visit Starbucks."

Costa Rica's sixty-seven volcanoes are discussed in Forth's article:

> Most of them are dormant or extinct (yet still scenic), but there are several active ones that could conceivably blow at any time (including Irazu, Poas, Rincon De La Vieja, and Turrialba). Up until 2010, Costa Rica's famous Arenal volcano had almost daily activity and was one of the country's biggest tourist attractions. However, smoldering volcanoes and running lava are not just cool subjects for photographs. In 1968, a major Arenal eruption buried three villages and took 87 lives, so do not underestimate the power of Mother Nature. Just last year, an ashy plume caused Juan Santamaría International Airport to shut down temporarily. Volcanic activity is monitored, so there should be some advanced warning if an explosion is expected, and you should definitely pay attention to them.

Unlike in most countries, tipping in restaurants in Costa Rica is not expected; there is usually a 10 percent service charge included anyway. Unless you receive exceptionally good service, don't bother tipping in catering establishments. However, tipping tour guides, maids, and drivers is quite common, provided the service is excellent. Be generous, because they work hard and rely on tips to supplement their wages.

Costa Rica—literally meaning "Rich Coast," officially the Republic of Costa Rica—is bordered by Nicaragua to the north, Panama to the southeast, the Pacific Ocean to the west, the Caribbean Sea to the east, and Ecuador to the south of Cocos Island. It has a population of around 4.8 million, of whom nearly a quarter live in the metropolitan area of the capital and largest city, San José.

According to Wikipedia, "The country has consistently performed favorably in the Human Development Index (HDI), placing sixty-ninth in the world as of 2015, among the highest of any Latin American nation. It has also been cited by the United Nations Development Programme (UNDP) as having attained much higher human development than other countries at the same income levels, with a better record on human development and inequality than the median of the region. Its rapidly developing economy, once heavily dependent on agriculture, has diversified to include sectors such as finance, pharmaceuticals, and ecotourism."

As Wikipedia also says,

Costa Rica is known for its progressive environmental policies, being the only country to meet all five UNDP criteria established to measure environmental sustainability. It was ranked 42$^{nd}$ in the world, and third in the Americas, in the 2016 Environmental Performance Index, was twice ranked the best performing country in the New Economics Foundation's (NEF) Happy Planet Index, which measures environmental sustainability, and was identified by the NEF as the greenest country in the world in 2009. Costa Rica officially plans to become a carbon-neutral country by 2021. In 2012, it became the first country in the Americas to ban recreational hunting.

## The Wild Life

"Introducing Costa Rica" says that, "Such wildlife abounds in Costa Rica as to seem almost cartoonish: keel-billed toucans ogle you from treetops and scarlet macaws raucously announce their flight paths. A keen eye will discern a sloth on a branch or the eyes and snout of a caiman breaking the surface of a mangrove swamp, while alert ears will catch rustling leaves signaling a troop of white-faced capuchins or the haunting call of a howler monkey. Blue morpho butterflies flit amid orchid-festooned trees, while colorful tropical fish, sharks, rays, dolphins and whales thrive offshore—all as if in a conservationist's dream."

## Outdoor Adventures

"Introducing Costa Rica" also talks about the variety of outdoor adventure opportunities in Costa Rica. Rainforest hikes and brisk high-altitude trails, rushing white-water rapids, and world-class surfing: Costa Rica offers a dizzying suite of outdoor adventures in every shape and size, from the squeal-inducing rush of a canopy zip line to a sun-dazed afternoon at the beach. National parks allow visitors to glimpse life in the tropical rainforest and cloud forest, simmering volcanoes offer otherworldly vistas, and reliable surf breaks are suited to beginners and experts alike. Can't decide what to do? Don't worry, you won't have to. Given the country's diminutive size, it's possible to plan a relatively short trip that includes it all. All trails lead to waterfalls, misty crater lakes, or jungle-fringed, deserted beaches. Explored by horseback, foot, or kayak, Costa Rica is a tropical choose-your-own-adventure land.

## The Pure Life

Then there are the people. The above mentioned article also talks about Costa Ricans, or Ticos as they prefer to call themselves. They're proud of their little slice of paradise, welcoming guests to sink into the easygoing rhythms of the *pura vida* (pure life). The greeting, farewell, catchy motto, and enduring mantra gets to the heart of Costa Rica's appeal—its simple yet profound ability to let people relax and enjoy their time. With the highest quality of life in Central America, all the perfect waves, perfect sunsets, and perfect beaches seem like the *pura vida* indeed.

## The Peaceful Soul of Central America

Lastly, "Introducing Costa Rica" talks about Costa Rica as the eco- and adventure-tourism capital of Central America and its worth as a place in the cubicle daydreams of travelers around the world. "With world-class infrastructure, visionary sustainability initiatives, and no standing army since 1948 (when the country redirected its defense funds toward education, healthcare and the environment), Costa Rica is a peaceful green jewel of the region. Taking into account that more than a fourth of the land enjoys some form of environmental protection and there is greater biodiversity here than in the USA and Europe combined, a place that earns the superlatives."

## References

Carib Tours. "Introducing Costa Rica."
   https://www.caribtours.co.uk/news-and-reviews/introducing-costa-rica/.
Wikipedia. "Costa Rica." https://en.wikipedia.org/wiki/Costa_Rica.
Forth, Catherine. "20 Things You Should Not Do in Costa Rica." Destination Tips,
   February 20, 2016. https://www.destinationtips.com/destinations/20-things-you-
   should-not-do-in-costa-rica/?listview=all.

# Nowruz, the Persian New Year

*The only new year based on nature's revival.*

بیامد عید نوروز بار دیگر

برفتیم جملگی ره را فراتر

بیاورد با خودش شادی و دوستی

امید بر دیدن انسان بهتر

بپوش رخت نو یی فکرت عوض کن

بیارای خانهات جنست عوض کن

Nowruz (pronounced no-rooz), the Persian New Year Celebration, is an ancestral festivity marking the first day of spring and the renewal of nature. According to several articles about Nowruz "The name is a combination of two Persian (Farsi) words. The first word, 'now,' means new, and the second word, 'ruz,' means day; together they mean 'New Day.' The exact beginning of the New Year occurs when the season changes from winter to spring on the vernal equinox, which usually happens on the 20th or 21st of March each year." The celebrations share many similarities with other spring festivals, such as Easter and the Egyptian holiday called Sham Al-Naseem, which dates back to the time of the pharaohs.

Nowruz is recognized as an official United Nations observance because it promotes peace and solidarity, particularly in families, and focuses on reconciliation and neighborliness, contributing to cultural diversity and friendship among peoples and different communities. About 300 million people worldwide celebrate Nowruz, with traditions and rituals particularly strong in the Balkans, the Black Sea and Caspian Sea regions, the Caucasus, Central and South Asia, and the Middle East.

## Festivities

For Persians, Nowruz is the time for a fresh start. Preparations include cleaning the house, replacing old items with new or fresh ones, and buying new clothing. At the moment of the new year, everything worn must be brand new. During the festivities, with the help of fire and light, one hopes for enlightenment and happiness throughout the coming year. A few hours prior to the transition to the New Year, family and friends sit around the table set with seven special dishes, each one beginning with the Persian letter "S," which stands for the seven angelic heralds of life: rebirth, health, happiness, prosperity, joy, patience, and beauty. At the exact moment of the equinox, the oldest person present begins the well-wishing by standing up and giving out sweets, pastries, coins, and hugs. Events may include folk dance performances, special concerts, and tree planting ceremonies. In addition to the seven items listed above, some people include the holy Qur'an or a book of poetry by Hafez, the great Iranian poet.

According to Najmieh Batmanglij, in ancient texts, each of the twelve constellations in the zodiac governed one of the months of the year, and each would rule the earth for a thousand years, after which the sky and the earth would collapse into each other. The festivities, therefore, last twelve days, plus a thirteenth day (representing the time of chaos) celebrated by going outdoors, putting order aside, and having parties.

## The Origin

Although Nowruz is partly rooted in the religious tradition of Zoroastrianism, it is enjoyed by people of several faiths. Articles about Nowruz states that Zoroastrianism emphasizes broad concepts such as the corresponding work of good and evil in the world and the connection of humans to nature. Its practices were dominant for much of the history of ancient Persia, centered in what is now Iran. Today, there are a few Zoroastrian communities throughout the world, with the largest in southern Iran and India. While the physical region called Persia no longer exists, the traditions of Nowruz are strong among people in Azerbaijan, Afghanistan, Canada, India, Iran, Iraq, Pakistan, Tajikistan, the United States, Turkey, Uzbekistan, and some European countries.

## References

Batmanglij, Najmieh. "Nowruz Cards: Celebrate the Persian New Year." Mage Publishers: Persian Literature and Culture, January 1, 2004. http://magepublishers. com/nowruz-cards-celebrate-the-persian-new-year/.

"Happy Nowruz." Hi Persia, February 26, 2017. http://hipersia.com/en/news.cfm?id=179.

Michael, Jaclyn. "Celebrating Nowruz: A Resource for Educators." The Outreach Center, Center for Middle Eastern Studies, Harvard University. https://cmes.fas.harvard.edu/files/NowruzCurriculumText.pdf.

R., Annie. "Nowruz 1396 & the ACAA." Afghanistan and Central Asian Association. https://acaa.org.uk/2017/03/26/nowruz-1396-the-acaa/.

"History." Center for Middle Eastern Studies, cmes,fas.harvard.edu/history.

# Chapter 3
## Faith/Religion

*Faith is the backbone of the society that is easy to see*
*Without it there would be no hope, we cannot let it be*
*We need something to keep our spiritual body upright*
*Without it we fall, we get lost and give up easily.*

- Hinduism: "Treat others as you would yourself be treated. Never do to others what would pain you." (Panchatantra 3.104)
- Buddhism: "Hurt not others with that which hurts yourself." (Udana 5.18)
- Zoroastrianism: "Do not to others what is not well for oneself." (Shayast-na-shayast 13.29)
- Jainism: "One who neglects existence disregards their own experience." (Mahavira)
- Confucianism: "Do not impose on others what you do not yourself desire." (Analects 12.2)
- Taoism: "Regard your neighbor's loss or gain as your own loss or gain." (Tai Shang Kan Ying Pien)
- Baha'I: "Desire not for anyone the things you would not desire for yourself." (Baha'Ullah 66)
- Judaism: "What you yourself hate, do to no man. What is hateful to you do not do to your neighbor." (Talmud, Shabbat, 31a)
- Christianity: "Do unto others as you would have them do unto you." (Matthew 7:12)
- Islam: "Do unto all men as you would wish to have done unto you. Do unto all people as you would they should do to you." (Mishkat-el-Masabih)
- Sikhism: "Treat others as you would be treated yourself." (Adi Granth)
- Native American: "Live in harmony, for we are all related."
- Sacred Earth: "Do as you will, as long as you harm no one."

## References

"Golden Rule." *Wikipedia*, Wikimedia Foundation, 25 June 2019, en.wikipedia.org/wiki/Golden Rule.

## Christmas, Time to Go Beyond Oneself

I hear the jingle bells, and I wonder what could be the message?
I see the clouds dancing, I see the snow falling,
and I wonder what could be the message?
I go through rainy days and frosty nights, and I wonder what could be the message?

I know that it is more than what I see, what I think;
it is like a feeling, it is like a concept,
It is certainly not just about presents, it is not about the food, and it is not about Santa,
It is not about a year ending, it is not about a year beginning,
It is about remembering, it is about understanding,
it is about changing, it is about accepting,
It is about a new start, it is about giving, it is about forgiving, it is about forgetting,
It is about family and friends, it is about gathering, it is about living, it is about loving,
It is about learning, it is about joining, it is about growing, and it is about appreciating.

# Christianity and Islam

*The same ideas, only different times and places.*

I would first like to mention that my knowledge about religion is limited. However, while working on a related topic, I came across some interesting information about the similarities between these two major religions and their beliefs. I hope this will not offend anybody, as I would hate to do that. In this article, I will concentrate on Christianity and Islam and their holy books, the Bible and the Qur'an. While Islam considers the Bible to be God's word and Jesus as God's messenger, the same cannot be said about Christianity regarding the Qur'an and Mohammad.

The Qur'an includes a large number of stories that originally came from the Bible. Here are a few examples from "Christian View of Why There Are So Many Similarities Between Qur'an and Bible":

- Creation of earth in seven days (Bible). God created earth in seven days (Qur'an).
- We are children of Adam and Eve (Bible). We are children of Adam and Eve (Qur'an).
- Noah's flood happened (Bible). Yes, Noah's flood happened (Qur'an).
- The flood was global (Bible). Indeed, it was global (Qur'an).
- Noah's ark set on a mountain (Bible). Noah's ark set on a mountain (Qur'an).

Many other Qur'an stories are different versions of Biblical stories, such as the crucifixion of Christ. According to the Qur'an, Jesus Christ was raised up to heaven before his crucifixion. Both religions are monotheistic, and both hold that there is only one God, the creator and sustainer of the universe. God sent prophets such as Noah, Abraham, Ishmael, and Isaac. In both religions, people should follow the holy scriptures of God and teachings of the prophets. They both also agree that Mary, the mother of Jesus, was a virgin; therefore, Jesus was born miraculously. However, in

Christianity, Jesus Christ is a messiah who performed miracles, and he will descend from Heaven to earth and kill the Antichrist. In Islam and Christianity, Satan is evil, so people should not follow him. In the Qur'an and the Bible, it is mentioned that an Antichrist will appear on Earth before the Day of Judgment when everyone will be judged. Hell and Paradise (Heaven) exist in both religions.

Here are a few differences between Christianity and Islam. Most Christians believe in the Trinity, meaning that God has three forms—Father, Son, and Spirit. However, some early Christians were Unitarians. Even today, there are Christian Unitarian churches that do not accept the Trinity. In Islam, the Trinity is totally rejected. Jesus is neither God nor the Son of God. Jesus was a human prophet and therefore not divine. Islam teaches that God is the sovereign creator and ruler of all that is. In fact, the will of God is more basic to who He is than His love or mercy. God can choose not to be merciful, and He can choose not to love; thus, God's mercy and love are not intrinsic to His nature, but are choices He makes. Submitting to God's will is more important than loving or knowing God. Muslims consider Moses, Jesus, and Mohammad as prophets and messengers sent by God. Islam and Christianity both trace their roots to Abraham or, as he is referred to in the Qur'an, Ibrahim. According the Qur'an, Ibrahim is a "friend of God" and father of the prophets. He is father to Ismail or, as he is known in the Bible, Ishmael, and Ishaq, who is alternatively known as Isaac. In the Qur'an and the Bible, Abraham is grandfather to Yaqub, or Jacob. Ibrahim is also one of the ancestors of the Prophet Mohammad. In Christianity, all Jews, including Jesus, are descended from Abraham. Abraham is considered the main patriarchal figure in both Islam and Christianity and he is thought of as the father of both Arabs and Israelites.

It is not surprising that the Bible's Old Testament and the Qur'an have a lot in common, given the fact that the two religions both trace their origins to Abraham. Interestingly, some Muslims consider the Bible to be Holy Scripture, so long as it is translated to not contradict the Qur'an. There are several instances in which both sacred texts relay similar events, although with slightly dissimilar narrations. The Bible and the Qur'an both mention a number of the same people, including everyone from Saul and Gideon to Xerxes and Pharaoh. They both venerate the early prophets, such as David, Noah, and Moses.

The two religions share a similar creation story as well. In the Old Testament, the creation story occurs in Genesis as one cohesive story. In the Qur'an, the creation story is told throughout the text and appears in fragments. Both texts begin with God creating the heavens and the earth out of nothing, and both texts describe the moment when God decided to create humankind. Genesis and the Qur'an tell of God creating Adam, the first man, out of clay. While the Qur'an does not go into as much detail as Genesis does, both texts show the creation of the first woman, Eve or Hawwa. There is a tempter in both texts, Lucifer in the Bible and Ilbis in the Qur'an. Another similarity that exists in the Bible and the Qur'an is the veneration of Jesus Christ. Jesus Christ is the cornerstone of the Christian faith and the literal Son of God, a perfect sacrifice to atone for the sins of humankind. While the Qur'an does not consider Jesus to be of divine origin, it does honor Christ as a great prophet, mentioning his name twenty-five times. Honor also is showered upon Jesus's mother, the Virgin Mary, as well. Jesus is given many titles, including the "Word of God" and the "Spirit of God."

The Qur'an and the Bible share many of the same values. In the Bible, God gives Moses the Ten Commandments, a list of general life rules to which the Israelites must adhere. These rules include honoring one's parents and never taking the Lord's name in vain. In the Qur'an, one can find similar commands scattered throughout, and the text describes the sins of adultery and murder as being particularly profane. Muslims are told in the Qur'an to honor the daily calls to prayer, similar to Christians being directed to uphold the Sabbath as a day of worship. Both religions encourage modesty among their faithful followers, and both texts describe the human body as deserving respect. Muslim women wear a veil to cover parts of their bodies, including their hair and chests. A passage in the Bible, located in the First Corinthians, tells Christian women to cover their heads when they are praying, as the faithful should focus on God's beauty instead of the physical beauty of women.

I hope you find this information interesting. Let us wish that someday, all believers will join forces and fight those who cause so much destruction in the name of God.

## Reference

"Christian View of Why There Are So Many Similarities Between Qur'an and Bible?" Christianity Stack Exchange. https://christianity.stackexchange.com/questions/11675/christian-view-of-why-there-are-so-many-similarities-between-quran-and-bible.

# Islam: The Fastest Growing Religion

*It seems that the world is heading toward Muslim majority.*

According to "The Future of the Global Muslim Population," as of 2010, Christianity was by far the world's largest religion with an estimated 2.2 billion adherents, nearly a third (31 percent) of all 6.9 billion people on Earth. Islam was second with 1.6 billion adherents, or 23 percent of the global population. Vanessa Molina tells us that around 62 percent of the world's Muslims live in South and Southeast Asia, with over one billion adherents. "The Future of the Global Muslim Population" details the Muslim population and expectations for its growth. The country with the largest Muslim population is Indonesia, which is home to 12.7 percent of the world's Muslims, followed by Pakistan (11 percent), India (10.9 percent), and Bangladesh (9.2 percent). Most Muslims are of two denominations: Sunni (85 to 86 percent) or Shia (12 to 13 percent).

The Pew Research Center has also produced research on the growth of religious groups. In "Why Muslims Are the World's Fastest-Growing Religious Group," Michael Lipka and Conrad Hackett discuss growth across the world. According to them, Muslims are expected to grow more than twice as quickly as the world's population between 2015 and 2060. With the current trend, Islam is expected to surpass Christianity in numbers by the end of the century. This is partly because Muslim populations are concentrated in some of the fastest-growing parts of the world. Adnan Khan points out that in this population, the fertility rate is higher than that of the seven other major religious groups. Muslim women have an average of 3.1 children, which is significantly higher than the next-highest group (Christians at 2.7) and the average of all non-Muslims (2.3). Additionally, in all major regions where there is a sizable Muslim population, Muslim fertility rates exceed non-Muslims. Recall, for example, that Osama Bin Laden, who was sick and in hiding, had twenty-two children, and his father had fifty-two.

Also, according to Khan, the growth of the Muslim population is helped by the fact that Muslims have the youngest median age of all other major religious groups (23 in 2010), seven years younger than the median age of non-Muslims (30). That means that a larger share of Muslims will soon be at the point in their lives to begin having children. This, combined with high fertility rates, is expected to accelerate Muslim population growth. Lipka and Hackett claim that Muslims are expected to grow as a percentage in every region except Latin America and the Caribbean, where relatively few Muslims live. Studies show that the same dynamics hold true in many countries where Muslims live in large numbers alongside other religious groups. According to Conrad Hackett, in India, where the Muslim population is growing at a faster rate than the country's majority Hindu population, it is projected to rise from 14.4 percent of the 2010 population to 18.4 percent (311 million people) by 2050. Hackett also says that while there were roughly equal numbers of Muslims and Christians in Nigeria as of 2010, Muslims are expected to grow to a solid majority of Nigeria's population (58.5 percent) in 2050.

Lipka and Hackett argue that even the switching of religions, which is expected to hinder the growth of some other religious groups, is not expected to have a negative net impact on Muslims. By contrast, between 2010 and 2050, Christianity is projected to have a net loss of more than sixty million adherents worldwide because of switching.

Other factors affecting the growth rate include the following:

- Muslims are not generally allowed to leave the faith.
- Muslim men may marry non-Muslim women, but Muslim women may not marry outside the faith. Moreover, women who marry Muslim men are supposed to convert.
- Most Muslims either have no access to or don't use birth control.

## References

"The Future of the Global Muslim Population: Projections for 2010-2030." Pew Research Center. http://www.pewforum.org/The-Future-of-the-Global-Muslim-Population.aspx.

Hackett, Conrad. "By 2050, India to Have World's Largest Populations of Hindus and Muslims." Pew Research Center. Fact Tank: News in the Numbers, April 21, 2015. http://www.pewresearch.org/fact-tank/2015/04/21/by-2050-india-to-have-worlds-largest-populations-of-hindus-and-muslims/.

Khan, Adnan. "Extract from *Global Trends for the 21ˢᵗ Century* by Adnan Khan." *The Khilafah*, October 18, 2016. http://www.khilafah.com/extract-from-global-trends-for-the-21st-century-by-adnan-khan/.

Lipka, Michael, and Conrad Hackett. "Why Muslims Are the World's Fastest-Growing Religious Group." Pew Research Center. Fact Tank: News in the Numbers, April 23, 2015. http://www.pewresearch.org/fact-tank/2017/04/06/why-muslims-are-the-worlds-fastest-growing-religious-group/.

Molina, Vanessa. *Gal in the Gulf: A Different View of the Middle East.* Bloomington, IN: AuthorHouse, 2016.

# Contemporary Views about Faith

*Should I believe in God?*

I am a fellow of the Alexander von Humboldt Foundation, a German scientific organization with offices in many countries around the world. Humboldt fellows include many American scientists and distinguished people with extraordinary achievements. Before 2005, forty fellows were among the elite group of Nobel Prize winners, and I'm sure that number is greater now. In one of the foundation's most recent publications, several German scientists expressed their views regarding science and faith, which I found interesting and informative. This essay includes a summary of their views.

Many scientists believe that our brains search to understand the world around us and, in the process, drive us to believe in God, astrology, extraterrestrials, or string theory. This happens because of our ability to link cause and effect. Once we understood the connection between cause and effect, we could not stop searching for reasons why the world is as it is. We wanted to know the cause of things such as disease and death, but we also found it impossible to apply the principle of "no effect without a cause" to strokes of fate without resorting to the supernatural. When our ancestors reached the limits of their understanding, they came to the conclusion that an invisible God must be responsible, a solution that was so compelling—and still is—that a lot of societies developed it quite independently. This line of thought answers our major questions and gives us something to hold on to. After all, humans are weak, fragile, and not equipped with tools or intelligence to uncover the major secrets of this complex world.

Some scientists believe that when faced with uncertainties, we feel lost and tend to panic. To comfort ourselves, we either ignore, deny, avoid, or try to understand those uncertainties. Some of us find believing in fate or even conspiracy more comforting than admitting ignorance.

## Should I Believe in God?

For reasons mentioned above, most people believe in some form of supernatural power, but there are other arguments for believing as well. For example, here is Blaise Pascal's philosophical argument regarding God. Think about two events: (1) the event that God exists, and (2) the event that a person believes that God exists. Suppose that p is a number between zero and one, the probability that God exists. Each person has the option of being a believer or nonbeliever, which leads to four disjointed (mutually exclusive) possibilities: (1) God exists and the person is a believer, (2) God exists and the person is a nonbeliever, (3) God doesn't exist and the person is a believer, and (4) God doesn't exist and the person is a nonbeliever.

Suppose that the payoffs of these options can be expressed in dollars. Using the numbers and through calculating the expected payoffs, Pascal concludes that believing in God results in a better payoff—no matter how small the probability that God really exists.

## How Many Gods? Non-Euclidean Geometries/Statistical Physics

One frequently cited empirical discovery is the general theory of relativity and its adoption to non-Euclidean geometry. Recall that Euclid developed the idea of geometry around 300 BC. In his book, he starts with five main postulates, axioms, or assumptions from which he drove theorems of geometry. The postulates were as follows:

1.  Given two points, there is a straight line that joins them.
2.  A straight-line segment can be prolonged indefinitely.
3.  A circle can be constructed when a point for its center and a distance for its radius are given.
4.  All right angles are equal.
5.  From a point outside a line, only one line can be a parallel to it.

The last postulate, number 5, is more complicated than the other four. Over the years, many mathematicians have tried to derive it from the first four, but nobody has come up with a proof.

# Details

Geometry is the realm of mathematics in which we talk about things such as points, lines, angles, triangles, circles, squares and other shapes, as well as the properties and relationships between all these things. For centuries, it was widely believed that the universe worked according to the principles of Euclidean geometry where parallel lines never crossed, and this was the only kind of geometry taught in schools. In fact, for a long time this was my favorite joke: "Parallel lines have a lot in common. It's unfortunate that they can never meet."

The early nineteenth century would finally witness decisive steps in the creation of non-Euclidean geometry. Non-Euclidean geometry arises when the parallel postulate is replaced with an alternative one. Doing so, one obtains hyperbolic geometry and elliptic geometry, the traditional non-Euclidean geometries. The essential difference between the geometries is the nature of parallel lines. Euclid's fifth postulate, the parallel postulate, states that within a two-dimensional plane, for any given line $\ell$ and a point A, which is not on $\ell$, there is exactly one line through A that does not intersect $\ell$. In hyperbolic geometry, by contrast, there are an infinite number of lines through A not intersecting $\ell$, and in elliptic geometry, any line through A intersects $\ell$.

Another way to describe the differences between these geometries is to consider two straight lines, both perpendicular to a third line and indefinitely extended in a two-dimensional plane:

- In Euclidean geometry, the lines remain at a constant distance from each other and are known as parallels. This means that a line drawn perpendicular to one line at any point will intersect the other line and the length of the line segment joining the points of intersection remains constant.
- In hyperbolic geometry, they curve away from each other, increasing in distance as one moves further from the points of intersection with the common perpendicular.
- In elliptic geometry, the lines curve toward each other and intersect.

In my view, the story of geometries somehow relates to the story of three statistics regarding particles in physics; Fermi-Dirac, Bose-Einstein, and Maxwell-Boltzmann. If we have indistinguishable particles, we apply Fermi-Dirac statistics. To identical and indistinguishable particles, we apply Bose-Einstein statistics. And to distinguishable classical particles, we apply Maxwell-Boltzmann statistics.

Finally, based on our knowledge about geometry and the fact that none of them—Euclidian, hyperbolic, or elliptic—is incorrect, we could infer that assuming no god, or one god, or many gods as our postulate would not necessarily lead to any inconsistency or contradiction.

## References

"Geometry." *Wikipedia*, Wikimedia Foundation, 2 May 2019, en.wikipedia.org/wiki/Geometry.

*Humboldt Network*, www.humboldt-foundation.de/web/humboldt-network.html.

"Non-Euclidean Geometry." *Wikipedia*, Wikimedia Foundation, 6 May 2019, en.wikipedia.org/wiki/Non-Euclidean geometry.

# Santa: Giving for the Sake of Giving

*Kindness is both a gift and a reward.*

When I hear "Jingle Bells," Christmas carols, and "Happy New Year," I wonder about the message they carry. Clearly it is not about presents, food, or Santa. It is not even about the end of one year and the beginning of another. So I ask myself, what *are* they about?

I think Christmas is about lots of things, notably leaving self and touching hearts. It's about reflecting on the past year, evaluating, examining, and adjusting. It's about another opportunity for bold moves and fresh starts. It's about giving, receiving, forgiving, and forgetting. About family, friends, love, and care. About making an effort to become nicer and kinder. About trying to become a pillar of support for those who need us. About learning to enjoy the simple pleasures of life and paying attention to nature's astonishing beauty. About welcoming modesty, amity, and humility, while letting go of jealousy, ego, hate, and anger. About loving generously, caring deeply, and learning to be mindful. And above all, Christmas is about accepting, appreciating, and growing. In sum, it's about becoming kinder to yourself and to others.

## Kindness

Kindness, a simple gift that touches every heart,
Something appreciated by all, never mind how culturally apart.
A present made up of happiness, confidence, and strength,
It gives direction to happy land and a point to start.
It brings hope and joy to all and every needy heart,
It gives a measurable advantage, an enjoyable head start.
At the end, the giver and receiver appear in the same chart,
It is easily realized, no need to be genius or even smart.

People remember you for your kindness, it is an exceptional art,
Their hearts become a resting place, never let your memories depart.
A kind word may not be enough to warm a room, a house, or a car,
But even in the coldest winters, it warms both our body and our heart.
Children outgrow their toys and material things, never mind rich or poor,
But they always cherish families' help and kindness, that's for sure.
—Reza Noubary

## Quotes about Kindness

- "Kindness is a language which the deaf can hear and the blind can see." (Mark Twain)
- "Kindness in words creates confidence. Kindness in thinking creates profoundness. Kindness in giving creates love." (Lao Tzu)
- "Kind hearts are the gardens. Kind thoughts are the roots. Kind words are the blossoms. Kind deeds are the fruits." (Kirpal Singh)
- "Kindness has converted more sinners than zeal, eloquence or learning." (Frederick W. Faber)
- "Kindness is the light that dissolves all walls between souls, families, and nations." (Paramahansa Yogananda)
- "Kindness gives birth to kindness." (Sophocles)
- "There is no need for temples, no need for complicated philosophies. My brain and my heart are my temples; my philosophy is kindness." (Dalai Lama)
- "Genuine kindness is no ordinary act, but a gift of rare beauty." (Sylvia Rossetti)
- "Kind words can be said in a second but their effect can last forever." (Reza Noubary)
- "Kindness can accomplish things force cannot." (Reza Noubary)
- "Kindness is a way to show people they matter to you." (Reza Noubary)

## My Promise

Look at me one last time, before you say goodnight, before you fall asleep,
Look at me one last time, before you close your eyes, before you lose me to a dream,
Promise to live, promise to love,

Promise to care, promise to share,
Promise to think, promise to seek,
Then I promise wonderful surprises and pleasant dreams.
—Reza Noubary

# Chapter 4
## Health/Medicine

*Body and mind connection, the puzzle of the centuries.*

### *MY THOUGHTS IN ANNIVERSARY OF MY SURGERY*

*A few years ago I had a serious health problem that opened my eyes to life's peculiarities*
*I became a changed person with different thoughts, values, and priorities*
*I now cry more often, appreciate more, and admire nature's superiorities*
*I love with intensity, hope desperately, and make decision with more authority*
*I value the family and friends, I notice the nature's order and irregularities*
*I appreciate time, I practice kindness, I accept people's abnormalities.*

### *Thank Doctors and Nurses*
*Sometimes we are sick, tired, or do not feel well*
*Sometimes with no reason we see the world as hell*
*We may say things we are not supposed to tell*
*Even to our doctors and nurses who are like angel.*

# Medical Errors: The Third Leading Cause of Death in the United States

*If the United States health care were a country,*
*it would be the sixth largest economy in the world.*

They are hard to believe, but here are some disturbing findings regarding health and treatments:

- As many as 440,000 people die each year from medical errors, according to "A New, Evidence-Based Estimate of Patient Harms Associated with Hospital Care" by John T. James.

- Only heart disease and cancer kill more Americans than preventable medical errors in hospitals, according to "Medical Mistakes are 3rd Leading Cause of Death in U.S."

- The United States has the most expensive health care in the world, according to "Health Care Spending in the United States and Other High-Income Countries." We spend more on health care than the next ten biggest spenders—Japan, Germany, France, China, United Kingdom, Italy, Canada, Brazil, Spain, and Australia—combined. If our health care system were a country, it would be the sixth largest economy on the entire planet. Compared with the rest of the world, our health care is ranked about average, but our high spending is not buying us particularly safe care, said Dr. Ashish Jha of the Harvard School of Public Health.

- Articles such as "The 'Underperforming' US Health Care System: Revisiting the Conventional Wisdom" present reasons why health care in the United States is not performing well. According to some experts, the two significant causes of such mediocre performance are overreliance on technology and a poorly developed primary care infrastructure. After Japan, the United States is second in the availability of technological procedures such as CAT scans and MRIs, but this has not translated into a higher standard of care. The

United States has a superior system for treating acute surgical emergencies, but it is an unmitigated failure at treating chronic illnesses. With its focus on diagnostic tests, drugs, and surgical interventions for most ills, conventional medicine harms an unexpectedly large number of patients. The lethality of our system is in part caused by side effects, whether expected or not, but preventable errors also account for a staggering number of deaths. The problem may also be linked to a cascade effect in which diagnostic procedures lead to more treatment, more symptoms, and hence more complications and deaths, according to "Cascade Effects of Medical Technology."

- Some managers think that our tort law adds to the staggering cost of medical care. But making the legal system less receptive to medical malpractice lawsuits will not significantly affect the costs of medical care, according to Tom Baker, professor of law and health sciences at the University of Pennsylvania School of Law and author of *The Medical Malpractice Myth*. Others think that the problem is partly due to a large number of unnecessary medical and surgical procedures and hospitalizations. Around 7.5 million unnecessary medical and surgical procedures and 8.9 unnecessary hospitalizations occur annually, according to "Death by Medicine."

## Remarks

1. Most do not blame the physicians for all that is happening. Chris Kresser argues that in many ways, doctors are just as victimized by the deficiencies of the healthcare system as patients and consumers are. With increased numbers of patients and HMO-mandated time limits for each patient's visit, as well as the required paperwork, most doctors are trying their best to cope with the situation.

2. Some find the current situation not at all surprising. Homoeopathic practitioners, for example, believe that medical science has gone too far in the wrong direction, and that the more we go down that path, the worse things will become.

3. Another view is that change may not be entirely necessary because these statistics could rely on conjecture. The cause/effect relationship between the number of deaths while undergoing medical treatment may not be clear. When a person dies during medical treatment, that does not necessarily mean

their death resulted from their choice of treatment. In some cases, the person might have died with no treatment at all.

## Is There an Alternative?

Most experts agree that there is no easy fix. Discussion about Kresser's article includes an array of viewpoints, with some people arguing that any profession operates within a for-profit system and that to suggest a solution outside this reality is naïve. Within the medical field, someone should always profit, but how do we align this with patients' interests and benefits?

Some people suggest minimizing interactions with the conventional system, which, at least in the case of chronic diseases, has little to offer. Some blame conventional strategies, which often target symptoms rather than underlying causes of disease. They suggest a gradual transition to integrated medicine based on mind-body connection. Integrated medicine combines the most scientifically validated and least harmful therapies from both high-tech and holistic medical practices. Some doctors and patients accept this philosophy and its whole-person approach—designed to treat the person, not just the disease. They think that therapies that take advantage of the subtle interactions between a person's state of mind and basic physiological functions are a reasonable alternative. This approach includes the mind-body medicine that uses relaxation techniques and the power of thoughts and emotions.

## References

Baker, Tom. *The Medical Malpractice Myth*. Chicago, IL: Univiversity of Chicago Press, 2007.

Brown, Lawrence D., and Michael S. Sparer. "The 'Underperforming' US Health Care System: Revisiting the Conventional Wisdom." *Journal of Health, Politics and Law* 43, no. 5 (2018): 731–738. https://read.dukeupress.edu/jhppl/article/43/5/731/134938/Introduction-The-Underperforming-US-Health-Care.

Deyo, Richard A. "Cascade Effects of Medical Technology." *Annual Review of Public Health* 23, no. 1 (February 2002): 23–44. https://com-radiology.sites.medinfo.ufl.edu/files/2010/03/Oct-09-1.pdf.

James, John T. "A New, Evidence-Based Estimate of Patient Harms Associated with Hospital Care." *Journal of Patient Safety* 9, no. 3 (September 2013): 122–128. https://

journals.lww.com/journalpatientsafety/fulltext/2013/09000/A_New,_Evidence_based_Estimate_of_Patient_Harms.2.aspx.

Kresser, Chris. "Medical Care Is 3rd Leading Cause of Death in U.S." January 19, 2019. https://chriskresser.com/medical-care-is-the-3rd-leading-cause-of-death-in-the-us/.

"Medical Mistakes Are 3rd Leading Cause of Death in U.S." Bernie Sanders: U.S. Senator for Vermont, July 17, 2014. https://www.sanders.senate.gov/newsroom/press-releases/medical-mistakes-are-3rd-leading-cause-of-death-in-us.

Mercola. "Preventable Medical Mistakes Account for One-Sixth of All Annual Deaths in the United States." October 9, 2013. http://www.quantumhealing.co.za/preventable-medical-mistakes.html.

Null, Gary, Carolyn Dean, Martin Feldman, Debora Rasio, and Dorothy Woods Smith. "Death by Medicine." *Semantic Scholar*, 2010. https://www.semanticscholar.org/paper/Death-by-Medicine-Null-Dean/805177164c0c17c09c3a1646c0e61a7f711b6537.

Papanicolas, Irene, Liana R. Woskie, and Ashish K. Jha. "Health Care Spending in the United States and Other High-Income Countries." *Journal of the American Medical Association* 319, no. 10 (2018): 1024–1039. https://jamanetwork.com/journals/jama/fullarticle/2674671.

*The probability of a woman being tested positive for breast cancer is, surprisingly, very low. Not every test works as we wish or expect.*

Diagnostic tests are frequently used to detect the presence or absence of a disease. Ordinarily a positive test result indicates presence, and a negative test result indicates absence of the disease. How often do test results match reality? What percentage of people who test positive for a disease actually have it, and what percentage of people who test negative actually do not? It turns out that in some cases, the answers to these questions surprise even medical professionals. In fact, when only a small percentage of the population has a specific disease, the probability of a positive test result accurately indicating the presence of that disease can be surprisingly low. This is the case even for a test with acceptable accuracy. Hard to believe? Here are a few examples:

## Mammograms

Mammograms are used to detect breast cancer, and the statistics about mammograms' accuracy vary widely. The Society of Breast Imaging, for example, estimates that of women who get a mammogram at any given time, only 1 percent truly have breast cancer. Note that 1 percent presents the probability of breast cancer in a one-time test and should not be confused with the probability of breast cancer in a woman's lifetime. Mammograms typically produce positive test results for 86 percent of women with breast cancer and negative test results for 88 percent of women without it. With these specifications, the probability of a woman who has tested positive for having breast cancer is, surprisingly, less than 8 percent.

Why is this probability so low? Consider a random sample of a hundred women having mammograms at a given time. Here, one woman is expected to have breast cancer, which represents 1 percent of the sample. For the woman with breast cancer, the chance of detection is 86 percent, so we would expect a positive test result for her. For each of the ninety-nine women without breast cancer, the likelihood of a negative test result is 88 percent. So for this group, we would expect about 0.88 x 99 = 87 negative and twelve positive (false positive) test results. This means that out of the thirteen women with positive test results, only one actually has breast cancer (1/13 < 8 percent).

## ELISA Test

Next, consider HIV testing using the standard Wellcome ELISA (enzyme-linked immunosorbent assay) test. According to the Food and Drug Administration, the ELISA test picks up approximately 99.3 percent of HIV positives and 99.99 percent of HIV negatives, making it an accurate test. The incidence of HIV positive in the general population without known risk factors is estimated to be twenty-five in a million. That is, in a group of ten million people without known risk factors, about 250 are expected to actually be HIV positive. Applying the ELISA test to this group of 250, about 250 x 0.993 = 248 of them are expected to have positive tests. Also from the remaining 9,999,750 true HIV-negatives, about 9,999,750 x (1 – 0.9999) = 9,999,750 x 0.0001 = 1000 are expected to have positive tests (false positive). This means that about 1000/1248 (80 percent) of the positive test results would actually come from people who are not HIV positive!

Before judging the ELISA test a waste of time, we should note that the test has dramatically increased the likelihood of detection. Although only 0.0025 percent of people with no known risk factors are HIV positive, the test will identify almost 20 percent of them correctly—an increase by a factor of almost eight thousand! Still the number of false positives is high. As explained earlier, this is the problem with testing for a rare disease. A study in the United Kingdom in the late 1980s confirms these numbers. Out of 3,122,556 blood samples taken from people without known risk factors for HIV, 373 tested positive based on the ELISA test. These samples were then retested using the much more specific (and expensive) Western Blot test, and sixty-four cases were confirmed. This means that 83 percent of the positive test results were, in fact, false positives.

## PSA

Finally, consider the prostate specific antigen (PSA) blood test for prostate cancer in men. Studies such as "Prostate Cancer in Elderly Men" suggest that about 30 percent of men over fifty have cancerous cells in their prostate, though few of them die of prostate cancer. The PSA test has high rates of false positive and false negative results; about 50 percent of men with high PSA readings do not have prostate cancer. When a person tests positive, other tests are usually considered, though they are often inconclusive. Given that cancerous prostate cells might never pose a health threat, deciding whether PSA tests should be routinely administered is not easy. The current recommendation by the American Cancer Society is that men over the age of fifty should have an annual PSA test, along with a digital rectal exam, although a statistical analysis published in the Journal of the American Medical Association suggests that the benefits of such screening are marginal at best.

## Overuse of Diagnostic Tests

The article "7 Medical Tests and Treatments You May Not Really Need" addresses the problems related to the overuse of diagnostic tests. Recently the Choosing Wisely campaign, which represents some 375,000 doctors and includes *Consumer Reports*, has acknowledged that many popular medical tests, though critical, are overused. The tests used to detect heart disease are good examples. According to Dr. Elliott Fisher, director of the Dartmouth Institute, which studies health care issues, stress tests and EKGs are among the most overused tests for people over the age of fifty with no symptoms. A *Consumer Reports* survey found that in 2010, 44 percent of people with no symptoms of heart disease had a screening test, exercise stress test, EKG, or ultrasound. Millions of healthy people each year get tests that they really do not need. According to Steven Nissen, a prominent cardiologist at the Cleveland Clinic, for people at low risk for heart disease, these tests are ten times more likely to show a false positive than a real problem. Moreover, like EKGs, stress echocardiograms, which create pictures of the heart during exercise, frequently yield misleading results. In fact, although for several years cardiology guidelines have discouraged use of these tests for people who have no symptoms, their use has been common, says Dr. James Fasules of the American College of Cardiology.

## Final Words

Both patients and doctors rely too much on tests and their outcomes. Doctors often order tests to satisfy patients. Doctors may also order tests to protect themselves from malpractice suits, according to "7 Medical Tests and Treatments You May Not

Really Need." Additionally, patients often expect doctors to order some sort of test. It's hard to believe, but an estimated thirty thousand Medicare patients die each year from unnecessary care, according to Fisher. He also estimates that up to one-third of our spiraling health care costs is wasted on unnecessary tests and treatments. Based on such information, the Choosing Wisely campaign concluded that by not choosing wisely, doctors could actually hurt more people than help.

## References

Pure Home Care Services. "7 Medical Tests and Treatments You May Not Really Need," June 18, 2012. http://purehomecareservices.com/2012/06/7-medical-tests-and-treatments-you-may-not-really-need/.

Society of Breast Imaging. "Guidelines for Breast Screening." https://www.sbi-online.org.

Stangelberger, Anton, Matthias Waldert, and Bob Djavan. "Prostate Cancer in Elderly Men." *Reviews in Urology* 10, no. 2 (Spring 2008): 111–119. https://www.ncbi.nlm.nih.gov/pmc/articles/PMC2483315/.

Bell, Douglas S, et al. "A Test of Knowledge about Prostate Cancer Screening. Online Pilot Evaluation among Southern California Physicians." Journal of General Interal Medicine, Blackwell Science Inc, Apr. 2006, www.ncbi.nlm.nih.gov/pmc/articles/PMC1484731/.

# Cancer: Biological Bad Luck

*Luck, an invisible player in the game of life.*

People who get cancer often view it in terms of cause and effect: How did this happen, and more importantly, how could I have avoided it? This is understandable based on what we hear and read. However, a recent study by oncologist Bert Vogelstein and bio-mathematician Cristian Tomasetti, published in the journal *Science*, concluded that most cancers are not influenced by lifestyle or environment, but that cancer is the result of bad luck. In "Biological Bad Luck Blamed in Two-Thirds of Cancer Cases," which summarizes Vogelstein and Tomasetti's study results, Will Dunham notes that two-thirds of cancer incidents can be blamed on random mutations accumulating in various parts of the body during ordinary cell division, rather than on heredity or risky habits.

Vogelstein and Tomasetti looked at thirty-one cancer types and found that twenty-two of them, including leukemia and pancreatic, bone, testicular, ovarian, and brain cancers could be explained largely by these random mutations—essentially biological bad luck. The other nine types, including colorectal, skin (known as basal cell carcinoma), and smoking-related lung cancers were more heavily influenced by heredity and environmental factors such as risky behavior or exposure to carcinogens. Overall, they attributed 65 percent of cancer incidents to random mutations in genes that can drive cancer growth. They examined the extent to which stem cell divisions in healthy cells—and the random mutations, or "bad luck" accumulations—drive cancer in different tissues.

What else can be said about bad luck? This question was highlighted when researchers tried to sort out environmental versus inherited causes of cancer. Their effort implied that cancer is harder to prevent than previously hoped and that early detection is under-appreciated. This sparked controversy and confusion among people who had believed that, though it's a complex topic to put numbers on, many cancers could be prevented, largely through lifestyle changes. This concern has also been addressed by Michael Walsh in "Reports That Cancer Is 'Mainly Bad Luck' Make a Complicated Story a Bit Too Simple."

To reexamine the luck theory, Vogelstein and Tomasetti did further study and again published their findings in *Science*, and again the media picked up their results. The second study addressed some of the original concerns about approach by boosting sample size and adding data from more countries and cancer types. The results supported their original conclusions, adding further evidence to their theory that cancer risk is most strongly associated with how quickly specialized cells, called stem cells, replicate. They predict that mutations in two out of three cancers are due to bad luck.

Although *Science* is a well-respected journal, some people still wonder whether this message does more to confuse than inform. According to Walsh, one of the biggest problems is that trying to get a clear answer to the cause-and-effect question from this analysis might oversimplify things. When cancer develops, many other real-world factors are at play, and it's critical to understand how those factors affect both the progression and the prevention of cancer. Mutations that can lead to cancer can be caused by environmental and lifestyle factors, such as cigarette smoke, but they can also be inherited or happen by chance. These chance mutations occur when errors are made as a cell copies and divides its DNA. Vogelstein and Tomasetti believe that this third factor is a major player in cancer cases, and in their model it accounts for around two in three mutations in cancer. This, they say, is the bad luck factor—and they want that to be acknowledged more often.

## Final Remarks

We learn about the world around us by collecting and analyzing data. Unfortunately, the world around us is so complex—and our knowledge so limited—that our views and understanding of data hardly match reality. For example, scientific modeling takes the data as a message and tries to model them using the basic decomposition.

> Datum = Smooth Part (Trend) + Rough Part
> = Systematic (Deterministic) Part + Random Part
> = Signal + Noise

Mathematics is used to model the systematic part, whereas probability and statistics are used to analyze the random part. Models developed are often judged on their signal-to-noise ratio. When the ratio is bigger than one, the smooth part is dominant.

This allows us to use the smooth part for prediction and the rough part for assessing our model and its precision. In the opposite case, where the random part is dominant, we often do not know much about the phenomenon under consideration—and so we attribute them to luck or chance.

## References

Dunham, Will. "Biological Bad Luck Blamed in Two-Thirds of Cancer Cases." *Daily Star*, January 4, 2015. http://www.dailystar.com.lb/Life/Health/2015/Jan-04/283044-biological-bad-luck-blamed-in-two-thirds-of-cancer-cases.ashx.

*I-Digest: Indonesia Digest.* www.indonesia-digest.net

Walsh, Michael. "Reports That Cancer Is 'Mainly Bad Luck' Make a Complicated Story a Bit Too Simple." *Cancer Research UK.* https://scienceblog.cancerresearchuk.org/2017/03/24/reports-that-cancer-is-mainly-bad-luck-make-a-complicated-story-a-bit-too-simple/.

# Obesity: An Epidemic of the Century

*FLAT stomach is what I want. FAT part is no problem*
*I have that. I only need L to cooperate.*

Obesity is now approaching epidemic proportions globally. According to the World Health Organization, in 2014 there were more than 1.9 billion overweight adults and more than 600 million obese adults. A recent comprehensive study by the NCD Risk Factor Collaboration revealed that in the last forty years, the average body mass index has risen by the equivalent of 3.31 pounds per person each decade. High-income English-speaking countries account for some of the biggest rises and more than a quarter of severely obese people. The United States and China have the most obese people, and the United States has more severely obese people than any other country.

As reported in "The State of Obesity: Better Policies for a Healthier America 2016," based on data collected in September 2018, the US obesity rate exceeds 35 percent in three states, 30 percent in twenty-two states, 25 percent in forty-five states, and 20 percent in every state. The annual health costs of obesity are now around 21 percent of our total medical costs, mainly because of the link between obesity and more than sixty chronic diseases, including diabetes and cardiovascular diseases. The only bit of good news is that the trend of increasing obesity in the United States has slowed since 2000.

No one has succeeded in finding a definite answer for the chronic weight problem in America, according to "Why Are Americans Obese?" but many theories include the contributions of genetics, age, and lifestyle. According to PublicHealth.org, the preponderance of evidence points to the two causes most of us already suspect—too much food and too little exercise—but the role of food and diet is obviously complex. We receive mixed messages when it comes to what to eat and how much. As a result, we have developed a culture that includes both fast food and fast weight loss options, partly because we spend more time at work and less time in our homes and kitchens than our parents.

"The State of Obesity" report contains other information about obesity and present-day eating and activity habits in the United States. For example, we consume 31 percent more calories now than forty years ago. Compared with people in any other industrialized country, we walk or bike much less, and this is true even for our youngsters. Fewer than 15 percent of our school-aged children walk or bike to school, compared with 48 percent in 1969. For these and other reasons, it shouldn't surprise us that 13.9 percent of our high school students are obese and an additional 16 percent are overweight.

Considering the negative effects of obesity, we should be concerned not only for our own health, but for the health of our children and grandchildren, as well as of our country and the rest of the world. Research shows that many problems related to obesity can be avoided by simple changes in lifestyle, such as staying active and eating more healthful food and smaller portions. Of course, we should also realize that being overweight is a medical problem and that nobody can deal with it individually.

## References

NCD Risk Factor Collaboration (NCD-RisC). "Trends in Adult Body-Mass Index in 200 Countries from 1975 to 2014: A Pooled Analysis of 1698 Population-Based Measurement Studies with 19.2 Million Participants." *Lancet* 387, no 10026 (April 2016): 1377–1396. https://doi.org/10.1016/S0140-6736(16)30054-X.

World Health Organization. "Obesity and Overweight," February 16, 2018. http://www.who.int/news-room/fact-sheets/detail/obesity-and-overweight.

"The State of Obesity: Better Policies for a Healthier America 2016." https://stateofobesity.org/wp-content/uploads/2018/08/stateofobesity2016.pdf.

*The State of Obesity: Better Policies for Healthier America.* https://stateofobesity.org/.

"Why Are Americans Obese?" *Public Health.* https://www.publichealth.org/public-awareness/obesity/.

# Body Fat: Treasure or Trash?

*You may not like your fat, but your body certainly does.*

Body fat has a bad reputation, and most people try to hide it or exercise it away. But for scientists, fat is one of the most fascinating and least understood components of the human body.

## Benefits of Fat

Fat serves a variety of important purposes, and our bodies are endowed with many self-defense mechanisms to hold on to it. In addition to storing excess calories and releasing hormones to control metabolism, fat can use stem cells to regenerate, increase appetite if threatened, and use bacteria, genetics, and viruses to expand itself. Fat triggers puberty, enabling the reproductive and immune systems, and it even affects brain size. We need fat for warmth and insulation, for cushioning our bones and internal organs, for energy, and even to think. Fat also bolsters immunity and helps produce a slew of hormones crucial to our health, including estrogen, leptin, angiotensin, and tumor necrosis factor-alpha to help keep cells healthy.

## A Little Fat Does the Body Good

Some experts claim that being slightly overweight increases one's longevity and that overweight people with certain chronic diseases often live longer and do better than normal-weight people with the same conditions. Some experts even believe that fat helps guard the body from damage, particularly as we age. Anytime the body fights illness or deals with a chronic disease, it requires more energy stored as fat. Studies such as "Association of All-Cause Mortality with Overweight and Obesity Using Standard Body Mass Index Categories" say that being overweight is associated with lower rates of mortality. Fat seems to have particularly helpful effects if it is around the butt and thighs, according to one Oxford University study published in the *Journal of Obesity*. It is thought that this fat traps potentially harmful fatty acids that can travel through the bloodstream to the heart.

## Different Types of Fat

Although the amount of body fat does matter, the type and where it is stored matters much more.

- White fat: Compared with other types of fat, white fat is more plentiful. Its home is mostly around the hips and thighs, but it's found almost anywhere in the body. It settles under the skin like padding and creates curves. Its second role is to burn energy and produce the hormone adiponectin. In "Adiponectin As an Anti-Inflammatory Factor," Noriyuki Ouchi and Kenneth Walsh suggests that adiponectin has anti-inflammatory and "insulin-sensitizing" properties that may help reduce risk for developing Type 2 diabetes. When people become fat, the production of adiponectin slows or shuts down, setting them up for disease. Fortunately, regular exercise increases adiponectin.
- Brown fat: Also known as "good fat," brown fat acts more like muscle and burns energy even when we are inactive. When activated, brown fat burns white fat. Lean people tend to have more brown fat than overweight or obese people do. Brown fat can be increased with regular aerobic exercise.
- Visceral (deep) fat: People with large waists or bellies have this toxic fat, which drives up the risk of diabetes, heart disease, stroke, and even dementia. Visceral fat accumulates around the organs deep inside the abdominal cavity. Even thin people with no apparent belly fat can have dangerous amounts of visceral fat. Visceral fat causes problems because it churns out stress hormones, such as cortisol, and inflammatory substances, called cytokines, that affect the body's production of insulin. The result is increased risk of both Type 2 diabetes and heart disease.
- Subcutaneous fat: This fat is found directly under the skin. In terms of overall health, subcutaneous fat in the thighs and buttocks isn't necessarily bad and may have some potential benefits.
- Belly fat: Belly fat is both visceral and subcutaneous. Abdominal fat is viewed as a bigger health risk than hip or thigh fat.

## Concluding Remarks

The full story of body fat reveals that the shape or composition of the body does not define how healthy the person is. An overweight or slightly obese person can certainly be fit and metabolically healthy, although the picture changes if the person becomes obese. In other words, our level of health has everything to do with the way we treat our body—not with its size.

Experts believe that we should not stress too much over fat, but should stay committed to our activities and nutrition. We should also not be dissuaded by advertising and images that show perfectly proportioned clones. All we need is to understand how our body works and set achievable goals for ourselves.

## References

Flegal, Katherine M., Brian K. Kit, Heather Orpana, and Barry I. Graubard. "Association of All-Cause Mortality With Overweight and Obesity Using Standard Body Mass Index Categories." *Journal of the American Medical Association* 309, no. 1 (Jan. 2013): 71–82. https://www.ncbi.nlm.nih.gov/pmc/articles/PMC4855514/.

*Journal of Obesity.* https://www.hindawi.com/journals/jobe/.

Manolopoulos, K N, et al. "Gluteofemoral Body Fat as a Determinant of Metabolic Health." Nature News, Nature Publishing Group, 12 Jan. 2010, www.nature.com/articles/ijo2009286.

Ouchi, Noriyuki, and Kenneth Walsh. "Adiponectin As An Anti-Inflammatory Factor." *Clinica Chimica Acta* 380, nos. 1–2 (May 2007): 24–30. https://www.ncbi.nlm.nih.gov/pmc/articles/PMC2755046/.

Sims, Stacy T. "The 3 Body Types—And How They Affect Your Weight Loss." July 29, 2016. https://www.prevention.com/weight-loss/g20434758/the-3-body-types-and-how-they-affect-your-weight-loss/.

# Medical Science Is Not an Exact Science

*Doctors are not supposed to have an answer to every health problem, and they do not.*

Most patients expect doctors to know exactly what their problem is and how to fix it. However, people who deal with medical-related issues point out that it is impossible, even for specialists, to figure out the cause of every health problem.

A recent study performed by researchers at Johns Hopkins University estimates that in the United States, medical errors are responsible for more than a quarter million deaths per year. Medical error is defined by John Bohnen and Ethan Grober as "an act of omission or commission in planning or execution that contributes or could contribute to an unintended result." According to Shannon Haymond in "What Everyone Should Know About Lab Tests," medical error is the third leading cause of death in the United States. Only heart disease and cancer kill more people. This is frightening and points to a much larger problem, since many medical errors are not lethal.

We know that medical science is neither an exact science like mathematics nor a hard or pure science like physics. Therefore we cannot always rely on the results obtained from sophisticated tools, since they could show considerable variation. S. C. Panda reminds us that one pathologist may opine about a particular case as malignant, which may not be corroborated if another colleague examines it. Additionally, scientific truths are not necessarily true for all time; the life of *truth* in medicine is short. There is a saying: "Half of what is true today will be proven incorrect in the next five years and unfortunately, we do not know which half that is going to be."

As pointed out by Haymond, lab tests producing false positives or false negatives is one important factor that contributes to delayed or wrong diagnoses and, as a result, unnecessary costs and care. Christopher Cheney, in "Tapping Patient Engagement to Reduce Diagnostic Errors," estimates that in the United States, diagnostic errors happen about 12 million times per year for outpatients alone. "The Path to Improve Diagnosis and Reduce Diagnostic Error" concludes that most people will experience at least one diagnostic error in their life. Errors related to lab tests are more common than we might think, high precision tests are not affordable, and most classical tests have a relatively high percent of false alarms. Haymond says that more than thirteen billion tests are performed in over 250,000 certified clinical laboratories each year in the United States. These include tests for genetic disorders, lead poisoning, and diabetes, and the results routinely guide diagnostic and therapeutic decisions. Despite all this, many people have the misperception that diagnostic tests are always correct.

As mentioned earlier, all lab tests have limitations, such as mistakes in ordering lab tests at the right time and problems with the accuracy, availability, and interpretation of their results. Another problem is the cost of tests. We could use more accurate tests, but we'd need to pay significantly more for them, which isn't always possible or practical.

There are other causes for uncertainty. For example, I take several medications, and I've noticed that some of my friends who take the same medications talk about side effects that I do not experience. No two people respond to disease or drugs precisely the same way. Our knowledge about the complex connection between our bodies and our minds is limited. Not much is known about the reactions of our bodies to certain chemicals in drugs or the interactions between various drugs. The medical field concentrates on curing the symptoms, as integrated medicine is not yet well developed. Doctors have limited time, a large number of patients, and lots of paperwork. We also have a lot to learn about disease management, and even diagnostic methods and ideas on causation of particular diseases change over time.

To account for the uncertainties, the medical profession has had to become adept at estimating and interpreting probability. In fact, almost all advice given by the medical field to the public is based solely on an expert's assessment of the probabilities involved. Depending on the situation, these probabilities are arrived at either empirically or by educated guess, and the information doctors receive is typically determined empirically. Take, for instance, clinical trials used to determine side effects. Here one needs to account for uncertainties related to missing data created by subjects who don't complete their logs, don't properly follow the protocol, or drop out of the study.

Similar methods are used to determine the probability of a patient experiencing a given symptom. Even when a disease has been accurately diagnosed, exactly how it will manifest itself is difficult to predict. For example, HIV can lead to cognitive impairment in its victims, referred to as HIV dementia, but this condition occurs in fewer than half of those infected. So how do doctors know who will get it? The answer is that they don't know for sure, so they use empirical data gathering.

In any situation, doctors weigh the probabilities when providing care to their patients. They look not only at the probability of the disease occurring in a typical person, but also at the probability that a certain patient will get the disease, experience given symptoms, or suffer from certain side effects. Not only is medical care always going to be slightly unreliable, but a doctor's preconceptions will always bias the care received by the patient. No matter what, most patients are at the mercy of the probability and odds.

## Final Words

Diagnostic methods and ideas about the causes of particular diseases change over time, especially with further use of technology, and tending to sick people goes beyond science and art to require humanity. This work involves knowledge and devotion that cannot be found in textbooks. Every patient is different, and an effective treatment for some patients might not work for others. In sciences such as physics or chemistry, we first create a simulated model with a least number of variables, and experiments can be performed under controlled conditions. In medicine this is not possible, because we are dealing with humans, who are amazingly complex.

## References

Haymond, Shannon. "What Everyone Should Know about Lab Tests." *Scientific American*, 9 May 2016. https://blogs.scientificamerican.com/guest-blog/what-everyone-should-know-about-lab-tests/.

"Medical Errors: The Third Leading Cause of Death in the United States." In this book.

Panda, S. C. "Medicine: Science or Art?" *Mens Sana Monographs* 4, no. 1 (2006): 127–138. https://www.ncbi.nlm.nih.gov/pmc/articles/PMC3190445/.

"The Path to Improve Diagnosis and Reduce Diagnostic Error." In *Improving Diagnosis in Health Care*, edited by E. P. Balogh, B. T. Miller, and J. R. Ball, pp. 355–402. Washington DC: National Academies Press, 2015. https://www.ncbi.nlm.nih.gov/books/NBK338589/.

"Study Suggests Medical Errors Now Third Leading Cause of Death in the U.S." *Johns Hopkins Medicine*, May 3, 2016. https://www.hopkinsmedicine.org/news/media/releases/study_suggests_medical_errors_now_third_leading_cause_of_death_in_the_us.

Grober, Ethan D, and John M A Bohnen. "Defining medical error." Canadian journal of surgery. Journal canadien de chirurgie vol. 48,1 (2005). 39-44.

Cheney, Christopher. "Tapping Patient Engagement to Reduce Diagnostic Errors." Tapping Patient Engagement to Reduce Diagnostic Errors | HealthLeaders Media. November 5, 2018. https://www.healthleadersmedia.com/clinical-care/ tapping-patient-engagement-reduce-diagnostic-errors.

# Artificial Intelligence Transforms the Future of Medicine

*Today doctors badly need help from artificial intelligence.*

Health care now has to deal with the ever-growing problems related to the acquisition, analysis, and application of the extensive knowledge needed to solve complicated clinical problems. People are living longer and a larger population has access to medical care, so many new diseases and medical conditions are being added to the list of known problems. The situation makes it harder and harder to keep up with new knowledge produced, analysis presented and results published. Fortunately, artificial intelligence (AI), a branch of computer science, is now capable of analyzing large, complex data sets and helping physicians save, find, and apply them.

AI is a field of science and engineering concerned with the computational understanding of what is commonly called intelligent behavior, and it has many areas of application. The British mathematician Alan Turing, who published the groundbreaking article "Computing Machinery and Intelligence" in 1950, is one of the founders of AI. Turing defines intelligent behavior in a computer as the ability to achieve intelligent, human-level performance in a cognitive task, which means it has the potential to find meaningful relationships within a data set for the field to which it is applied. It can, for example, be used in the medical field for diagnosis and treatment, as well as for predicting outcomes in various clinical scenarios. In recent years, one of the most fascinating and headline-making applications for AI in medicine has been the development of surgical robots.

## Future of Medicine

According to Kim Krisberg in "Artificial Intelligence Transforms the Future of Medicine," as of November of 2017, about seven thousand clinicians from five hundred institutions worldwide were building and using a diagnostic and management tool that uses AI to glean useful information from the world's collective medical knowledge. This online tool, known as the Human Diagnosis Project (Human Dx), lets physicians ask the community a clinical question and upload supporting information.

Abby Norman, in "Your Future Doctor May Not Be Human," points out that the applications for AI in medicine go beyond administrative drudgework. From powerful diagnostic algorithms to finely tuned surgical robots, the technology is making its presence known across medical disciplines. Is AI better than a real doctor? Could it take the place of the human mind? Clearly when it comes to human touch and emotions, the answer is no. However, the question goes deeper than that. Imagining a future in which AI is an established part of a patient's care team requires a better understanding of how AI measures up to human doctors, with their feelings, emotions, and many other capabilities.

## AI versus Human Doctors

According to Norman, AI's capability, although not yet fully developed, is comparable to that of doctors when it comes to diagnosing conditions. In fact, this is confirmed by researchers at the John Radcliffe Hospital in Oxford, England, who have developed an AI system for diagnosing heart disease that is at least 80 percent more accurate than doctors. To support her view, Norman refers to an advancement by researchers from Harvard University, who have created a "smart" microscope that can detect potentially lethal blood infections. This AI-assisted tool was trained using a series of 100,000 images garnered from 25,000 slides treated with dye to make the bacteria more visible. The AI system can already sort those bacteria with 95 percent accuracy. Also as is reported in futurisim.com, a study from Showa University in Yokohama, Japan showed that a new computer-aided endoscopic system could reveal signs of potentially cancerous growths in the colon with 94 percent sensitivity, 79 percent specificity, and 86 percent accuracy. This is great, considering that regular tests are not really better.

## Final Words

Time has changed. In a not-so-distant future, we are going to be visited and examined by a new kind of doctor who might not look like our present-day physicians. Reading these articles, I was wondering how lawyers are going to sue these new doctors. One positive change will be that AI doctors won't refuse to practice in remote or otherwise challenging areas of the United States. The goal of AI is not to create competition for human doctors, but to make their jobs less stressful so that they can concentrate on the aspects of health care that AI doctors are not yet capable of doing.

Abby Norman predicts that AI's role in medicine will continue to grow, although we need to avoid relying on them completely for decision making. We should integrate AI only where it makes sense to human doctors. After all, the key of medical decision-making is to make sure that the benefit of a recommended treatment outweighs the risk. In short, physicians need to decide how to employ AI in their practices so that it will be helpful to them and their patients.

## References

Jiang, Kevin. "Microscope's 3-D Movies of Cells Open New Frontier for Researchers." Harvard Gazette. April 24, 2018. https://news.harvard.edu/gazette/story/2018/04/microscopes-3-d-movies-of-cells-open-new-frontier-for-researchers/.

Krisberg, Kim. "Artificial Intelligence Transforms the Future of Medicine." Association of American Medical Colleges, November 14, 2017. https://news.aamc.org/research/article/artificial-intelligence-transforms-future-medicine/John Radcliffe Hospital. https://www.ouh.nhs.uk/hospitals/jr/.

Leary, Kyree. "AI Can Diagnose Heart Disease and Lung Cancer More Accurately Than Doctors." *Futurism/The Byte*, January 3, 2018. https://futurism.com/ai-diagnose-heart-disease-lung-cancer-more-accurately-doctors/.

Norman, Abby. "Your Future Doctor May Not Be Human. This Is the Rise of AI in Medicine." *Futurism/The Byte*, January 31, 2018. https://futurism.com/ai-medicine-doctor.

Mori, Yuichi et al., (2018). Real-Time Use of Artificial Intelligence in Identification of Diminutive Polyps During Colonoscopy: A Prospective Study. Annals of Internal Medicine. 169. 10.7326/M18-0249.

# Artificial Sweetener or Sugar?

*It is all about risk versus reward.*

For people concerned with diabetes and obesity, sweetener without calories seems like a dream come true. "The Nutrition Source" tells us that a regular can of soda contains about 150 calories, all of which come from sugar, but the same size can of diet soda contains zero calories. For a soda drinker, the choice seems like a no-brainer. However, as with so many things, there is more to the story than calories. According to the American Heart Association (AHA) and the American Diabetes Association (ADA), we should be careful when using artificial sweeteners in place of sugar to combat health issues such as obesity, metabolic syndrome, and diabetes, all of which are risk factors for heart disease. Additionally, many well-known obesity and weight-loss specialists have expressed concerns about artificial sweeteners.

## Are All Artificial Sweeteners the Same?

There's a variety of artificial sweeteners on the market. Those approved by the FDA include saccharin, acesulfame, aspartame, neotame, and sucralose, and the only natural low-calorie sweetener approved is stevia. One puzzling problem is the way our bodies respond to these substances, and the other problem is that people who use artificial sweeteners often choose to replace the lost calories with other sources. There's a standing joke about the guy who went to a fast food restaurant, ate a hamburger and french fries, but drank a Diet Coke to make up for the burger and fries. We'll fool ourselves by saying, "I'm drinking diet soda, so it's okay to have a hamburger or even something sweet."

According to Holly Strawbridge in "Artificial Sweeteners: Sugar-Free, But At What Cost?" artificial sweeteners could change the way we taste food. I've tried several brands of such products, because sometimes we're forced to use the only brand offered in a restaurant or coffee shop. Several are far more potent than table sugar or high-fructose corn syrup; the taste of a small amount is comparable to regular sugar, without comparable calories. "Overstimulation of sugar receptors from frequent use of these hyper-intense sweeteners may limit tolerance for more complex tastes," explains Dr. David Ludwig, obesity and weight-loss specialist at Boston Children's Hospital, as quoted in Strawbridge's article. I have noticed that after eating sugar-free cake or ice cream, I find natural sweets much less appealing or satisfying, which could turn into an excuse to avoid eating fruit and vegetables.

Strawbridge says that artificial sweeteners also trick us by preventing us from associating sweetness with caloric intake, and I have personally experienced this. I seldom feel full and constantly crave more sweets, so I have developed a tendency to choose sweet food over nutritious food. Several times I've given up diet drinks and gone back to healthy beverages such as water, and I can proudly report that this has helped me a lot. However I still cannot imagine having certain foods—pizza, for example—with water, so I can't honestly say that I can always pass up diet drinks. I've also read that studies performed on animals suggest that artificial sweeteners may be addictive.

## Back to Sugar?

So giving up artificial sweeteners and going back to sugar may not be such a bad idea. If that's your decision, remember to note how foods are packaged. You might find Dr. Ludwig's explanation useful, again as quoted by Strawbridge: "Sugar-containing foods in their natural form, whole fruit, for example, tend to be highly nutritious—nutrient-dense, high in fiber, and low in glycemic load. On the other hand, refined, concentrated sugar consumed in large amounts rapidly increases blood glucose and insulin levels, increases triglycerides, inflammatory mediators and oxygen radicals, and with them, the risk for diabetes, cardiovascular disease and other chronic illnesses." This is what Suzanne Somers discusses in her book *Knockout: Interviews with Doctors Who Are Curing Cancer—And How to Prevent Getting It in the First Place.* She points out that artificial sweeteners contain harmful substances that trick our bodies.

Here's another interesting issue: It seems that cancer loves sugar as much as we do. The idea that dietary sugar and cancer are linked dates back to the 1920s. Dr. Otto Warburg, a Nobel laureate who studied cancer cell metabolism, noted that cancer cells were glutinous consumers of glucose. The observation that some cancer cells are naturally sugar hungry came to be known as the Warburg effect.

Thankfully there are products made with stevia, which is approved by the FDA and can replace sugar naturally. Stevia is different from sugar in many ways, and there are several reasons why it's a better option than sucrose, whether you are diabetic or just looking to adopt a healthier lifestyle. Ideally it will replace sugar in diet soft drinks and thus help all of those addicted to drinks such as Diet Coke. The key is to eat healthy and eat lots of fruit, vegetables, and dairy, which will reduce our hunger and keep us from craving sweets loaded with sugar. We can also use honey from bees as a sweetener in baking.

## Final Words

Artificial sweeteners may seem like a healthful alternative to regular sugar, but the risk may be greater than the benefit. Everybody knows the importance of using products that help us stay healthy, but artificial sweeteners do not fall in that category. They have harmful effects on the body, thus violating sound principles of nutrition.

The Wikipedia article "Sugar Substitute" points out another factor, which is that the profit margin on artificial sweetener is extremely high for manufacturers. I was surprised to learn that artificial sweeteners cost the food industry just a fraction of the cost of sugar and corn syrup, which was introduced as a low-cost alternative to sugar. It's not hard to infer that the food industry chooses to promote its "diet" or "light" products heavily, directing customers to a more profitable product, artificially sweetened.

It should be pointed out that the studies about a potential relationship between artificial sweeteners and chronic disease are observational, so cause and effect should not be assumed. In addition, the increased risk quoted in some studies is relative risk, not absolute risk.

## References

Harvard T. H. Chan School of Public Health. "The Nutrition Source." https://www. hsph.harvard.edu/nutritionsource/healthy-drinks/sugary-drinks/.

Strawbridge, Holly. "Artificial Sweeteners: Sugar-Free, but at What Cost?" *Harvard Health Publishing*, July 16, 2012. https://www.health.harvard.edu/blog/ artificial-sweeteners-sugar-free-but-at-what-cost-201207165030.

Wikipedia. "Sugar Substitute." https://en.wikipedia.org/wiki/Sugar_substitute.

# Good Things Come to Those Who Sweat

*Sweat, an unwanted fat crying.*

The human body is equipped with an amazingly effective cooling system, as described by Kellie Davis in "The Not-So-Obvious Benefits of Sweat": "Our skin is covered with approximately two to five million sweat glands that run like ductwork in an attic." Sweating indicates that our cooling system is doing its job. How much a person sweats is determined by physiological characteristics such as age, gender, and weight, as well as factors such as temperature, the level of exertion, and how anxious we feel. On average, a healthy person can produce one to three liters (two to six pints) of sweat per hour. As we age, our skin changes and our sweat glands produce less sweat, which sometimes makes it harder to cool off and may increase the risk of heatstroke.

Studies such as "Sex Differences in the Effects of Physical Training on Sweat Gland Responses During a Graded Exercise" have concluded that women are at a disadvantage when it comes to cooling off during heavy bouts of exercise or during hot conditions. Davis points out that this is because women, compared with men, carry less body fluid and may sweat less to prevent dehydration. Because of this, women are advised to take more precautions in extreme heat conditions or during long bouts of exercise.

## Our Cooling System

Davis writes the following (see also Paramedicmike.ca):

> The human body hosts two different types of sweat glands: eccrine and apocrine. Eccrine sweat glands work like ducts on the skin's surface and produce a watery substance. These glands are mostly concentrated on the brow, hands, and feet, and they function primarily as the body's air conditioning unit. Apocrine sweat glands are found

in the hair follicles located in and around the scalp, armpits, anus, and genitals. Apocrine sweat glands produce a thicker, plasma-like substance that also contains fatty acids and protein byproducts, including urea and ammonia. Emotional stress triggers apocrine glands to expel fatty sweat into the skin, where bacteria break it down. This turns into an odorous fatty acid substance, which makes certain types of sweat smell and causes unsightly underarm stains. These glands remain inactive until puberty, which explains why preteen children suddenly smell after recess.

Davis also explains, "Sweat is primarily made up of water, but it also contains salt and, depending on a person's diet, other chemicals. One of the highest mineral concentrations in sweat is sodium, which explains why sweat tastes salty. In addition, sweat contains moderate amounts of potassium, chloride, calcium, and magnesium, as well as small amounts of trace minerals including copper, zinc, and iron."

## Hyperhidrosis

There is general agreement that sweating is necessary and healthy. However, excessive sweating can lead to a condition known as hyperhidrosis, in which the body sweats when there is no need, dripping perspiration from the head, feet, palms, or underarms. Although not harmful, excessive sweating can interfere with daily activities and stress, and maybe even more sweating.

## Benefits of Sweating

Sweating has a number of incredible health benefits. The examples listed here come from Davis and other sources:

- Healing powers: Sweat glands play a role in the wound-healing process, including recovery from scrapes, burns, and ulcers.
- Happiness defenders: The act of sweating alone does not ward off bad moods, but a good sweat in the gym or outdoors increases endorphin levels—those feel-good hormones that contribute to a runner's high. Endorphins are related to positive mood and an enhanced sense of overall well-being.

- Kidney protectors: Sweating limits the accumulation of salt and calcium in the kidneys and urine, which can reduce the risk of kidney stones. In addition, it increases thirst and water consumption, making it less likely for kidney stones to form.

Knowing that our body is equipped with such an amazing cooling system with healing power, it is wise to take advantage of it and avoid some critical health problems with a little perspiration.

## References

Davis, Kellie. "The Not-So-Obvious Benefits of Sweat." *Sail By the Masses*, June 24, 2015. http://bythemasses.sailemagazine.com/author/kelliedavis/.

Ichinose-Kuwahara, Tomoko, Yoshimitsu Inoue, Yoshiko Iseki, Sachi Hara, Yukio Ogura, and Narihiko Kondo. "Sex Differences in the Effects of Physical Training on Sweat Gland Responses During a Graded Exercise." *Experimental Physiology* 95, no. 10 (October 2010): 1026–1032. https://physoc.onlinelibrary.wiley.com/doi/full/10.1113/expphysiol.2010.053710.

Paramedicmike.ca.

## Concluding Note to This Chapter

I have suffered chronic health problems my whole life, and I've learned that opening up about our problems is a great challenge. People don't want to be seen as sick or disabled, and we don't want to be pitied. This is especially true when other people have no idea that anything is even wrong with you.

There are pros and cons to living with chronic health problems in silence, but sharing our stories can give new meaning to them and be a huge release for us. Chronic illnesses are not like the flu or cancer—we don't suddenly wake up and feel better, but they won't necessarily kill us either. Some people have to cope with chronic health problems every single day, which can be a big part of a person's life. But we can also choose not to let chronic health problems define us.

# Chapter 5
## Math/Mind

*The book of nature is written in the language of mathematics.*
*—Galileo Galilei*

*Mathematics has its own kingdom*
*The key to enter it is called wisdom*

*Some fear mathematics for its complexity*
*Others enjoy it for its truth and explicitly*
*For me, it is the beauty, elegance and simplicity*
*For the world, it is the usefulness and necessity*

*There is a secret in everything named x*
*Seeking to reveal itself to wisdom*
*It is a closed door waiting to be opened*
*Wishing a smart mind to enter its kingdom*

*In a math book there is wisdom*
*In a theorem a provable thing*
*No reasoning can be faked here*
*The logic needs to be made clear*

*Mathematics does not have a season*
*It is valued for its logic and its reason*
*It gives direction to the land of perfect truth*
*Following it saves us from the ignorance prison*

*There is a secret in every equation, seeking curiosity and passion*
*If you note its beauty and depth, it certainly meets your expectation*

# Mathematics, a Symbolic Language

*I was doing great in my math class until the alphabet appeared in the equation.*

Estimates of the number of languages spoken in the world vary widely, partly because wars have caused many to disappear. According to Ethnologue's latest report, 7,111 known languages or dialects are being spoken, and almost all of them have one thing in common—they are instruments for communication based on the use of sounds or conventional symbols, words, and sentences. Most also have a category for words representing nouns or objects, and a category for words representing verbs or actions. The more developed languages are also described in terms of a vocabulary of symbols or words, a grammar of rules for how they may be used, and a syntax or propositional structure that places the symbols in linear structures.

As noted in *Literacy Strategies for Improving Mathematics Instruction*, by Joan M. Kenney et al., what the major languages have in common provides an interesting way for looking at the language of mathematics. One model proposed in 1995 suggests that we may think about mathematical nouns, or objects, as being numbers, measurements, shapes, spaces, functions, patterns, data, and arrangements—items that comfortably map onto commonly accepted mathematics content strands. The four predominant actions that we ascribe to problem solving and reasoning—modeling and formulating, transforming and manipulating, inferring, and communicating—may be regarded as mathematical verbs. Taken as a whole, these four actions represent the processes we go through to formulate and solve a problem.

## Symbolic Language

As we know, part of the English language is used for making formal mathematical statements and communicating definitions, theorems, proofs, word problems, and examples. Although the English language is a source of communication, it is not designed for mathematics and most other hard sciences. Mathematics is usually written in a symbolic language designed to express mathematical and complex scientific ideas and thoughts. In other words, the symbolic language developed to present and communicate mathematics is a special-purpose language with its own symbols and rules of grammar, quite different from a language such as English. This special-purpose language consists of symbolic expressions written as mathematicians traditionally write them. A symbol is a typographical character. The symbolic language also includes symbols that are specific to mathematics. We can usually read expressions in this language in any article about mathematics written in almost any languages. Both English and this symbolic language are used in mathematics writing and mathematical lectures.

An example of the elements of symbolic language includes ten digits: 0, 1, 2, … 9. We also have symbols for operations that include +, -, x, and /; symbols that stand for values such as x, y, and z; and special symbols such as $\pi$, =, <, and ≤. In the language of mathematics, nouns can be fixed things such as numbers or expressions with numbers: 73, 5(3-1/7). The verb could be the equals sign of = or an inequality sign such as < or >. Pronouns could be variables such as x or y, 5x-6, $x^2y$, or 8/x, which could be put together into a sentence such as $5x + 14 = 22$.

## Let's Simplify

Language is a type of abstraction (first order) used for communication, which enabled humans to pass their knowledge to future generations and end up controlling the world. Although useful, most languages have their own shortcomings and limitations in that they can furnish only a finite number of names and words. Ordinary languages are not designed for describing, expressing, or explaining complex scientific ideas and concepts.

The symbolic language of mathematics, on the other hand, is equipped with tools for expressing and communicating complex scientific ideas and relationships. For example, unlike words, numbers have no limit. That is why we are better at identifying people by their social security numbers than by their names. In fact, numbers are now used more for identification than for numeration. Just think about the many different items in a grocery store, each of which has its own unique identification that includes a great deal of information about it.

# References

Kenney, Joan M., Euthecia Hancewicz, Loretta Heuer, Diana Metsisto, and Cynthia L. Tuttle. *Literacy Strategies for Improving Mathematics Instruction*. http://www.ascd.org/publications/books/105137/chapters/Mathematics-as-Language.aspx.

"The Language of Mathematics." https://www.mathsisfun.com/mathematics-language.html.

Eberhard, David M., Gary F. Simons, and Charles D. Fennig (eds.). 2019. *Ethnologue: Languages of the World*. Twenty-second edition. Dallas, Texas: SIL International. Online version: http://www.ethnologue.com.

"Summary by Language Size." Ethnologue. https://www.ethnologue.com/statistics/size.

"Last Words: The Dying of Languages." Last Words: The Dying of Languages | Worldwatch Institute. June 2001. http://www.worldwatch.org/node/500.

# Can Mathematics Help My Love Life?

*Maybe this time my heart would seek help from my brain.*

When students ask me why they need to learn algebra, I try to demonstrate the use of mathematics in their everyday lives, but many who are not mature enough to think about the future do not buy that. Students often see things from a narrow perspective, generally confusing mathematics with number manipulation and mathematicians with people who are good with numbers. When I tell them, for example, that mathematics is a symbolic language developed to express complex scientific ideas, they are surprised. When I add that algebra is like the grammar of that language, they are even more surprised. To make it more convincing I joke with them that a calculator is not a mathematician, but still a great number manipulator.

I have learned that to demonstrate the usefulness of mathematics, I really need to find an unexpected application, something that is of interest and concern to young students, such as their love lives.

## Dating

Admittedly, the roller coaster of romance is hard to quantify. Nevertheless, mathematics can help with dating problems. Consider, for example, the following questions:

1. How many people should you date before committing?
2. How can you maximize your chance of finding "the one"?

Suppose that you're in a situation in which you can date people and rank them according to your personal preferences. Let's assume that after each date, you have two options: to commit, or to break up permanently. Here are a couple of mathematical strategies to maximize your chance of finding the best partner.

Suppose that dating occurs in a random order, and your wish is to find the best partner (record winner). After each date, you may (a) commit or (b) continue dating and hope to meet a better partner. Both decisions involve risk. If you commit, you might miss better future dates, but if you continue, you might pass up the best.

Let's see how mathematics could help. Clearly, your first date is the best so far (first record). Any future date better than the first date—whether it's the second, third, or final date—would be the second record. If your first date was really the best, you only encounter one record in your dating history (no better future date). If your second date was really the best (better than the first), you encounter two records, and so on. So if you date ten people, you will encounter between one and ten records. Given the number of potential dates, the probabilities of encountering a given number of records can be mathematically calculated.

For ten potential dates, these probabilities are presented in the table below. From the table, the chance of encountering only one record—that is, the chance that your first date is the best—is 10 percent. The chance of encountering two records—that is, the chance that there would be only one future date better than your first date—is 28.29 percent. As we see, the occurrence of three records in ten potential dates has the highest chance (31 percent). This implies that if you keep dating until you meet the third best record (partner), you maximize your chance of finding the one with the highest rank in your list. This means that your chance of meeting the best date is largest if you wait until you meet the third record date.

| No. of Records | Probability |
|:---:|:---:|
| 1 | 0.10000 |
| 2 | 0.28290 |
| 3 | 0.31316 |
| 4 | 0.19943 |
| 5 | 0.07422 |
| 6 | 0.01744 |
| 7 | 0.00260 |
| 8 | 0.00024 |
| 9 | 0.00001 |
| 10 | 0.0000 |

## Strategy 2

Here you first date a certain number of people (initial group) and break up with them permanently. Then you date more people until you find the first partner better than the best of the initial group. If you cannot find such a person, you commit to the last one. For ten potential dates, this strategy maximizes your chance of finding the best (77.4 percent) if you include three people in the initial group. For five and fifteen dates, your chance is maximized if you respectively include two and five people in the initial group.

# Counting, Simple But Surprising

*There are more options than you could imagine.*

I clearly remember the day my mother expressed her admiration for the different appearances the Lord has given us for identification and differentiation. As a child, I was surprised at the thought that God must make an exception when he creates twins. However, I was even more surprised years later, when I learned about counting techniques.

Suppose you have two books, A and B, and a shelf that holds only two books. To place the books on the shelf, you have two choices: AB and BA. With three books, your choices are ABC, ACB, CAB, ACB, BCA, and BAC. 3 x 2 x 1 = 6 = 3! (3 factorial), which means you have three choices for placing the first book, two choices for the second book, and one choice for the third. With four books, it is 4 x 3 x 2 x 1 = 24 = 4! and so on. With fourteen books, your choices (combinations) are 14! = 87,178,291,200, which is more than twelve times the world's population. Amazing. Think about a big shelf in a library. The number of choices is unbelievably large and mind boggling.

To clarify further, think about a room with only fourteen seats. The first person who enters the room has fourteen choices to pick a seat. The second person has thirteen choices, the third person has twelve, and so on. Therefore, there are a total of 14! Permutations. Think about a large class, movie theater, or football stadium. Even more surprising is the fact that we're talking about integers that are countable (discrete variables). Imagine what happens with continuous variables or cases such as the human face and all the possibilities. They are simply countless. I'm not sure if I could explain this to my mom and, more importantly, if she would believe it. However, I'm still fascinated by the fact that there are infinite possibilities even in discrete cases.

Here's an example in sports. In table tennis (old rules), to win a standard game, a player must either be the first to reach 21 points with a margin of 2, or win 2 consecutive points following a tie at 20 before the opponent does. For the first case, for the game to finish, the score should be one of these 21-0, 21-1, …, 21-19 combos. The number of possibilities are given in the table below. For example, for 21-1, the winner should take the last point plus 20 points out of 21 points played. That 1 point taken by the loser could be the first, second, or twenty-first point. Also, for the game to end, for example, at 21-4, the winner should take the last point plus 20 points from the first 24 points played. If you like challenges, try to calculate the number of possibilities for the second case (going through 20-20).

| 21–0 | 1 |
|------|--:|
| 21–1 | 21 |
| 21–2 | 231 |
| 21–3 | 1,771 |
| 21–4 | 10,626 |
| 21–5 | 53,130 |
| 21–6 | 230,230 |
| 21–7 | 888,030 |
| 21–8 | 3,108,105 |
| 21–9 | 10,015,005 |
| 21–10 | 30,045,015 |
| 21–11 | 84,672,315 |
| 21–12 | 225,792,840 |
| 21–13 | 573,166,440 |
| 21–14 | 1,391,975,640 |
| 21–15 | 3,247,943,160 |
| 21–16 | 7,307,872,110 |
| 21–17 | 15,905,368,710 |
| 21–18 | 33,578,000,610 |
| 21–19 | 68,923,264,410 |

## Bridge Hands

There are as many as 635,013,559,600 possible combinations of thirteen-card hands in the popular card game of bridge. Dealing all the possible hands could easily take several million years, or maybe a day if several billion people do it together. For fair cards, each of these possibilities are equally likely/equally probable, or in fact, equally unlikely/equally improbable, noting that the probability of occurrence for each possible hand is only 1/635,013,559,600. In other words, any hand is just as improbable as a hand of thirteen diamonds. When dealing any hand, one of these possibilities will occur, which illustrates the daily occurrence of highly improbable events. It's interesting that some hands surprise us more than others, even though they are all equally unlikely.

# Mathematical Humor

*My teacher thinks that I'm an average student. I think he's mean.*

A mathematician is a blind man in a dark room looking for a black cat that is not there.

> —Charles Darwin? Lord Bowen? Confucius? E. R. Pearce?
> William James? Ralph Waldo Emerson? Anonymous?

1. What did 0 say to 8? Nice belt.
2. What 70 did we felt hungry? 78.
3. "Why should I learn subtraction, Dad?"
   "Well, son, to make a difference."
4. There are three types of people in the world, those who can count and those who cannot.
5. As long as mathematics is part of a school's curriculum, prayer will be part of it too.
6. "Sir, do you want me to cut the pizza for you?"
   "Yes, please."
   "Six pieces or eight?"
   "Six pieces is good. I'm not very hungry."
7. Why is pizza round, its box square, and its slices triangular?
8. The golden rule for mathematics teachers: You must tell the truth, nothing but the truth, but not the whole truth.
9. My teacher thinks that I'm an average student. I think he's mean.
10. "My mom is half British, half German, and half Italian."
    "Well, Little John, that's not possible. There are too many halves there."
    "But teacher, my mom is a big woman."
11. Only a fraction of people note that there's a fine line between a numerator and a denominator.

12. Mathematicians never die. They just lose some of their functions.

13. Mathematicians never die. They just lose their identities.

14. Mathematicians never go crazy. They just become irrational.

15. When a statistician passes through airport security check, an explosive is discovered in his bag. He explains: "Studies shows that the chance of one explosive on an airplane is 1 in 1,000 and the chance of two explosives on an airplane is 1 in 1,000,000. So I decided to bring an explosive myself to decrease the odds of any unfortunate incident."

16. A statistician was drowned trying to cross a river. He was 5 foot 9 inches, and the average depth of the river was 5 foot 8 inches.

17. Mathematicians believe nothing until it's proven. Physicists believe everything until it's proven wrong. Chemists don't care. Biologists don't understand the question.

18. A mathematician put a two-dollar stamp on a letter. To be sure that was sufficient, he went to the post office to check. The clerk said, "Sir, you only need a one-dollar stamp." So he purchased a one-dollar stamp and put it on the same envelope with a negative sign in front of it to make it one dollar ($2 - $1 = $1).

19. Why do mathematicians sit in the corner of the room during the winter? Well, because it's 90 degrees there.

I could go on and on. Once a joke enters the public domain, it can be modified by anyone. I often change the personalities in jokes to make them funnier or more relevant, so it's difficult for me to credit the source for any particular joke. "Mathematical Jokes" is a collection of math humor gathered by Andrej and Elena Cherkaev.

## Mathematical Folklore

In the study of folklore, a *folk* is defined as any group of people who have at least one thing in common, such as nationality, race, or profession. Mathematicians, as a folk, share a common core of mathematical folklore that, like other folklore, exists in multiple forms and variations. A part of this folklore consists of different versions of classic jokes, such as the absent-minded mathematics professor joke, that are attached to various mathematics legends. For example, a famous mathematics professor, after finishing a conversation with a student, asked her which direction he was going. "Toward the library, professor," she answered. "Oh, thanks. In that case, I had my lunch," he said. The collection of mathematical folklore is often enjoyed not only by mathematicians and their students, but also by nonmathematicians, because every joke contains a portion of truth or falsehood about mathematicians and mathematical pop culture.

## What Makes Us Laugh?

Applying the logic commonly used to explain our sense of humor, scientists have tried to determine how our brains react to jokes that make us laugh. Several hypotheses about humor have been proposed in an attempt to explain this. For example, take words or sounds like the number 8, which can also sound like the verb *ate*. These multiple meanings can allow for the context a joke requires. Ask a five-year-old, "Why was 6 afraid of 7? Because 7-8-9!" and watch as you suddenly become their favorite standup comic. Then ask, "Why was 10 nervous then? Because 10 thought that after 9, it was his turn!" Jokes about special people, whom we should respect, in different roles are usually considered funny.

Some studies have attempted to explore the core elements of humor and apply a new way of mapping and evaluating the components of humor to determine exactly what makes a joke funny. "Funniness is not a pre-existing 'element of reality' that can be measured; it emerges from an interaction between the underlying nature of the joke, the cognitive state of the listener, and other social and environmental factors," says Liane Gabora from the University of British Columbia, as quoted in "Can Quantum Theory Explain Why Jokes Are Funny?" Mathematics cannot describe physical properties of our brains. To test theories of humor, researchers have broken the construct of a joke down into its components, including the setup, the person who is telling the joke, their relationship with the audience, and the culture and surroundings.

Using the resulting formula, various scores were applied to weigh a joke's components and predict how people might find the overall structure funny. Then the jokes were listed and a number of variants created for each one, such as delivering the punchline without a setup or presenting it with a modification on its script. The jokes and their variants were tested on people, such as undergraduate students, who gave them each a rating based on how funny they thought the joke was. For the most part, variants were not considered as funny as the original jokes, but they did help pinpoint exactly what the audience found funny. Previous attempts to understand why puns make our lips pull back into a grin, our diaphragms spasm in laughter, and our brains release endorphins assumed that the sudden change in meaning as the joke resolved was to blame.

## References

Cherkaev, Andrej, and Elena Cherkaev. "Mathematical Humor." http://www.math. utah.edu/~cherk/mathjokes.html.

Frontiers. "Can Quantum Theory Explain Why Jokes Are Funny?" *Science Daily,* March 17, 2017. http://www.sciencedaily.com/releases /2017/03/170317102438.htm.

# The Wonderful World of Numbers

*You are 1. Without you 10, 100, 1,000, 1,000,000, and 1,000,000,000 are nothing—just 0.*

## In Poems

*When you are a small child one dollar is a lot of money*
*In a year or two a ten dollar bill looks like a beautiful bunny*
*When a teenager a hundred dollar bill is as sweet as honey*
*As you grow older zeros increase and makes your dark days sunny*
*Then one day you see the reality and discover a fact of great value*
*You find that you are the one on the front, without you*
*all that zeros mean nothing just a dummy.*

It seems inconceivable how much we rely on numbers in our daily lives and how natural it feels. Our birth is announced by a set of numbers representing the time, date, and our height and weight. We become a functioning member of society only after a Social Security number is assigned to us. Our health and fitness are evaluated using numbers representing our blood pressure, heart rate, body temperature, and so on. From that point onward, every action performed and every life encountered becomes part of our ongoing use of numbers. Some numbers live and die with us, and some even live long after we are gone. Numbers resonate with our personal and social lives in a greater way than we might imagine.

## A Brief History

Numbers and numeration systems have played a key role in human development. Throughout history, our understanding of numbers has gone through a dramatic change and reached a high level of sophistication. A number is an abstract concept used to describe a quantity. A numeration system is a set of basic symbols called numerals—such as 0, 1, and 2—and some rules—such as addition and subtraction—for making other symbols from them. The invention of a precise, workable numeration system is one of the greatest accomplishments of humanity. The numerical digits that we use today are based on the Hindu-Arabic numeral system developed over a thousand years ago, except for the decimal system and base 10 system that uses just ten symbols (0, 1 … 9). The most popular system is the binary or base 2 system, which uses only the two symbols 0 and 1. Because computers use a sequence of switches that can be only on or off (bit), base 2 works well there. In recent years, several other systems have been developed for identification of items, letters and packages, tickets, and others.

## Some Interesting Representations

Among many other applications, numbers are used for numeration, identification, and representation. For example, catch-22 is a noun representing a problematic situation and the number 007 represents a name. The numbers 5, 7, 12, 13, 40, and 666 represent mystical, unlucky, or religious icons, and pi indicates a geometric object.

- Number sense: One billion is 1,000 times one million, so how much bigger is one billion than one million? Well, one thousand millionaires have as much money as only one billionaire. Some of my students prefer this one: One million seconds is about 11 days, while one billion seconds is about 31.5 years.
- Golden ratio: The golden ratio (approximately 1.618) is a number used to create aesthetically pleasing designs and artworks, such as Leonardo da Vinci's *Mona Lisa*.
- Fibonacci numbers: Fibonacci numbers are 0, 1, 1, 2, 3, 5, 8, 13, 21, 34, 55, where each number in the sequence is the sum of the two preceding numbers. They are related to the golden ratio and appear frequently in nature. For example, the spiral shapes of sunflowers follow a Fibonacci sequence. It also appears in the foundation of aspects of art, beauty, music, and life.
- Google: The name of this popular search engine came from a misspelling of the word *googol*, which is a large number (a one followed by one hundred zeroes).
- 9/11 and 11: Conspiracy theories based on numbers have been around for a long time. Here is a relatively recent one related to the 9/11 disaster that involves the number 11. First recall that the beautiful twin towers of the World Trade Center looked like the number 11. The first flight to hit the twin towers was flight number 11 with 92 people on board: 9 + 2 = 11. September 11 is

the 254th day of the year: $2 + 5 + 4 = 11$ and $365 - 254 = 111$. 911 is the emergency number and $9 + 1 + 1 = 11$. 119 is the area code to Iraq and $1 + 1 + 9 = 11$. New York was the 11th state admitted to the union. There are 11 letters in "New York City," "Afghanistan," "the Pentagon," and "George W. Bush." The flight 77 that crashed in Pennsylvania had 65 people on board, $6 + 5 = 11$. Finally, recall the March 11 (2004) attack in Spain. There are exactly 911 days between this date and the September 11 (2001).

## What Is a Numeration System?

A numeration system is a set of basic symbols and rules for making other symbols from them. They may be used to represent quantities or to identify objects. The symbols of a numeration system are called numerals. A number is an abstract concept used to describe quantity. The invention of a precise and workable numeration system is one of the greatest accomplishments of humanity. Although various civilizations have approached the problem using different paths, they all finally arrived at the same point. Here are some examples of numeration systems:

- Decimal or base 10. Uses ten symbols 0, 1, … 9.
- Binary or base 2. Uses only two symbols, 0 and 1. Because computers use a sequence of switches that can be only on or off (also called a bit), base 2 works well there. Mathematics in base 2 is pathetically simple, but (unlike the decimal system) incredibly time consuming.

## Numbers Are Our Friends

Social Security numbers, telephone numbers, credit card numbers, and many more numbers serve important functions in our lives. Our houses, cars, and workplaces are full of numbers that make life easier and help us better understand the world around us. Unlike names, numbers are unlimited and thus a great tool for unique identification of people and items regardless of the population size. They are also fascinating and mystical.

## Reference

"Numeral System." *Wikipedia*, Wikimedia Foundation, 25 June 2019, en.wikipedia. org/wiki/Numeral_system.

# Living and Dying with Numbers

*Numbers, friends for life and beyond.*

Throughout history, numbers have played a key role in human development, and many civilizations have contributed to their advancement. Like human beings, numbers have grown, changed, matured, and achieved a high level of sophistication. Advances in this field are apparent to anybody who shops at grocery stores and malls. Every item we buy, piece of mail we receive, ticket we purchase, and so on has an identification number. Like people, there are some extraordinary, famous, and beautiful numbers that amaze us. Some numbers are celebrated on certain days of the year. For example, March 14 is celebrated as Pi Day since 3.14 is the beginning of this special number. A lot can be said about pi. For example, it has a decimal representation that never stops or repeats, although modern computers have now computed it to over a trillion decimal places!

Like people, some numbers belong to groups with given names, such as integers, rational, irrational, real, complex, and so on. Many numbers are given specific names because of their unique properties. It seems inconceivable how much we rely on numbers in our daily lives and how natural it feels. Without a Social Security number, we cannot even become a functioning member of modern society in the United States. Every action performed and every life encountered has become a part of the ongoing use of numbers. Some numbers are born and die with us, and some even live long after we are gone.

## What Are Numbers?

According to Yahoo! Answers, the primitive notion of numbers, requiring thousands of years to be extracted from repeated concrete situations, appears to have evolved from the many physical contrasts prevalent in nature—the difference between one tree and a forest, or one sheep and a herd. Likewise, objects within a group could be placed in one-to-one correspondence with objects from other groups. For example, our hands can be matched (placed in one-to-one correspondence) with our feet. Consequently, there was recognition of an abstract property shared by some group—the ability to be placed in one-to-one correspondence with each other. This property is what we now call numbers. Those groups that could not be placed in one-to-one correspondence did not share this property and are thus said to be different in numbers. The concept of numbers in mathematics was born out of this realization of sameness.

## What Is a Numeration System?

A numeration system is a set of basic symbols and rules for making other symbols from them. They may be used to represent quantities or numbers or to identify people or objects. The symbols of a numeration system are called numerals. A number is an abstract concept used to describe quantity. The invention of a precise and workable numeration system is one of the greatest accomplishments of humanity. Many nations have made contributions to this invention, approaching the problem on different paths but arriving at the same point. The history of approaches used by different civilizations is fascinating.

## References

"How's the Numbers Originatreed?" https://nz.answers.yahoo.com/question/index?qid=20070610023500AA3VHeb.

# Brain vs. Supercomputer

*I wonder why my unparalleled brain admires supercomputers.*

Most of us are impressed by the abilities of modern computers. A supercomputer can add, multiply, or compare a million large numbers in less than one second. According to "The 5 Fastest Supercomputers in the World," by Kevin Jackson, the capability of Sunway TaihuLight, previously the fastest supercomputer in the world (now third), is 93 petaflops, where one petaflop equals four quadrillion calculations/second. This article also describes the two supercomputers that have recently surpassed Sunway TaihuLight: Sierra, which has been optimized to 94.6 petaflops, and Summit, the current leader in supercomputers at 143.5 petaflops. Several million transistors can be accommodated in one square centimeter, and each can switch in less than one billionth of a second. Steady advances are being made in both hardware and software.

Compared with the capabilities of the human brain, even the latest supercomputers are still stupid. The brain's high ability for quick calculations is primarily attributable to the fact that all its nerve cells operate in mutual association as a neuronal network. Physicists have now succeeded in quantifying the inter-cooperation of these neurons on a mathematical basis. Given appropriate examples, a network of this nature can learn to store and retrieve information independently. Both neurobiology and computer science can profit from this knowledge.

Therefore, it is even more surprising that a child possesses abilities that a modern supercomputer cannot even approach. It is no problem for us to recognize the passing face of someone we know as we rush down a busy street. In a fraction of a second, we have recognized the person quite independently of the crowd of people, or any movements, size and orientation, light or shade, or a new hat. At the same time, memories and many other items of information about this person wake within us. Our brain achieves all this without any effort; even a child can do it. Although a computer can record images electronically, it is able to understand their content only in simple cases and after a long calculation.

The material basis of man's ability to recognize what he sees depends on the nerve cells. The human brain contains some hundred billion such neurons; the grey matter comprises a dense, extremely heterogeneous, and apparently random network of strongly ramified cells. These neurons, just like the transistors in computers, can be regarded as tiny electronic switches; each cell emits electrical pulses and thus controls other cells.

One essential difference between a computer and the brain is the mode of operation of the switch elements. In a computer, orders previously fed in by an operator are processed step by step. This involves the participation of only a few available transistors. The neurons, in contrast, function as a network: a vast number of nerve cells are simultaneously activated to process the information.

The current theory is that the basic difference lies in this network structure. Using simple models, we are now beginning to understand why the properties of a network differ so radically from those of a conventional computer.

A neural network comprises more than one hundred billion neurons. Each of these neurons is directly linked to some tens of thousands others. The point of contact between the nerve cells—the synapses—are responsible for learning and memory.

In recent decades, neurobiologists have made important discoveries regarding the functioning of the neurons, so that we now have a sound understanding of the individual cell, and research is being concentrated on the complicated biochemical processes that occur in the points of contact of the nerve cells, the synapses. However, the higher functions of the brain are still mostly a closed book to us, even today. How do neurons cooperate to recognize a person? Is there a single cell that sends electrical impulses only if you see your grandmother? How is your grandmother stored in your brain, in one synapse or distributed over the whole brain? How does the brain call up all the associations that manifest themselves when you think of someone you know? All these points are still essentially unknown, and some scientists doubt that the brain can even understand itself.

In this way, the network of neurons adopts a mathematical form. The exchange of signals between the nerve cells via the synapses becomes a series of nonlinear mathematical equations with a large number of unknowns and feedback. Such equations are normally difficult or impossible to solve, but in this case, physicists have succeeded by applying the methods used in theoretical solid-state physics. We can now convert the properties of the network into a mathematical form, which will permit many things to be quantified and understood.

The mathematical solution reveals that a neuronal network can operate as an associative memory, which means that a mass of data can be stored by selecting the appropriate synaptic strength. The system is now able to complete incomplete information, and thus to associate data. A faded picture can now be fully restored.

Alternatively, the system is independently capable of finding all the personal data relating to a name, even if it is incorrectly written. This functions simultaneously with a vast number of images. Each image provides a pattern for the activation of the neurons, into which the complete network can be firmly locked. Any deviations from this return automatically into the stored pattern.

The remarkable thing is that a network operates quite differently from a computer. A computer stores data like in a storage depot—each shelf has a number, and anyone searching for data must know the number, or he will have to search through all the shelves individually. If the data is incomplete, all the shelves will have to be compared with the available information. A program will control the entire operation step by step. In the brain, all of the data is stored over the entire system, with each synapse containing a small portion. In other words, the store extends over the whole network. Retrieval of incomplete or incorrect data is affected according to content; the network completes and corrects information itself. Doing this, all the neurons work simultaneously in accordance with the simple rules of the model.

## Final Remarks

According to Wikipedia, in philosophy, the computational theory of mind (CTM) refers to a family of views that hold that the human mind is an information processing system and that cognition and consciousness together are a form of computation.

The computational theory of mind holds that the mind is a computational system that is realized (i.e. physically implemented) by neural activity in the brain. The theory can be elaborated in many ways and varies largely based on how the term *computation* is understood. Recent work has suggested that we make a distinction between the mind and cognition networks, avoiding counter-arguments that center around phenomenal consciousness.

## References

"Computational Theory of Mind." https://en.wikipedia.org/wiki/Computational_theory_of_mind.

Jackson, Kevin. "The 5 Fastest Supercomputers in the World." *Science Node*, November 19, 2018. https://sciencenode.org/feature/the-5-fastest-supercomputers-in-the-world.php.

"John Searle." https://en.wikipedia.org/wiki/John_Searle#Artificial_intelligence.

# Pi, the Superstar of Numbers

*Pi, a sensational celebrity in the world of numbers.*

If there's one day that screams "mathematics party," it has to be Pi Day. The superstar of numbers, pi begins with 3.14—thus March 14th. It is also the best day to celebrate and promote mathematics and talk about its role in our lives.

Pi has a long and interesting history. The Egyptians and Babylonians were the first cultures to discover it, about four thousand years ago. The number is even mentioned in the Bible. In addition to its first three digits, during the decade 2010–19 its fourth digit also matched the common way of writing the date (3.141). In 2015 there was a five-digit match (3.1415).

Although enthusiasts have been celebrating Pi Day for more than three hundred years, only recently—on March 11, 2009—did the House of Representatives pass a resolution making March 14 officially the national Pi Day. According to an article titled "Pi Jokes," in honor of Pi Day, enthusiasts often amuse or enervate themselves and others by telling jokes involving pi. Most pi jokes are a pun on the name of the dessert know as pie.

Pi is the ratio of a circle's circumference to its diameter. It is also the ratio between a circle's area and its radius squared. Pi is an irrational number that takes an infinite number of digits to give its exact value, which means that we can neither get to the end of it nor find the next digit using a pattern in its previous digits. To date, with the help of supercomputers and a clever algorithm, pi has been tracked out to several billion digits after the decimal place. The pi algorithm, classified as one of the ten most important algorithms of the twentieth century, allows a computer to rapidly determine a digit at any desired position in the expansion of pi without first having to determine all of the preceding digits. The ideas that inspired the algorithm have already revealed a number of other surprising relations in both mathematics and physics.

So, enjoy Pi Day. If you want to celebrate like the rest of the world, make a circular pie with a diameter of 4 and cut it into four equal pieces. Then you have four pieces of pi-sized pie. If you have lots of friends, make the diameter 8 and cut the pie into sixteen pieces of pi-sized pie. Have a piece and think about the role of mathematics in your life for 3.1415926535897932 … minutes. Also, if you see a mathematician, give them a hug or kiss for luck.

To see why pi is so special, consider the following:

1. Pi has its own day, officially designated as such by the US House of Representatives.
2. Pi is mentioned in the Bible.
3. The celebration of pi goes back more than three hundred years.
4. Pi's digits have been recoded to more than several trillion decimal places.
5. Pi is a member of the big family of real numbers, irrational numbers.
6. Pi has more tees, hats, ties, etc. emblazoned with its sign than any other number.
7. Pi has a close friend, the circle, that appears everywhere and reminds us of it.

## References

"Pi Jokes." https://web.archive.org/web/20160520064517/http://www.mahalo.com:80/pi-jokes/.

# Can a Monkey Type *Hamlet?*

*Not even one page of it, not even if it outlives the universe.*

Well, although the answer is a no-brainer, the question is a reasonable one. A well-known philosophical argument states that if a large group of monkeys sit in front of a large number of computers and hit the keys randomly, they will eventually create all famous books, including Shakespeare's play *Hamlet.* In literature, this is now known as "the infinite monkey theorem," and its associated imagery is considered a popular and proverbial illustration of the mathematics of chance and probability. The infinite monkey theorem is widely known to the public because of its transmission through popular culture.

I first heard about the infinite monkey theorem when I was a high school student and found it fascinating. Years later, I realized that this statement oversimplifies important concepts such as infinity, probability, and time spans beyond average human comprehension. Here's why: Let's calculate the time it takes a monkey to reproduce *Hamlet.* The English language includes twenty-six letters, ten numbers, one space, and eight punctuation marks. That's forty-five unique characters, not counting capital letters, so suppose that monkeys are given keyboards with forty-five characters. The probability that a monkey types the first character correctly is 1 in 45 (0.022222) since there are forty-five possibilities. What is the chance that the monkey would type the second character correctly? It's the same as the first character, 1 in 45. So the chance that monkey would type the first two characters correctly is 1/45 x 1/45. The same applies to the third, fourth, and so on.

So what is the chance of this monkey typing the first hundred characters in order? It's the probability of typing the first character correctly, times the probability of typing the second character correctly, and so on. This is 1/45 times itself a hundred times, which would give us a number that is almost zero. The number of possible permutations is 45 times itself one hundred times, or 2,095 with 162 zeros, because to fill each position there are forty-five choices.

The universe is roughly fourteen billion years old, or 4400 with 15 zeros seconds old. Even if we let billions of billions of billions of monkeys each type one hundred characters per second, they will never finish the task. Therefore, it is clear that randomness is not enough to create *Hamlet*. We would need much, much, much more than that.

According to the tool at www.wordcounter.net, there are 169,541 characters in *Hamlet*. This includes all twenty-six letters of the alphabet, spaces, periods, commas, apostrophes, question marks, exclamation points, colons, semicolons, ampersands, and hyphens. Altogether, that is thirty-six possible characters. Just the chance of typing *Hamlet*, the name of Shakespeare's play, is 1 in 2,176,782,336. Even if a hundred monkeys work together, that gives them only slightly better odds: 1 in 21,767,823, which is not likely. The odds of monkeys randomly typing 169,541 characters correctly are 1 in $36^{169,541}$, a number hard to even imagine.

Here is a simpler example. What's the probability that a monkey types the following passage? "I cannot think about life without sports." With twenty-six letters plus spaces, there are twenty-seven choices for each of the forty positions. Thus the number of possibilities is 27 times itself 40 times, or 1,797 with 54 zeros. The above passage is just one option. Therefore, the probability we are seeking is one in 5564 with sixty-one zeros.

## Summary/Final Example

One line of this article in my computer has around eighty characters. Suppose there are only thirty choices for each position. So there are 30 times itself 80 times, or 1,478 with 115 zeros different possible permutations—which is greater than the number of atoms in the universe.

## References

"Infinite Monkey Theorem."
   https://en.wikipedia.org/wiki/Infinite_monkey_theorem

# Mathematics of Diversity

*Not only is mathematics diverse; it is capable of quantifying diversity,*
*A subject that plays significant role in institutions like university,*
*Some consider diversity as a source of strength,*
*Some prefer homogeneity as a form of defense,*
*It seems most pros and cons are reasonable, make sense,*
*However, either choice is not free but comes with an added expense.*

In recent years, diversity has become an issue of great concern and importance, and many studies, investigations, discussions, and publications have been devoted to it. This has been triggered by the realization that most new jobs in our economy will require a postsecondary education, and that women and racial/ethnic minorities will comprise of a majority of the workforce. Because of this awareness, a transformation has taken place that links diversity in the student body with the development of new teaching and learning practices. Moreover, diversity in student enrollments has led to the development of new academic support programs and the revision of education policies and curricula to reflect the diversity of the human experience.

To address questions regarding diversity, it is necessary to quantify it so that we can compare communities. To clarify, consider the following examples and the questions they pose:

1. Two universities have two thousand students each. The first consists of a thousand white, five hundred black, and five hundred Hispanic students. The second consists of eight hundred white, eight hundred black, and four hundred Hispanic students. Which university is more diverse?

2. A university is part of a system of higher education. The racial composition of the student body of the system as a whole is 40 percent white, 35 percent black and 25 percent Hispanic. The corresponding proportions of this university are 60 percent, 20 percent, and 20 percent. To what extent does the composition of

this university differ from that of the system as a whole? If another university in this system is 50 percent white, 30 percent black, and 20 percent Hispanic, which university has a racial composition closer to that for the system?

## Variety vs. Variability

Suppose that two classes, each with ten students, are given a true-false test with ten questions. In one class, four students score 3 and six students score 8. In the other class, four students score 5 and six students score 7. In both classes, the variety of grades is two—there are only two types of grades. The variations, on the other hand, measured by standard deviation, are respectively 2.79 and 1.63.

## Information Measure

Consider a university that is made up of two equally represented types, such as male and female or black and white. This can be represented by two options or binary case, like flipping a fair coin. When flipping a fair coin, we are uncertain about the outcome. There are only two possible outcomes, each with a 50 percent probability of occurrence. If we guess the outcome (heads or tails), then we are 50 percent uncertain about our guess. If we receive a message that the outcome was heads, then our 50 percent uncertainty will be removed. Removing this uncertainty is equivalent to one bit of information. In this sense, information is the same as uncertainty. If we flip the coin twice, there are four possibilities—HH, HT, TH, and TT. Then whatever our guess, we are 75 percent uncertain about it since there are four possible outcomes. To remove the uncertainty, we need two bits of information, one bit for each coin. This is equivalent to counting options or logical alternatives by the exponents of two rather than by their number. For one coin, the number of options is $2^1$. For two coins, we have $4 = 2^2$.

Information gained from a message is obtained by finding the minimum number of yes-or-no questions required to identify the message. In general, the amount of information a message—say, a—of the set of possible messages A conveys is the difference between two states of uncertainty, the uncertainty U(A) before or without knowledge of that message and the uncertainty U(a) after or with knowledge of that message. In this algebraically equivalent form, information is seen as a measure of the difficulty of making appropriate (to a degree better than chance) decisions, and because a less-expected message is more informative, information can also be interpreted as a measure of the surprise value of a message.

So if a decision maker must pick one of the eight alternative courses of action and is given a report that shows that six of them lead to certain failure, there remains 8 − 6 = 2 options to choose from, making the report worth two bits of information (difference between the exponents of $2^3$ and $2^1$). This is now equivalent to receiving the answers to yes-or-no questions. To remove the remaining uncertainty, the decision maker will have to gather one more bit of information or risk, a 50 percent chance of failure. The risk is, of course, considerably less than the risk that existed before receiving the report (87.5 percent).

## Entropy

Entropy may be defined as a measure of observational variety or of actual (as opposed to logically possible) diversity. Unlike the measure of selective information, entropy takes into account that messages or categories of events may occur with unequal frequencies or probabilities.

To see how these ideas may be related to diversity, consider two populations that are each made up of two types. Suppose that one population has 80 percent of type 1 and 20 percent of type 2, while the other population has 50 percent of each type. Deciding or guessing the type of a randomly selected member involves less uncertainty for the 80-20 case than for the 50-50 case. In fact, guessing that a randomly selected member is of type 1 involves 20 percent uncertainty for the 80-20 case and 50 percent uncertainty for the 50-50 case.

## Summary

The answer to yes-or-no questions is taken to convey one bit of information, which constitutes a basic unit of measurement. A convenient measure in a binary system with additive property is the logarithm to base 2. This is equivalent to counting options by the exponents of 2 rather than by their number. Mathematically,

$$U(A) = \log_2 N_A$$

where $N_A$ is the number of logical alternatives. For one coin, $N_A = 2$ and $\log_2 2 = 1$. For two coins, $N_A = 4$ and $\log_2 2^2 = 2$. The amount of information a message—let's say, A—of the set of possible messages A conveys then becomes the difference between two states of uncertainty, the uncertainty U(A) before or without knowledge of that message and the uncertainty U(a) after or with knowledge of that message, that is

$$I(a \, \varepsilon' \, A) = \log_2 N_a = \log(N_a / N_{A)} = \log_2 P_a$$

where $P_a = N_a / N_A$ is the logical probability of the alternative relative to A. In this algebraically equivalent form, information is seen as a measure of the difficulty of making appropriate (to a degree better than chance) decisions, and because a less expected message is more informative, information can also be interpreted as a measure of the surprise value of a message. Putting all these things together, the diversity D can be calculated as:

$$D = p \log (1/p) + (1 - p) \log (1/ (1 - p))$$

where p is the percentages of type 1 members in the population under consideration. For the examples above, we have p = 0.80, D = 0.87 and p = 0.50, D = 1. As expected, the 50-50 population is more diverse than the 80-20 population. In other words, guessing is harder in the first case than the second.

## References

Noubary, Reza. "Measuring Diversity Using Entropy." *Fields Institute for Research in the Mathematical Sciences, Vol. 6*, Canadian Workshop on Information Theory, 1999, 139–143.

# Coincidences

*Life without coincidences is simply dull.*

An unusual day is a day when nothing unusual happens. Most people are fascinated and often puzzled by notions such as randomness, uncertainty, and the related phenomena of risks and coincidences. Many people realize that without risk and uncertainty, life would be dull and boring. Understandably, there are also misconceptions and misunderstandings about these concepts and everything related to them. My several years of teaching at the collegiate level have given me a clear picture of the high degree of student naiveté about these concepts. To help students understand them, I often talk about well-known coincidences and present elementary analyses. I ask students to participate, discuss, and defend their views.

To lay the ground for a deeper discussion, I sometimes use statements like the following and ask students to express their views about them:

1. Faced with uncertainty, most people panic. To comfort themselves, some people deny, avoid, or try to understand the uncertainty. Some people find believing in religious fate or even conspiracy more comforting than admitting ignorance. People who try to understand often appeal to many different means. According to John Allen Paulos, "Human beings are pattern-seeking animals." It might be part of our biology that conspires to make phenomenon such as coincidences more meaningful than they really are. For example, basketball fans notice certain patterns such as sequences of successive hits and ignore equally probable unfamiliar patterns.

2. *What do you think about this definition?[2] "A coincidence is a surprising concurrence of events, perceived as meaningfully related with no apparent causal connection."

   What do you think about this definition? "Coincidences are occurrences of events that happen at the same time by accident but seem to have some connections."

3. Which of the following do you consider a reasonable statement?[3]
   A. Religious faith is based on the idea that almost nothing is coincidence.
   B. Science is an exercise in eliminating the taint of coincidence.
   C. Police work is often a feint and parry between those trying to prove co-incidence and those trying to prove complicity.
   D. Without coincidence, there would be few movies worth watching, and literary plots would grind to disappointing halts.
   E. Coincidences feel like a loss of control. Believing in fate, or even conspiracy, can sometimes be more comforting than facing the fact that sometimes things just happen.
   F. The really unusual day would be one when nothing unusual happens.

4. Do you consider the following a coincidence? Think about September 11th (9/11). Let's try to give it a meaning through a pattern-seeking approach. First, we notice that 911 is the number used for emergency $(9 + 1 + 1 = 11)$. That's a good start. The twin towers looked like the number 11, so perhaps everything that happened had something to do with the number 11. Here's more evidence. The first flight to hit the twin towers was flight number 11 with ninety-two people on board $(9 + 2 = 11)$. September 11 is the 254th day of the year $(2 + 5 + 4 = 11$ and $365 - 254 = 111)$. There are eleven letters in "New York City," "Afghanistan," "the Pentagon," and "George W. Bush." Now we're getting somewhere. New York was the eleventh state admitted to the Union. 119 $(1 + 1 + 9 = 11)$ is the area code for both Iraq and Iran, and flight 77 that crashed in Pennsylvania had 65 people on board $(6 + 5 = 11)$. Here's another

---

[2] Definition suggested by Persi Diaconis and Frederick Mosteller, "Methods for Studying Coincidences," *Journal of the American Statistical Association* 84, no. 408 (Dec. 1989): 853–861.

[3] Discussions presented in Lisa Belkin, "The Odds of That," *New York Times* (Aug. 11, 2002).

confirmation. There were exactly 911 days between the March 11, 2004, attack in Spain and the September 11, 2001 attack.

Next I present some classical and popular examples of coincidences. My goal is to get the students' attention and increase their level of interest. I start with the well-known set of similarities between the life and death of two United States presidents.

5. Abraham Lincoln and John F. Kennedy connections: Just a coincidence?
   - Abraham Lincoln was elected to Congress in 1846, and John F. Kennedy in 1946.
   - Lincoln was elected president in 1860, and Kennedy in 1960.
   - The names *Lincoln* and *Kennedy* each contain seven letters.
   - Both Lincoln and Kennedy were particularly concerned with civil rights.
   - Both Lincoln and Kennedy lost children while living in the White House.
   - Both Lincoln and Kennedy were shot on a Friday and in the head.
   - Lincoln's secretary was named Kennedy, and Kennedy's secretary was named Lincoln.
   - Both Lincoln and Kennedy were assassinated by Southerners.
   - Both Lincoln and Kennedy were succeeded by Southerners named Johnson.
   - Both Lincoln and Kennedy were Democrats and former senators. (Lincoln was a "Republican" but the parties swapped platforms between Kennedy and Lincoln's time)
   - Andrew Johnson, who succeeded Lincoln, was born in 1808. Lyndon Johnson, who succeeded Kennedy, was born in 1908.
   - Both *Andrew Johnson* and *Lyndon Johnson* have thirteen letters.
   - John Wilkes Booth (JWB), who assassinated Lincoln, was born in 1839. Lee Harvey Oswald (LHO), who assassinated Kennedy, was born in 1939.
   - Both assassins were known by their three names, comprising fifteen letters.
   - In the names of the two assassins, replacing 1 for A, 2 for B, etc. JWB = LHO=35.
   - Booth ran from a theater and was caught in a warehouse. Oswald ran from a warehouse and was caught in a theater.
   - Lincoln was assassinated in Ford's Theatre. Kennedy was assassinated in an automobile made by the Ford Motor Company.

- Booth and Oswald were both assassinated before their trials.
- A week before being assassinated, Lincoln was in Monroe, Maryland. A week before being assassinated, Kennedy was with Marilyn Monroe.
- Both presidents wore glasses.
- The digits of 11/22 (November 22) add to 6, and Friday has six letters.
- Take the letters FBI, shift each forward six letters in the alphabet, and you get LHO.
- Oswald has six letters. He shot from the sixth floor of the building where he worked.
- The triple shift of FBI to LHO is expressed by the number 666, the infamous number of the devil.

## FIFA World Cup 2018 Coincidence

In the 2018 World Cup quarterfinals, eight teams remained. The following observations were made for the teams facing each other on July 6 and July 7:

- *France* has six letters and *Uruguay* has seven letters.
- *Brazil* has six letters and *Belgium* has seven letters.
- *Sweden* has six letters and *England* has seven letters.
- *Russia* has six letters and *Croatia* has seven letters.

## Personal Coincidences

As pointed out earlier, different people have different perceptions about coincidences. Dylan Wynn, author of *The History of Coincidences*, considers the following events in history that happened on or near his birth date of May 31, 1970, coincidences:

- Joan of Arc was burned at the stake on May 30, 1415.
- William Shakespeare's first daughter was baptized on May 26, 1583.
- Austrian composer Wolfgang Mozart's father died on May 25, 1761.
- President George Washington's wife died on May 29, 1787.
- The first steamship to cross the Atlantic Ocean from the United States to England arrived on May 27, 1819.
- The first message transmitted on a telegraph line was on May 24, 1844.
- Adolph Hitler's brother, Gustav, was born on May 17, 1885.

- Mt. Everest, the tallest mountain in the world, was first climbed on May 29, 1953.
- The first woman to drive in the Indy 500 car race was on May 30, 1977.
- Patricia Harris, the first black woman to serve as a US ambassador and to hold a cabinet post, was born on May 31, 1924.
- Serial killer Jeffrey Dahmer was born on May 21, 1960.
- Nicole Simpson, ex-wife of O. J. Simpson, who was murdered in 1994, was born on May 19, 1959.
- Ted Kaczynski, the infamous Unabomber, was born on May 22, 1942.
- Serial killer Robert Lee Yates, arrested in 2000, was born on May 27, 1952.
- Eric Robert Rudolph, guilty of the 1996 bombing in Atlanta, was arrested on May 31, 2003.

## References

Wynn, Dylan. *The History of Coincidences*. West Conshohocken, PA: Infinity, 2003.

# Fibonacci, Art, Music, and Nature

*From nature to brilliant architectures.*

Where did the decimal numbering system we use come from? When did we change from Roman numerals to a decimal numbering system? Well, it was in the thirteenth century when Fibonacci published his *Liber abaci*.

According to "Who was Fibonacci?" by J. J. O'Connor and E. F. Robertson, Leonardo Pisano, better known by his nickname Fibonacci, was born in Pisa in 1175 A.D. He was the son of Guilielmo, a Pisan merchant and member of the Bonacci family. Fibonacci, who sometimes used the name Bigollo, was educated in North Africa. His father's job was to represent merchants trading in Bugia. Fibonacci was taught mathematics in Bugia and traveled widely with his father to Egypt, Syria, Greece, Sicily, and Provence. He could see the colossal advantages of the mathematical systems used in the countries they visited.

In 1200, Fibonacci returned to Pisa and used the knowledge he had gained on his travels to write *Liber abaci*, which translates as *The Book of Calculations*. In *Liber abaci*, he introduced the Latin-speaking world to the decimal system, as well as the Fibonacci numbers and Fibonacci sequence for which he is best remembered today. The resulting sequence is 1, 1, 2, 3, 5, 8, 13, 21, 34, 55, … This sequence, in which each number is the sum of the two preceding numbers, has proved extremely useful and appears in many different areas of mathematics and science. For example, some plants branch in such a way that they have a Fibonacci number of growing points. Flowers often have a Fibonacci number of petals, and sunflowers have a Fibonacci number of spirals in the arrangement of the seeds. By taking the ratio of successive terms in the Fibonacci series, the special value of 1.61803, called the golden ratio, is obtained. The ratio was used in Greek architecture, such as the Parthenon in Athens, and in geometry to form a star used in many flags of the world.

Fibonacci then wrote a number of important texts that played an important role in reviving ancient mathematical skills and making significant contributions of his own. Of his books we still have copies of *Liber abaci* (1202), *Practica geometriae* (1220), *Flos* (1225), and *Liber quadratorum* (1225), although he wrote other texts as well. His text on commercial arithmetic, *Di minor guisa*, and his commentary on Book X of Euclid's *Elements* unfortunately are lost.

Fibonacci was a sophisticated mathematician and his achievements were clearly recognized. His practical applications rather than the abstract theorems made him famous among his contemporaries. His most impressive work overall is *Liber quadratorum*, which translates as *The Book of Squares*, according to O'Connor and Robertson. This number theory book examines methods for finding Pythagorean triples.

According to O'Connor and Robertson, "After 1228 there is only one known document which refers to Fibonacci. This is a decree made by the Republic of Pisa in 1240 in which a salary is awarded to: 'the serious and learned Master Leonardo Bigollo.' This salary was given to Fibonacci in recognition for the services that he had given to the city, advising on matters of accounting and teaching the citizens."

Fibonacci's contribution to mathematics has been largely overlooked, and his work in number theory was almost wholly ignored and virtually unknown during the Middle Ages. At the age of 75, Fibonacci passed away, but his theories and applications of mathematics are still used today.

## Music

It is well known that the Fibonacci sequence of numbers and the associated "golden ratio" are manifested in nature and certain works of art. It is less well known that these numbers also underlie certain musical intervals and compositions. As is presented in numerous publications, music has a foundation in the mathematical study of sequences and series. There are thirteen notes in the span of any note through its octave. A scale is composed of eight notes, of which the fifth and third notes create the basic foundation of all chords, and are based on a tone which are combination of two steps and one step from the root tone, that is the first note of the scale. In a scale, the dominant note is the fifth note of the major scale, which is also the eighth note of all thirteen notes that comprise the octave. This provides an added instance of Fibonacci numbers in key musical relationships. Interestingly, $8/13 = 0.61538$, which approximates the golden ratio minus one.

Here is another view of the Fibonacci relationship presented by Gerben Schwab in his YouTube video. First, number the eight notes of the octave scale. Next, number the thirteen notes of the chromatic scale. The Fibonacci numbers, in red on both scales, fall on the same keys in both methods (C, D, E, G, and C). This creates the Fibonacci ratios of 1:1, 2:3, 3:5, 5:8 and 8:13.

## Nature and Golden Angle

The golden ratio φ is an irrational number (infinite decimal representation with no pattern) equal to $(1 + \sqrt{5})/2 = 1.61803 \ldots$ It has many properties such as $1.61803 \ldots = 1 + 1/1.61803$. A golden rectangle is a rectangle so that the ratio of the longer side to the shorter side is φ. Credit cards are a typical example. The golden angle is about 137.5° and is related to the golden ratio. It is $1/\varphi^2$ of a circle. Also

$$\varphi = 1 + (1/(1+(1/(1+(1/(1+\ldots))))))$$

$$\varphi = 1 + \cfrac{1}{1 + \cfrac{1}{1 + \cfrac{1}{1 + \cdots}}}$$

Many plants display Fibonacci phyllotaxis, featuring Fibonacci numbers and the golden angle. Based on a survey of the literature encompassing 650 species and 12,500 specimens, R. Jean (1994) estimated that among plants displaying spiral or multijugate phyllotaxis, about 92 percent of them have Fibonacci phyllotaxis

## References

Meisner, Gary. "Music and the Fibonacci Sequence and Phi." *Phi: The Golden Number*, May 4, 2012. https://www.goldennumber.net/music/.

O'Connor, J. J., and E. F. Robertson. "Who Was Fibonacci?" http://nurvirtamonarizqa. blogspot.com/2010/05/kisah-om-fibonacci-who-was-fibonacci.html.

*Phi: The Golden Number.* www.goldennumber.net.

Schwab, Gerben. https://www.youtube.com/user/astrosoundvids/videos?disable_polymer=1.

Roger V. Jean (1994). *Phyllotaxis: A systemic study in plant morphogenesis.* Cambridge University Press: Cambridge.

# Is Air Travel Safer Than Car Travel?

*Well, I am a great driver.*

Some people think that traveling by plane is inherently more dangerous than driving a car. According to the National Safety Council, the odds of dying in a motor vehicle accident versus air and space transport are 1 in 114 and 1 in 9,821 respectively, which indicates that flying is far safer than driving. However, flying may feel more dangerous because our perception about risk is usually based on factors beyond mere facts. For example, most people think they are good drivers and feel safer because driving affords personal control. Additionally, a car crash does not often lead to death, whereas plane crashes are often catastrophic, killing many people at once and grabbing the attention of the media.

## How Do We Measure Risk?

In general, there is a lot more to calculating and comparing risk than we might think. According to Austin Jesse Mitchell in "How Do People Survive Plane Crashes?" the annual risk of an average American being killed in a plane crash or a motor vehicle is about 1 in 11 million and 1 in 5,000 respectively. What does this mean to you and me? First, most of us are not average; some people fly more than others, while some do not fly at all. Simply dividing the total number of people killed in commercial plane crashes into the total population gives us a good general guide, but it's not specific to our personal risk. Here are useful numbers we may prefer to use (considered altogether):

1. Risk per person: dividing the number of people who die into the total number of people. (This was described before. It serves as a good baseline.)
2. Risk per flight: dividing the number of victims into the total number of flights passengers took.
3. Risk per mile: dividing the number of victims into the total number of miles they all flew.

## Example

In 1995, according to "Motor Vehicle Traffic Fatalities, 1900–2007," out of every 100,000,000 people, about 16,300 died in automobile accidents and 111 were killed in commercial flight accidents. The number of deaths per 100 miles were respectively 3 and 100 for 100,000,000 miles traveled and 30 and 20 for every 100,000,000 trips made.

This shows that the risk of death per mile is 33 times higher for car travel. However, the risk of death per trip is about 1.5 times higher for planes.

## Discussion

In "How Risky Is Flying?" David Ropeik provides an interesting discussion on air travel versus car travel. The calculations just mentioned are useful and accurate, but the one most relevant to us depends on our personal flying patterns. Some of us take many short flights, while others fly less frequently but take longer flights. Since according to the available data, most plane crashes take place in connection with takeoffs and landings, we may conclude that the risk is more a matter of how *often* one flies and less a matter of how *far*. If you are a frequent flier, the risk per flight means more to you. For people who fly occasional long-distance, the risk per mile means more. A frequent long-distance flier may consider both.

Ropeik also says that the number of plane crash fatalities varies widely from year to year, so a calculation of risk based on one year versus an average of five, ten, or twenty years may vary significantly. In some years, few if any plane crashes occur, which makes the value of the risk per year misleading. If we average things over five or ten years, other factors will muddy the water. In the last five years, for example, safety factors have changed, which could make a ten-year average misleading.

According to Ropeik, despite all these variables, numbers are a great way to put risk in general perspective. Whatever measure we use, flying is less risky than traveling by car. However, numbers are not the only way, nor are they even the most important way, because we judge what to be afraid of. Risk perception is not just a matter of facts. For example, consider the risk awareness factor. People who are more aware of a particular risk become more concerned about it. This explains why flying seems scarier to many of us when there is a plane crash in the news, even though that one crash has not significantly changed the overall statistical risk.

"Road Rage Statistics Filled with Surprising Facts" includes the following interesting statistics regarding road rage:

- Recent data from the National Highway Traffic Safety Administration shows that 94 percent of all road accidents are caused by driver error. Out of those accidents, 33 percent could be linked to behaviors typically assigned to road rage.
- In 1990, the AAA Foundation for Traffic Safety studied more than 10,000 traffic accidents related to driver violence. Over a seven-year period, more 12,500 injuries were linked to these acts.
- Road rage was also linked to 218 deaths, mostly caused by angry drivers. This number has been steadily increasing at a rate of 7 percent each year.
- Data gathered by the website SafeMotorist.com indicates that 66 percent of recent traffic fatalities were due to aggressive driving.
- More disturbingly, 37 percent of those fatalities were caused by a firearm, rather than a typical accident. This shines a light on the fact that road rage often does not end once a driver is off the road or outside their car. Half of drivers who shared road rage stories admitted to engaging in aggressive behavior in response.
- Finally, in recent years the use of cellphones while driving has become a contributing factor to accidents of all kind.

## References

"Aggressive Driving and Road Rage." http://www.safemotorist.com/articles/road_rage.aspx.

*Critical Reasons for Crashes Investigated in the National Motor Vehicle Crash Causation Survey.* DOT HS 812 115 (February 2015). http://www-nrd.nhtsa.dot.gov/Pubs/812115.pdf.

Dittmann, Melissa. "Anger on the Road." *American Psychological Association* 36, no. 7 (June 2005). http://www.apa.org/monitor/jun05/anger.aspx.

"Road Rage: How to Avoid Aggressive Driving." https://newsroom.aaa.com/wp-content/uploads/2016/07/AAAFTS-Road-Rage-Brochure.pdf.

Elite Driving School. "Road Rage Statistics Filled with Surprising Facts." https://drivingschool.net/road-rage-statistics-filled-surprising-facts/.

Mitchell, Austin Jesse. "How Do People Survive Plane Crashes?" *Curiosity Makes You Smarter*, August 2, 2017. https://curiosity.com/topics/how-do-people-survive-plane-crashes-o53cN3Xy/.

"Motor Vehicle Traffic Fatalities, 1900–2007," https://www.fhwa.dot.gov/policyinformation/statistics/2007/pdf/fi200.pdf.

National Safety Council. "Injury Facts Chart: What Are the Odds of Dying From ...."
https://www.nsc.org/work-safety/tools-resources/injury-facts/chart.

Ropeik, David. "How Risky Is Flying?" *Nova*, October 16, 2006. http://www.pbs.org/
wgbh/nova/space/how-risky-is-flying.html.

Ropeik, David. "How Risky Is Flying? It Depends." *Big Think*, February 12, 2013.
https://bigthink.com/risk-reason-and-reality/how-risky-is-flying-it-depends.

"USDOT Releases 2016 Fatal Traffic Crash Data." National Highway Traffic Safety
Administration. October 6, 2017. https://www.nhtsa.gov/press-releases/
usdot-releases-2016-fatal-traffic-crash-data.

# Euler's e = 2.7182818... : An Exceptional Number

*The limit of compound interest.*

There are many interesting numbers in mathematics, but only a few really special numbers pop up everywhere in science. One example is *e* (Euler's number). Although many people find pi (3.14 …) fascinating, most mathematicians find *e* even more amazing. Pi is easy to understand, as it is simply the ratio of a circle's circumference to its diameter. *e*, on the other hand, is not so easy to describe or explain. Both numbers appear in the complex equation representing the bell-curve or normal distribution. However, *e* appears in significantly more places and sometimes unexpectedly. For example, most of us are familiar with the decimal and binary numbering systems. We may also know that because of progress made in our use of technology, binary is a more efficient system. However, we may not know that base *e* numbering system is the most efficient.

There are now several books about the four most famous numbers in the world of mathematics, namely $\pi$, *e*, *i*, and 0. These quantities all appear in a famous equation ($e^{\pi i} + 1 = 0$) known as Euler's identity or Euler's equation, named after the Swiss mathematician who studied it. Some call it a beautiful equation or equality. Why famous? Well, here *e* is Euler's number, which is the base of natural logarithms; *i* is the imaginary unit, which satisfies $i^2 = -1$; $\pi$/pi is the ratio of the circumference of a circle to its diameter; and 0 and 1 are the identities of addition and multiplication respectively. The equation is a supreme example of mathematical beauty, as it shows how the most fascinating numbers in mathematics are connected. Only 1 still does not have its own book, but considering its importance, it might have one soon.

According to Brian Blank, it is not easy to convince readers that the number e is a natural subject for study, but knowing more about it will certainly persuade them. People familiar with the power of compound interest know that a leap from daily compounding to continuous compounding involves e. However, it is surprising that although records of compound interest date back to antiquity, e didn't appear until the introduction of the Naplerian logarithm.

## *e* and Compound Interest

An account starts with one dollar and pays 100 percent interest per year. If the interest is credited once, at the end of the year, the value of the account at year-end doubles to two dollars. What happens if the interest is computed and credited more frequently over the course of the year? If the interest is credited twice in the year, the interest rate for each six months will be 50 percent, so after the first six months of the year, the initial dollar is multiplied by 1.5 to yield $1.50. Reinvesting this by the end of the year, it becomes $1.50 x $1.50 yielding $1.00 x $1.50^2 = \$2.25$ at the end of the year. Compounding quarterly yields $1.00 x $1.25^4 = \$2.4414$ ... and compounding monthly yields $1.00 $\times (1+1/12)^{12} = \$2.613035$. Compounding weekly (n = 52) yields $2.692597 ..., while compounding daily (n = 365) yields $2.714567 ..., just two cents more. The limit is the number that came to be known as e; with continuous compounding, the account value will reach $2.7182818. Bernoulli, in 1683, was the first person to notice this.

In "Does the Number e Have Any Real Physical Meaning?" the answer is yes. It occurs naturally in any situation where a quantity increases at a rate proportional to its value, such as a bank account producing interest or a population increasing as its members reproduce. Obviously, the quantity will increase more if the increase is based on the total current quantity (including previous increases) than if it is based only on the original quantity (with previous increases not counted). How much more? The number e answers this question. To put it another way, the number e is related to how much more money you will earn under compound interest than under simple interest.

The more mathematics and science you encounter, the more you run into the number e. Since its discovery, e has shown up in a variety of useful applications including—but definitely not limited to—solving for voltages, charge buildups, and currents in dynamic electrical circuits; spring/damping problems; growth and decay problems; Newton's laws of cooling and heating; plane waves; and compound interest. e can also be used to help determine such things as the best applicant for a job and the wait time to the new record.

## References

Blank, Brian. "A Joint Review of *A History of Pi* (Petr Beckmann, Barnes and Noble, 1989), *The Joy of Pi* (David Blatner, Walker, 1997), *The Nothing That Is* (Robert Kaplan, Oxford University Press, 1999), *e: The Story of a Number* (Eli Maor, Princeton University Press, 1998), *An Imaginary Tale* (Paul Nahin, Princeton University Press, 1998), and *Zero: The Biography of a Dangerous Idea* (Charles Seife, Viking, 2000)." http://delivery.acm.org/10.1145/1170000/1165560/p19-blank.pdf.

Ellinor, Andrew, Patrick Corn, and Geoff Pilling. "The Discovery of the Number *e*." Brilliant.org. https://brilliant.org/wiki/the-discovery-of-the-number-e/.

University of Toronto, Mathematics Network, Answers and Explanations. "Does the Number *e* Have Any Real Physical Meaning, Or Is It Just a Mathematical Convenience?" http://www.math.utoronto.ca/mathnet/answers/ereal.html.

Wikipedia. "e (mathematical constant)." https://en.wikipedia.org/wiki/e_ (mathematical constant).

O'Connor, J. J., and E. F. Robertson. The Number E. http://www-history.mcs.st-and.ac.uk/HistTopics/e.h

# Repeating Decimals and Cyclic Numbers

*Numbers are more mysterious than we think.*

Think about 1/7 = 0.142857142857142857 ... 142857, which is an interesting number. For example, 142 + 857 = 999. Multiplying 999 by a number from 1 to 6 will give the result of the same numbers in the same order, but with a different offset. For instance:

$1 \times 142{,}857 = 142{,}857$
$2 \times 142{,}857 = 285{,}714$
$3 \times 142{,}857 = 428{,}571$
$4 \times 142{,}857 = 571{,}428$
$5 \times 142{,}857 = 714{,}285$
$6 \times 142{,}857 = 857{,}142$

This number also seems to have interesting relations with number 7. Multiplying it by 7 will give 999,999. Any number that isn't evenly divisible by 7 divided by 7 will give a result with decimals that end up with 142857 repeating itself endlessly.

$7 \times 142{,}857 = 999{,}999 \ (= 142{,}857 + 857{,}142)$
$1/7 = 0.142857142857142857 \ldots$
$43/7 = 6.142857142857142857 \ldots$
$74/7 = 10.57142857142857 \ldots$

142,857 is a Kaprekar number and a Harshad number (in base 10). According to the article "142,857," this is the best-known cyclic number in base 10. As we noted earlier, when multiplied by 2, 3, 4, 5, or 6, the answer will be a cyclic permutation of itself and will correspond to the repeating digits of 2/7, 3/7, 4/7, 5/7, or 6/7 respectively.

If we multiply it by an integer greater than 7, there is a simple process to get to a cyclic permutation of 142,857. Adding the rightmost six digits (ones through hundred thousands) to the remaining digits and repeating this process until we have only the six digits left will result in a cyclic permutation of 142,857.

$142,857 \times 8 = 1142,856$

$1 + 142,856 = 142,857$

$142,857 \times 815 = 116,428,455$

$116 + 428,455 = 428,571$

$142,857^2 = 142,857 \times 142,857 = 20,408,122,449$

$20,408 + 122,449 = 142,857$

Recall that multiplying it by a multiple of 7 will result in 999,999 through this process:

$142,857 \times 7^4 = 342,999,657$

$342 + 999,657 = 999,999$

If we square the last three digits and subtract the square of the first three digits, we also get back a cyclic permutation of the number:

$857^2 = 734,449$

$142^2 = 20,164$

$734,449 - 20,164 = 714,285$

It is the repeating part in the decimal expansion of the rational number $1/7 = 0.142857$. Thus multiples of $1/7$ are simply repeated copies of the corresponding multiples of 142,857:

$1 \div 7 = 0.142857$

$2 \div 7 = 0.285714$

$3 \div 7 = 0.428571$

$4 \div 7 = 0.571428$

$5 \div 7 = 0.714285$

$6 \div 7 = 0.857142$

$7 \div 7 = 0.999999 = 1$

$8 \div 7 = 1.142857$

$9 \div 7 = 1.285714$

## 1/7 as an Infinite Sum

Here are some interesting patterns of doubling, shifting, and addition that gives 1/7.

$1/7 = 0.142857142857142857 \ldots$

$= 0.14 + 0.0028 + 0.000056 + 0.00000112 + 0.0000000224 + 0.000000000448 + 0.00000000000896$

$= (14/100) + (28/100^2) + (56/100^3) + (112/100^4) + (224/100^5) + \ldots ((7 \times 2^N)/100^N) + \ldots$

$= \{(7/50) + (7/50^2) + (7/50^3) + (7/50^4) + (7/50^5) + \ldots + (7/50^N) + \ldots\}$

Each term is double the prior term shifted two places to the right. Another infinite sum is

$1/7 = 0.1 + 0.03 + 0.009 + 0.0027 \ldots = 1/10 + 3/100 + 9/1000 + 27/10000$

## Connection to the Enneagram

The 142,857 number sequence is used in the enneagram figure, a symbol of the Gurdjieff work used to explain and visualize the dynamics of the interaction between the two great laws of the universe, the Law of Three and the Law of Seven. The movement of the numbers of 142,857 divided by 1/7, 2/7, etc. and the subsequent movement of the enneagram are portrayed in Gurdjieff's sacred dances known as the movements.

## References

Wikipedia. "142,857." https://en.wikipedia.org/wiki?curid=576354.

# Averages or Extremes?

*Tired of being average? Join the extremes club and become a newsmaker.*

Should I worry about large earthquakes or average ones? A typical link or the weakest link? Traditionally, statistics have focused on the study of typical values with high frequencies and averages. The celebrated central limit theorem states that under certain conditions, for large samples, the distribution of sample mean is approximately (bell-shaped) normal, has given statistics its focus on averages—we do what we know how to do. The theories of extremes (large or small values) and record values are less simple, less unified, and more recent—but not less important.

However, as discussed in my article "It Is Time to Support Extremes," it is becoming increasingly impractical to focus on averages alone. Instead, it has become important to understand the distributions of rare events and extreme values, since they usually are accompanied by severe consequences. Moreover, events like these catch the attention of the media and therefore the general public. With natural disasters such as earthquakes, for example, it is not the average intensity but the most severe that concerns us most. In examining material strengths and systems reliability, it is the weakest links that we must worry about. In a study of a parallel or series system, components with maximum or minimum resistances or lifetimes are of greatest interest. In risk management, we need to prepare for the largest possible disasters, and our insurance must cover the largest claims.

## Extreme Values

As S. A. Frank points out in "The Common Patterns of Nature," reliability, time to failure, and mortality may depend on extreme values. When an organism or system relies on numerous components, failure of any component can cause the system to fail or the organism to die. We can think of failure for a component as an extreme value in a stochastic process; then overall failure depends on how often an extreme value arises in any of the components. In some cases, overall failure may depend on the breakdown of several components. The extreme value distribution is often used to describe these kinds of reliability and failure problems.

Frank also mentions that many problems in ecology and evolution depend on evaluating rare events. What is the risk of invasion by a pest species? For an endangered species, what is the risk of rare environmental fluctuations causing extinction? What is the chance of a rare beneficial mutation arising in response to a strong selective pressure?

An extreme value is the largest or smallest number in a data set. Every data set has extreme values, although in many cases these do not differ greatly from the rest of the data.

The first recognition of the importance of extreme value theory seems to have been in astronomy. Early astronomers were concerned with the problem of deciding whether to accept or disregard an observation that differed greatly from the rest of a data set. Following Fourier, statisticians have commonly refused to recognize as valid any sample values from a normal distribution that differ by more than three standard deviations from the mean. This refusal occurs despite the simple logic that if the distribution being sampled is unbounded, then the largest or smallest sample value is also unbounded. As sample size increases, there is more opportunity for values in the tails of the distribution to occur, though, of course, these values occur with low frequencies. The study of extreme values attempts to describe the relationship between sample size and the magnitude of observed extreme values as well as their distribution.

Applications of extreme value theory began in the 1930s with the pioneering work of E. J. Gumbel. His first application was for old age, considering the longest possible duration of life. Gumbel went on to show that the statistical distribution of large floods also could be understood through the use of extreme value theory. There exists a long list of areas in which extreme value theory plays a decisive role.

## Extreme Values Course

Several publications have discussed the extreme value theory in detail. See, for example, "Statistical Modeling of Extreme Values," by Nader Tajvidifor, for mathematical modeling of extreme events. According to www.research.chula.th, recent developments have introduced flexible and theoretically well-motivated models for extreme values, which now are at the stage where they can be used to address important technological problems in handling risks in areas such as wind engineering, hydrology, flood monitoring and prediction, climatic changes, structural reliability, corrosion modeling, and large insurance claims or large fluctuations in financial data (volatility).

In many applications of extreme value theory, predictive inference for unobserved events is the main interest. One wishes to make inference about events over a time period much longer than that for which data are available. For example, insurance companies are interested in the maximum amount of claims due to storm damage during, say, the next 30 days, based on data from the past 10 to 15 years. In bridge design, a major factor is the maximum wind speed that can occur in any direction during the life of the bridge. However, the dataset used to estimate a return value for high wind speeds is often recorded over a much shorter time period than the expected lifetime of the bridge.

Statistical modeling of extreme events has been the subject of much practical and theoretical work over the past few decades. Tajvidi says that the course he's teaching will provide an overview of a number of different topics in modern extreme value theory, including the following topics:

- Structural engineering: Modern building codes and standards provide information on extreme winds and other maximum forces expected to act on a structure in its lifetime.
- Ocean engineering: The designs of offshore platforms, breakwaters, and dikes rely on knowledge of the probability distribution of the largest waves and the periods associated with the largest waves.
- Pollution Studies: Codes to control pollution require that pollutant concentration (expressed as the amount of pollutant per unit volume of, say, air or water) remain below a given critical level. Here the largest value plays a fundamental role.
- Meteorology: Extreme meteorological conditions influence many aspects of human life, as well as the behaviors of some machines and the lifetimes of certain materials. In these cases, engineers are concerned with the accurate prediction of rare events rather than mean values.
- Sports: The estimation or prediction of future records, including the ultimate record, is of great importance since it sheds light on human strength, weakness, and limitations.
- Insurance: The future solvency of an insurance company depends on its ability to predict, with some degree of accuracy, the magnitude and frequency

of enormous claims. If a terrorist bombing destroys a client's skyscraper in Manhattan, or if hurricanes, floods, or earthquakes hit large numbers of a company's clients, the company must be prepared.

- Materials strength: An important application of extreme value theory to a material's strength is the analysis of size effect. In many engineering problems, the strength of actual structures must be inferred from the strengths of small elements or reduced-size prototypes or models, which are tested under laboratory conditions. Extreme value theory is used to make reliable extrapolation possible. In general, the minimum strength of the weakest sub-piece determines the strength of a piece.

## Summary

Traditionally, data values with high frequencies and averages have been the focus of statistical analysis and modeling. This approach has rested on the important and powerful central limit theorem. Extremes, rare events, and records have been neglected and treated as outliers rather than as important information. We have cited examples that point to the importance of these non-average values in the modern technological world. Every course in introductory statistics should introduce students to these, for not only are they important, but also the theory surrounding them is sufficiently elementary to be introduced to beginners.

## References

Frank, S. A. "The Common Patterns of Nature." *Journal of Evolutionary Biology* 22 (2009): 1563–1585. https://stevefrank.org/reprints-pdf/09JEBmaxent.pdf.

Noubary, Reza. "It Is Time to Include Extremes In Statistics Curriculum." Proceedings of the Annual Meeting of the Decision Science Institute (2008): 192–197. www.research.chula.ac.th

Noubary, Reza. "It Is Time to Support Extremes." *Mathematical Association of America Focus* 27, no. 9 (December 2007): 24–25.

Tajvidi, Nader. "FMSN55/MASM15: Statistical Modeling of Extreme Values." http://www.maths.lth.se/matstat/kurser/fms155mas231/.

# Do We Understand Correlation?

*There is more than 95 percent correlation between the import of bananas and the number of divorces in England. Whoa, what could that possibly mean?*

Are the per capita consumption of cheese in the United States and the number of people who died by becoming entangled in their bedsheets really related (correlation = 0.947)? What about the number of people who drowned after falling out of a fishing boat and the marriage rate in Kentucky (correlation = 0.952)? These are interesting questions that make us wonder whether correlation really means what we think it does. A few years ago, a study appeared in *The College Mathematics Journal* titled "Is Presidential Greatness Related to Height?" In the article, author Paul Sommers asked the following question: What makes a president great or near great? Apparently nothing in presidents' political backgrounds provides clues to their greatness. Instead, Sommers demonstrates that greatness depends on height; that is, height and greatness are correlated. In United States presidential elections, the taller candidate usually wins.

## Correlation or Causation?

As Michael Hiltzik points out in "See Some Hilarious Charts Showing That Correlation Is Not Causation," the idea that correlation does not imply causation is so widely understood in the abstract that it has become a cliché. When we see lines sloping together, bars rising together, or points on a scatterplot clustering, the data practically begs us to assign a reason, according to "Beware Spurious Correlations." Hiltzik explains that we want to believe a connection exists and that specious correlations, often drawn from publications, are mainstays of attention-grabbing headlines the world over. Based on the data, he adds, some people like to believe that the age of Miss America is closely related to murders by steam, hot vapors, and hot objects. Statistically, however, we cannot make that leap, says "Beware Spurious Correlations."

Charts that show a close correlation often rely on a visual parlor trick to imply a relationship. Tyler Vigen, a student at Harvard Law School and the author of *Spurious Correlations*, has made sport of this on his website, which charts farcical correlations.

## Apples and Oranges

According to "Beware Spurious Correlations," plotting unrelated data sets together can make it seem that changes in one variable are causing changes in the other. Y-axis scales that measure different values may show similar curves that should not be paired. This becomes pernicious when the values appear to be related but are not. Even when Y-axes measure the same category, changing the scales can alter the lines to suggest a correlation. Every time we see such a thing, we try to create a narrative. For example, although we might be tempted to think that if Pandora loses less money, more music is copyrighted, this is probably just coincidence.

Hiltzik also says the most powerful weapon that debaters wield against the unwary is causation—marijuana use leads to heroin addiction, pornography to rape, video games to mass murder, high consumption of margarine to divorces in Maine. Whoops! The first three of these are common juxtapositions of parallel trend lines, and the fourth is from the website Spurious Correlations.

Hiltzik also mentions that Vigen's site aims to underscore the common warning that correlation does not prove causation by providing charts of absurd correlations. As a dividend, the site allows you to make your own!

## What Is the Lesson?

It is completely evident that correlation does not imply causality. In addition to those already discussed, correlations can appear to be significant for several other reasons:

1. coincidence,
2. variables under consideration that might be directly influenced by some common underlying cause,
3. one of the variables that may actually be a cause of the other, or
4. the correlation coefficient might measure the degree of linear association (a small subset of possible fans of association) between the attributes considered and nothing more.

# References

"Beware Spurious Correlations." *Harvard Business Review* (June 2015): 34–35. https://elb.hbr.org/2015/06/beware-spurious-correlations.

Hiltzik, Michael. "See Some Hilarious Charts Showing That Correlation is Not Causation." *Los Angeles Times*, May 12, 2014. http://www.latimes.com/business/hiltzik/la-fi-mh-see-correlation-is-not-causation-20140512-column.html.

Sommers, Paul M. "Is Presidential Greatness Related to Height?" *College Mathematics Journal* 33, no. 1 (2002): 14–16. Published online January 30, 2018. https://www.tandfonline.com/doi/abs/10.1080/07468342.2002.11921912.

# Simpson's Paradox

*Never let Homer Simpson do the data analysis for you.*

I clearly recall my teacher's distinct voice telling the class this fraction fact: "Remember that a/b + c/d is not equal to (a + c)/(b + d)." I also remember a classmate questioning its importance, but I did not find the teacher's response convincing. Now, as a mathematics teacher for almost fifty years, I still get the same questions from students who feel that such little mathematical facts are not important.

In responding to students who care to listen, I start with a simple example that goes like this: Think about two young families with children living in a remote neighborhood. One family has a boy and two girls, and the other has two boys and a girl. Suppose that we want to calculate the ratio of boys to girls in that neighborhood. To do this, we may find the average number of boys ((1+2)/2) =1.5) and girls ((2+1)/2) = 1.5) in that neighborhood and calculate the ratio as 1.5/1.5 = 1. Alternatively, we may find the ratios of boys to girls in each family, ½ = 0.5 and 2/1 = 2 respectively, and calculate their average as (0.5 + 2)/2 – 1.25. As you see, we do not get the same answer. Why? In short, this is because the average of ratios is not the same as the ratio of the averages. Following are some more examples.

## Who Is the Better Free Throw Shooter?

During the last basketball season, Jim attempted one hundred free throws in the first half of the season and made thirty. His free-throw percentage was 30/100 = 0.300. He also attempted twenty in the second half of the season and made eight (8/20 = 0.400). His stats were better than Curt's stats—5/20 (0.250) for the first half of the season, and 35/100 (0.350) for the second half. For the season, however, Curt's free-throw percentage (40/120 = 0.333) was higher than Jim's (38/120 = 0.317).

Consider a disease for which there are two methods of treatment, A and B. The patient has to choose which treatment they wish to use. Suppose that in the past, out of a hundred male patients who chose A, twenty recovered (recovery rate $= 20/100 = 0.20$). Also, out of 210 male patients who chose B, fifty recovered (recovery rate $= 50/210 = 0.24$). These rates suggest that a male patient should prefer treatment B to treatment A (24 percent vs. 20 percent). Also, out of sixty female patients who chose A, forty recovered (recovery rate $= 40/60 = 0.67$). Out of twenty female patients who chose B, fifteen recovered (recovery rate $= 15/20 = 0.75$). These rates suggest that a female patient should prefer treatment B to treatment A (75 percent vs. 67 percent) as well.

When we combine the data, we see that the total number of people (regardless of their gender) who chose A was 160, out of which sixty recovered (recovery rate $= 60/160 = 0.38$). Also, the total number of people (regardless of their gender) who chose B was 230, out of which sixty-five recovered (recovery rate $= 65/230 = 0.28$). These rates suggest that it is wise to use or choose treatment A over treatment B (38 percent vs. 28 percent). This contradicts our earlier conclusion based on patient's gender.

The lesson here is that with only two numbers, as in this example, drawing a conclusion is not always straightforward. From a mathematical point of view, the conclusion based on details (higher dimensions/gender) should be preferred. In fact, breaking the data gives a two-dimensional view of it, which is better than a one-dimensional view based on collapsed data.

The above examples are cases of what is known as Simpson's paradox. The paradox occurs because collapsing the data can lead to an inappropriate weighting of the different populations.

# Coloring Maps

*No worries, all you need is four colors.*

If you have a coloring book with a map that includes all fifty states of the United States, how many colors would you need in order to color all the states in a way that the same color never touches itself?

Here's how the problem started. While coloring a map of the counties of England in 1852, a student named Francis Guthrie realized that only four colors were needed, and he wondered whether that was true for every map. The conjecture, sometimes referred to as Guthrie's problem, was then communicated to mathematician de Morgan and from there into the general community. In 1878, Cayley wrote the first paper about the conjecture, which attracted a large number of false proofs from both well-known mathematicians and a few interested amateur ones.

In Wikipedia's article titled "Four Color Theorem," we read that in mathematics, the four-color theorem—or the four-color map theorem—states that given any separation of a plane into contiguous regions producing a figure called a map, no more than four colors are required to color the regions of the map so that no two adjacent regions have the same color.

As mentioned above, numerous false proofs were presented, some more convincing than others. After fallacious proofs were given independently by two mathematicians in 1879 and 1880, it took a decade before an error was found in proof using a map with eighteen faces. Later it was shown that a map with nine faces suffices to show the fallacy.

In 1976, this was one of the first major theorems to be proved using a computer, which took 1,200 hours. Many mathematicians refused to accept a result that had not been checked by hand. Despite some initial worries, however, independent verification soon convinced everyone that the four-color theorem had finally been proved. Details of the proof appeared in two articles in 1977. Since then, several attempts have led to improvements in the algorithm. "The Four Colour Theorem" by Leo

Rogers refers to this as an outstanding example of how old ideas combined with new discoveries and techniques in different fields of mathematics can provide new approaches to a problem. It is also an example of how an apparently simple problem that was thought to have been solved gradually became more complex. And finally, this was the first spectacular example in which a computer was involved in proving a mathematical theorem.

## Summary

The year 1976 saw a complete solution to the four-color conjecture when it was to become the four-color theorem for the second—and final—time. The proof was achieved using methods on reducibility. It was carried through the ideas that constructed an unavoidable set with around 1,500 configurations.

## References

Wikipedia. "Four Color Theorem."
    https://en.wikipedia.org/wiki/Four_color_theorem.
Rogers, Leo. "The Four Colour Theorem." University of Cambridge, NRICH Project.
    https://nrich.maths.org/6291.

# Modeling of the State of Knowledge

*A good model treats the facts respectfully and the unknowns fairly.*

Assigning probability to the possible outcomes of an experiment is a complex task. One approach is based on a classical definition of probability. If we want to assign probabilities to a set of outcomes, and we see no reason for one outcome to be more likely than another, then we assign them equal probabilities. Called the principle of insufficient reason, or the principle of indifference, this goes back to Laplace. If we happen to know (or learn) something about the nonuniformity of the outcomes, how should the assignment of probabilities be changed? Fortunately we can apply an extension—the principle of maximum entropy—to the principle of insufficient reason.

The maximum entropy method states that given a set of facts, choose a model (assignments) that is consistent with all the facts, but otherwise is as uniform as possible with the unknowns. Its purpose is to find the probability distribution (rules of assignments) that makes the fewest assumptions about the data (has the maximum entropy) and best fits the given state of knowledge. The idea is similar to determination of the prior distribution in Bayesian inference.

As described in Wikipedia's "Entropy (information theory)," consider tossing a coin with known, though not necessarily fair, probabilities of coming up heads or tails. The entropy of the unknown result of the next toss is maximized if the coin is fair (that is, if heads and tails both have equal probability 1/2). This is the situation of maximum uncertainty since whatever our prediction, we are 50 percent uncertain. In other words, it is the most difficult case to predict the outcome of the next toss. Here the outcome of each toss of the coin delivers one full bit of information. However, if we know the coin is not fair, and that it comes up heads or tails with probabilities p and q, where $p + q = 1$, then our prediction is less uncertain. The reduced uncertainty is quantified in a lower entropy: on average, the outcome of each coin toss delivers less than one full bit of information. For example, if $p = 0.7$, our prediction will be heads every time and our uncertainty is only 30 percent. Using the formula for entropy given below, the coin delivers 0.8816 < 1 bit of information.

As explained in "Entropy (information theory)," the extreme case is that of a double-headed coin that never comes up tails, or a double-tailed coin that never results in a head. Then there is no uncertainty. The entropy is zero: each toss of the coin delivers no new information since the outcome of each coin toss is always completely predictable.

## Information Entropy

Information was originally defined in the context of sending a message between a transmitter and receiver over a potentially noisy channel. Think about a situation in which you are shouting messages to your friend across a large field. You are the transmitter, your friend is the receiver, and the channel is this large field. We can model what your friend is hearing using probability.

Suppose that you are shouting (transmitting) the letters of the alphabet, A to Z. First suppose that you and your friend agree that you will always first shout "A" (a priori) to get his attention. When you actually start shouting, no information is being transmitted because your friend knows exactly what you are saying. This is akin to modeling the probability of receiving A as 1 and all other letters as zero.

Next suppose that you and your friend agree, a priori, that you will be shouting letters in order from some English text. Which letter do you think would transmit more information, E or Z? Since E is the most common letter in the English language, we can usually guess when the next character is an E. We are less surprised when it happens; thus it transmits a relatively low amount of information. Conversely, Z is an uncommon letter. We would probably not guess that it is coming next and be surprised when it does, thus Z conveys more information than E. This is akin to modeling a probability distribution over the alphabet with probabilities proportional to the relative frequencies of letters occurring in the English language.

## Specific Example

Suppose a grocery store wants to find the probability distribution related to customers who buy apples, bananas, or oranges. First, $P_{apple} + P_{banana} + P_{oranges} = 1$ where P's represent percentages for each item. If apples cost a dollar each, bananas two dollars, and oranges three dollars, and if the average price of fruit in the grocery store is $1.75, then $1.75 = $1.00 \text{ P}_{apple}$ + $2.00 \text{ P}_{banana}$ + $3.00 \text{ P}_{oranges}$. These are the constraint equation. This might be all the information they have, but with two equations and three unknowns, it simply is not enough information to come up with a unique solution. That's where the maximum entropy principle comes in, because it narrows down the space of all the potentially possible solutions—and there are lots—to the one best solution: the one with the highest entropy.

As discussed below, the entropy of the system given below provides the third equation:

$$\text{Entropy} = \text{P}_{apple} \log_2 (1/\text{P}_{apple}) + \text{P}_{banana} \log_2 (1/\text{P}_{banana}) + \text{P}_{orange} \log_2 (1/\text{P}_{orange}).$$

Finding percentages for apples and bananas in terms of the percentage for oranges, and replacing it in the entropy equation, we get

$$\text{Entropy} = (\text{P}_{orange} + 0.25) \log_2 (1/(\text{P}_{orange+} 0.25)) + (0.75 - 2 \\ \text{P}_{orange}) \log_2 (1/(0.75 - 2\text{P}_{orange})) + \text{P}_{orange} \log_2 (1/\text{P}_{orange})$$

Now all that remains is to find the value of $\text{P}_{orange}$ so that the entropy is maximized. There are a number of methods for doing this. The entropy is maximized when $\text{P}_{orange} = (3.25 - \sqrt{(3.8125)})/6 = 0.216$, $\text{P}_{apple} = 0.466$, and $\text{P}_{banana} = 0.318$.

## Entropy and Expected Surprise

What does it mean to be surprised? Usually it means that something happened that was unexpected or unlikely to happen. Surprise is a probabilistic concept and can be treated accordingly. Take the particular case where something can happen or not. Suppose that the probability that it happens is $p$. If $p = 0.90$ and it happens, you're not surprised. But if $p = 0.05$ and it happens, you will find it somewhat surprising. If $p = 0.0000001$ and it happens, you will be very surprised. Therefore, a natural measure for the "surprise value of an outcome" should be a monotone decreasing function of its probability. It seems logical (and works well) to take the logarithm of probability and throw in a minus sign to get a positive number. If something is certain, then its probability is one and its surprise value is zero. If it's impossible that something will happen, its probability is zero and its surprise value is infinite. We can quantify the degree of surprise as

$$\text{Surprise (A)} = - \log \text{p(A)}$$

where A represents the event of interest and p(A) is its probability of occurrence. As base of the logarithm we can use 2, Euler's number e, or 10. The corresponding units of surprise are then bits for 2, nats for e, and bans for 10. For example, for a fair coin, if A is the event of observing a head, using base 2 we have

$$\text{Surprise (Head)} = - \log p \text{ (Head)} = - \log \tfrac{1}{2} = 1 \text{ bit}$$

Now, since surprise as defined as a random variable, we can calculate the expected surprise. Let X be a Bernoulli (two option, 0 or 1) random variable with probability of 1 being $p$. Then the possible surprise values are:

$$\text{Surprise (0)} = - \log (1{-}p) \quad \text{Surprise (1)} = - \log p$$

Also, the expected surprise is

$$p \left(-\log p\right) + (1{-}p) \left(-\log (1{-}p)\right)$$

That itself is a surprise, since it is the same as the entropy of X!

Next, let's explore the relationship between being maximally surprised and an important concept known as the maximum entropy. First, why is this important? Suppose that your goal is to learn about something, so you set up some learning experiments. If you already knew everything about this topic, everything is perfectly predictable and nothing surprising. In other words, you learn nothing new. In a more typical situation, you are unable to predict the outcome perfectly, so there is a learning opportunity! This leads to the idea that we can measure the "amount of possible learning" by the expected surprise (entropy). Therefore, maximizing entropy is nothing other than maximizing opportunity for learning.

That sounds like a concept useful in designing and carrying out experiments. Let's consider an example to clarify this. Suppose that you want to design an online test in which the questions are chosen dynamically depending on test takers' previous responses/answers, which means the questions are optimized or customized. If you make the questions too difficult, few will be answered and you'll learn nothing about the situation (the differences between the test takers). That indicates that you must make the questions less difficult. What is the optimal level of difficulty, meaning the difficulty level that maximizes the rate of response and learning? Let the probability of giving a correct answer to a question be $p$ . We want the value of $p$ that maximizes the Bernoulli entropy, and it's easy to show that that is $p = 0.5$. Therefore, you aim to state questions where the probability of a correct answer for a test taker is 0.5.

In the case of a continuous random variable, the probability of any particular outcome $\{X = x\}$ is zero, so the $-\log p$ definition is useless. But we will be surprised if the probability of observing $x$ is a small interval—that is, if the values of a density function $f(x)$ in that interval is small. This leads to

$$\text{Surprise}\,(x) = -\log f(x)$$

And the expected surprise of

$$-\int f(x) \log f(x)\, dx$$

Here's another surprise. We know there are infinite density functions, some more useful than others. One density function that is most practically useful is the bell curve or normal distribution. Here's why: among all densities function with mean zero and standard deviation σ, the normal density has the maximum entropy.

Additionally, most observable patterns of nature arise from aggregation of numerous small-scale processes. As the number of entities contributing to the aggregate increases, they converge in the limit to distributions that define the common patterns of nature. The best known of the limiting distributions, the Gaussian (normal/bell curve) distribution, follows from a celebrated theorem known as the central limit theorem. Hence, in this interpretation, the basic central limit theorem expresses the fact that the per symbol entropy of sums of independent random variables with mean zero and common variance tends to the maximum. This seems eminently reasonable; in fact, it is an expression of the second law of thermodynamics, which Eddington viewed as holding "the supreme position among the laws of Nature."

## References

Wikipedia. "Entropy (information theory)." https://en.wikipedia.org/wiki/Entropy_ (information_theory).

# Geometries That They Did Not Teach You in School

*Geometry is reality. If you do not know geometry, please do not enter.*

According to "Non-Euclidean Geometry," the idea of geometry was developed by Euclid around 300 B.C. when he wrote *The Elements*, his book about geometry. In the book, he starts with five main postulates, or assumptions, and from these, he derives all of the other theorems of geometry. The postulates are as follows:

1. Given two points, there is a straight line that joins them.
2. A straight line segment can be prolonged indefinitely.
3. A circle can be constructed when a point for its center and a distance for its radius are given.
4. All right angles are equal.
5. If a straight line falling on two straight lines makes the interior angles on the same side less than two right angles, the two straight lines, if produced indefinitely, will meet on that side on which the angles are less than the two right angles.

The fifth postulate is clearly the most complicated. We read in "Non-Euclidean Geometry" that over the years, many mathematicians were upset by this fact, believing that the fifth postulate derives from the first four. However, it is impossible to derive this solution, and mathematicians who attempted to do so ended up with several equivalent postulates. Two thousand years after Euclid introduced the problem, nobody had come up with a proof of the fifth postulate. This led to the introduction of non-Euclidean geometries, which share the first four postulates but contradict the fifth.

## Various Types of Geometries

In "Geometry and General Relativity," Scott McKinney says, "The Earth looks flat from our perspective, right? Yes, we're fooled by our perspective on the Earth's surface. If we fly into space it's obvious the Earth is not flat. Amazingly, we don't have to look at the Earth from outer space—or even resort to looking at its shadow on the moon—to determine that it has a curved surface. Tools developed by mathematicians working in the field known as 'Differential Geometry' make it possible to determine that the Earth is not flat simply by taking measurements on its surface."

McKinney also says, "These mathematical tools were in turn generalized to abstract, higher-dimensional surfaces sitting "inside" higher-dimensional spaces – and enabled physicists such as Einstein to develop accurate models of the geometry of space-time. Physicists in turn used this mathematical formulation to refine our understanding of gravitation." In fact, one of the most frequently cited arguments in favor of revision of mathematics in light of empirical discoveries is the general theory of relativity and its adoption of non-Euclidean geometry.

## References

McKinney, Scott. "Geometry and General Relativity." Science 4 All. http://www.science4all.org/article/geometry-and-general-relativity/?msg=fail&shared=email.

Robertson, E. F., and J. J. O'Connor. "Non-Euclidean Geometry." February 1996. https://www-history.mcs.st-and.ac.uk/HistTopics/Non-Euclidean_geometry.html.

# Need Mathematics/Science to Stay Competitive

*Finally, nerds are winning.*

In recent decades, we have witnessed many amazing inventions and breakthroughs, mostly by people who were educated in the United States. Proud of the performance and contributions of our higher education institutions, we might wonder whether this trend will continue, thus guaranteeing our competitiveness in the global world. Unfortunately, this might not be the case; recent studies point to a decline in basic knowledge of sciences and mathematics in our schools and universities. In fact, a large percentage of positions requiring advanced knowledge of sciences and mathematics are now filled by people who have recently moved to the United States from other countries. In 2017, Chinese inventors received 11,241 US patents, according to Susan Decker in "China Becomes One of the Top 5 U.S. Patent Recipients for the First Time." This was a 28 percent increase from the same period in 2016. This trend is likely to continue, since the two primary sources for graduate students in science and technology at US universities are China and South Korea.

To see where we stand, let's look at few more facts and statistics. In "Asia Tops Biggest Global School Rankings," Sean Coughlan refers to an extensive global school ranking published by the Organization for Economic Cooperation and Development. He says that the study may have some drawbacks, considering that (1) some countries have a more homogeneous population and schools than others and (2) students in some countries are better test takers than in others. Nevertheless the study is considered significant, as it enables participant countries to compare themselves against the world's education leaders, exposes their relative strengths and weaknesses, and shows what long-term economic gains an improved quality in schooling could provide. Coughlan says the top five countries were all Asian—Singapore, Hong Kong, South Korea, Taiwan, and Japan. The five lowest-ranked countries were Oman, Morocco, Honduras, South Africa, and Ghana. Out of the seventy-six countries included, the United States ranked twenty-eighth.

Coughlan says that standard of education is a powerful predictor of the wealth that countries can generate in the long run. According to the National Academies, among the twenty-nine wealthiest countries, the United States ranked twenty-seventh in the proportion of college students with degrees in science and engineering. Additionally, among developed countries, the United States was ranked thirty-first in mathematics and twenty-third in science. These rankings are not stellar, despite the fact that our schools and universities have, by far, the best facilities in the world. We could lose ground to foreign rivals unless we find a way to enhance the quality of our mathematics and science education and increase the number of students majoring in these disciplines. Of course, finding ways to motivate more students to major in science and mathematics requires long-term planning, as well as learning more about other countries' approaches and making necessary changes and adjustments.

## References

Coughlan, Sean. "Asia Tops Biggest Global School Rankings." *BBC News*, May 13, 2015. https://www.bbc.com/news/business-32608772?ocid=socialflow_twitter.

Decker, Susan. "China Becomes One of the Top 5 U.S. Patent Recipients for the First Time." *Bloomberg*, January 9, 2018. https://www.bloomberg.com/news/articles/2018-01-09/china-enters-top-5-of-u-s-patent-recipients-for-the-first-time.

National Academies of Sciences, Engineering, and Medicine. http://www.nationalacademies.org/.

Organization for Economic Cooperation and Development. "Programme for International Student Assessment." http://www.oecd.org/pisa/.

Zuckerman, Mortimer B. "Why Math and Science Education Means More Jobs." *U.S. News & World Report*, September 27, 2011. https://www.usnews.com/opinion/articles/2011/09/27/why-math-and-science-education-means-more-jobs.

# Using Technology and Learning Mathematics

*Does technology change our problem-solving ability and approach?*

Educators have studied the role and possible effects of technology, specifically computers, in teaching and learning mathematics. Such studies compare mathematicians trained using traditional methods (abstract thinkers) to mathematicians trained using computers (computer-assisted learners). Among experts and educators, opinions vary about the methods' outcomes, validity, interpretations, and comparisons.

There is general agreement that extensive use of computers change students' problem-solving approaches and abilities that are key to learning and applying mathematics. This makes any direct comparison difficult, so the query about effective teaching and learning should probably be replaced by the following questions: What kind of mathematician does our teaching method produce, and should we differentiate between the two (effective teaching and learning)?

Compared with the human brain, even the most advanced supercomputers are not really intelligent. The brain's vast capacity derives from the fact that all its nerve cells operate in mutual association as a neural network. Given appropriate examples, a network of this nature can learn to store and retrieve information independently. Few of us have difficulty recognizing the face of someone we know as we rush through a busy shopping mall. In a fraction of a second, we recognize the person and notice features that distinguish them from others. At the same time, we recall memories and other items of information about this person. Our brain achieves this without any effort. Even a child can do it. Although a computer can record images electronically, it is able to understand their content only in certain cases and after a long calculation. Should students, especially mathematics majors, use computers to learn, rely on their brain power, or do both? If we use both, to what extent should we use them?

This depends, of course, on how each individual student best learns mathematics. Computers allow a large numbers of users to retrieve the same or similar information at the same time. The human brain, on the other hand, is more portable and infinitely more powerful. Its neural network permits people to use their imagination, see patterns and associations, and think creatively in ways that computers can't.

Would the use of computers make the progress of mathematics faster or slower, and would it change the ways we think? Computers will certainly continue to affect the course of progress, including in new areas such as computational mathematics and computer graphics that are important in their own right. However, computers wouldn't have helped produce mathematicians such as Newton or Euler, who could develop extremely complicated theories in their heads.

Some ways of using a computer in teaching mathematics are considered appropriate, and others are not. For example, a student might use a computer as a tool to construct her own understanding of mathematical concepts. Generally, using a computer as a tool to simulate the real world—or at least the quantifiable part of it—is appropriate, but using it merely as a super calculator isn't appropriate. The first application would facilitate learning and understanding mathematics, but the second would only make life easier by saving time.

# Distribution-Free Statistics

*In 2014 the average income for an American household was $65,751,*
*but more than 50 percent of Americans earned $50,000 or less.*

Distribution-free or nonparametric statistics refers to a statistical method in which the data is not required to fit a particular distribution, such as normal or exponential. Nonparametric statistics does not rely on assumptions that the data are drawn from a given probability distribution. A large volume of literature exists on nonparametric theory and methods. "Educational Statistics" tells us that nonparametric statistics often uses ordinal data; it relies not on data values, but on their ranking or order. To clarify, consider that in geometry, certain results are true regardless of the size of the objects considered. For example, all triangles have three sides and their angles add up to 180 degrees. In the same way, distribution-free methods rely on common properties of probability distributions. To quantify the central tendency in parameter statistics, we add up all the measurements and divide that sum by the number of measurements to determine a sample mean. In distribution-free statistics, we order the measurements from smallest to largest and pick the one in the middle, which is called the sample median (50 percentile).

"Educational Statistics" also says that nonparametric methods are widely used for studying populations that take on a ranked order, such as football teams ranked by coaches or movies ranked one to four stars. The use of nonparametric methods may be necessary when data have a ranking but no clear numerical interpretation, such as when assessing preferences. In education, grades A, B, C, D, and F rank students as excellent, above average, average, below average, and failing, and this grading method compares students to each other.

Since nonparametric methods are based on fewer assumptions, their applicability is much wider than the corresponding parametric methods. In particular, they are applicable in situations where less is known about the area related to the data.

In addition, due to the reliance on fewer assumptions, nonparametric methods are more robust.

"Educational Statistics" adds that another justification for the use of nonparametric methods is their simplicity. In certain cases, even when the use of parametric methods is justified, it may be easier or more practical to apply nonparametric methods. Because of their simplicity and robustness, nonparametric methods are seen by some statisticians as leaving less room for improper use of data and misunderstanding results. To clarify, consider a situation where part of the available data is censored, known only to be bigger than or smaller than certain values. In this situation, it's impossible to find the sample mean, but the sample median can be calculated.

The wider applicability and increased robustness of nonparametric tests comes at a cost, according to "Educational Statistics." In cases where a parametric test would be appropriate, nonparametric tests have less power. In other words, a larger sample size can be required to draw conclusions with the same degree of confidence."

## When to Use Nonparametric Statistics

"Non Parametric Data and Tests" recommends that nonparametric methods be used

- for nominal or ordinal scales,
- for interval or ratio scales,
- when a distribution of data is skewed,
- when one or more assumptions of a parametric test are violated,
- when the sample is too small to run a parametric test,
- when the data has outliers that cannot be removed, and
- when testing for the median rather than the mean.

## References

DeNavas-Walt, Carmen, and Bernadette D. Proctor. *Income and Poverty in the United States: 2014.* US Census Bureau, September 2015. https://www.census.gov/content/dam/Census/library/publications/2015/demo/p60-252.pdf.

Frankel, Matthew. "Here's the Average American Household Income: How Do You Compare?" *USA Today*, November 24, 2016. https://www.usatoday.com/story/money/personalfinance/2016/11/24/average-american-household-income/93002252/.

Internal Revenue Service. "Tax Statistics." https://www.irs.gov/statistics.

Statistics How To. "Non Parametric Data and Tests (Distribution Free Tests)." January 20, 2014. https://www.statisticshowto.datasciencecentral.com/parametric-and-non-parametric-data/.

WikiEducator. "Educational Statistics." http://wikieducator.org/Educational_Statistics.

# 17 and 23

*Do some numbers have mystical side?*

## The Number Seventeen

Many coincidences are attributed to the number seventeen in history, because several events have taken place on the seventeenth day of the month. Wikieducator.org presents several of these coincidences:

- The first impeachment in the United States, of Senator William Blount, took place on December 17, 1798.
- The first child born in the White House, President Jefferson's grandson, was born on January 17, 1806.
- The Statue of Liberty arrived in the United States on June 17, 1885.
- The first plane flight, by the Wright brothers, happened on December 17, 1903.
- The first president of Israel was elected on February 17, 1949.
- The Bay of Pigs invasion took place on April 17, 1961.
- The Watergate break-in was on June 17, 1971.
- Watergate prosecutor Archibald Cox was born on May 17, 1912.
- Spiro Agnew, Nixon's vice president, died on September 17, 1996.
- Three major earthquakes have occurred on the 17th of the month: the San Francisco earthquake on October 17, 1989; the Northridge earthquake in Los Angeles on January 17, 1994; and the Kobe, Japan, earthquake on January 17, 1995.
- The youngest person to win the French Open tennis tournament was Michael Chang, who was seventeen years old.
- David Koresh, leader of the Branch Davidian cult in Waco, Texas, was born on August 17, 1959.

- O. J. Simpson was arrested for the murder of his ex-wife, Nicole, on June 17, 1994. Seventeen fingerprints were found at the murder scene. O. J. and Nicole had known each other for seventeen years, and their first child, Sydney, was born on October 17, 1985.
- President Bill Clinton was investigated by the seventeenth independent counsel, Ken Starr, which led to his impeachment proceedings.
- The only other president to be impeached so far was Andrew Johnson, the seventeenth president of the United States.
- Two space shuttles have exploded in flight, the *Challenger* in 1986 and the *Columbia* in 2003, seventeen years apart.
- Many analysts have pointed out that US presidential elections are decided by the results in seventeen states.

## The Number Twenty-Three

Many people think the number twenty-three has mystical properties. In "How Mystical 23 Changed Course of History," Ryan Parry and Rebecca Smith present several interesting examples.

- Saddam Hussein was the president of Iraq for twenty-three years.
- The controversial book *Satanic Verses*, by Salman Rushdie, is about twenty-three years of the prophet Mohammad's active life.
- Maynard Jackson, Jr., the first black mayor in Atlanta, was born on March 23, 1938, and died on June 23, 2003.
- Basketball legend Michael Jordan wore the number 23 for the Chicago Bulls, and his dad was murdered on July 23, 1993, during a botched robbery.
- William Shakespeare was born and died on April 23. His first plays came in 1623, and his wife, Anne, died in 1623.
- Car giant Nissan is touched by a numerical coincidence. In Japanese, *ni* means "two" and *san* means "three," so Nissan would be twenty-three.
- William Burroughs's final TV appearance was in U2's "Last Night on Earth" video. The letter *U* is the twenty-first in the alphabet and adding the two gives twenty-three.
- *Sesame Street*'s Bert is a member of the National Association of W Lovers, the twenty-third letter of the alphabet.

- The Latin alphabet has twenty-three letters.
- The German movie *23* explores an obsession with the number, based on a real-life story.

Here are several more twenty-three coincidences:

- When twenty-three or more people are in the same room, there is a better-than-even chance that at least two people share the same birthday.
- On average, every twenty-third wave crashing to shore is twice as large as normal.
- It takes twenty-three seconds for blood to circulate through the body.
- The average smoker gets through twenty-three cigarettes a day.
- Parents each contribute twenty-three chromosomes.
- Rock star Kurt Cobain was born in 1967 and died in 1994. Both years bizarrely add up to twenty-three if counted as individual digits: $1 + 9 + 6 + 7 = 23$ and $1 + 9 + 9 + 4 = 23$.
- Roman Emperor Julius Caesar was stabbed twenty-three times when he was assassinated.
- The human biorhythm is generally twenty-three days.
- The music group Psychic TV was obsessed with twenty-three. They released twenty-three live albums, each on the twenty-third day of twenty-three months running.
- In the final assault on the Death Star in *Star Wars*, Luke Skywalker is in Red 5. Red 2 and Red 3 start bomb runs at 23 degrees. The cellblock holding Princess Leia was AA-23.
- US Cavalry legend General Custer was promoted to the senior military rank at the age of twenty-three. He was the youngest general in the US Army at the time.

## References

Talk Paranormal Forum. "23." http://www.talkparanormal.com/thread-2389.html.
Parry, Ryan, and Rebecca Smith. "How Mystical 23 Changed Course of History." https://www.mirror.co.uk/news/ www.wwwriot.com.
Wynn, Dylan. *The History of Coincidences*. West Conshohocken, PA: Infinity, 2003.

# Mathematics Saved by Probability

*And one day, mathematics listened to probability's advice.*

It is well known that modern physics has overthrown the clockwork universe conceptions of earlier centuries, thanks to ideas of randomness. Mathematicians responsible for developing the laws of probability and statistics includes big names such as Fermat, Pascal, and Gauss. Their ideas received their first major application in physics in the kinetic theory of gases developed first by Maxwell and Boltzmann, and later by physicists including Fermi, Dirac, Bose, and Einstein.

As explained at www.geometry.net, here the use of probability is necessary because the number of particles involved is too large for a deterministic/mathematical calculation. Even the largest supercomputer cannot handle this. With the advent of quantum theory, physics seemed to be based on an essential randomness, whose reality was debated by Bohr and Einstein until the end of their lives. Only later, in the experiments of Alain Aspect, have we seen a convincing demonstration that the inescapable randomness of quantum theory is a fact of nature.

Since molecular collisions are so numerous and their molecular velocities so varied, and since our ignorance of the initial conditions is almost total, Maxwell postulated that positions and velocities are distributed at random. He was confident that this assumption would describe the gas adequately and would allow one to calculate the mean values of the macroscopic variables. His breathtaking intuition was confirmed half a century later by the work of Albert Einstein (1905) and by Jean Perrin (1908) on Brownian motion.

To clarify, think about one mole of gas. One mole of any molecular substance, such as $O_2$, contains $6.02 \times 10^{23}$ molecules. To construct the theory governing a deterministic system of $10^{23}$ molecules, physicists exploited probabilities through ignorance—and with complete success. The reason for this success deserves discussion. The Soviet physicist Lev Landau has shown that a classical system requiring infinitely many parameters would behave in a totally random fashion. In other words, it would be random unavoidably, and not merely by reason of our ignorance.

Boltzmann based his analysis on the following observation: the molecules are so fast, and their collisions so frequent, that the system rapidly loses or at least appears to lose track of the initial conditions. Typically, this leads us into the realm of probabilities through ignorance. Boltzmann based his theory on the following postulates:

1. Every molecule has equal a priori probability of being in region A.
2. The system evolves spontaneously from the less toward the most probable state.

This type of study led to model for phenomenon such as Brownian motion. The phenomenon was discovered and studied first by the botanist Robert Brown in connection with the erratic motion of pollen grains suspended in fluids. Einstein first presented a quantitative theory of the Brownian motion in 1905 based on kinematic theory and statistical mechanics. He showed that the motion could be explained by assuming that the immersed particle was continually being subjected to bombardment by the molecules of the surrounding medium. Wiener developed rigorous mathematical explanation in 1918 based on stochastic process called Wiener-Levy Process.

## References

Myrvold, Wayne. *Probabilities in Statistical Mechanics*. 10 Sept. 2004, philsci-archive. pitt.edu/11019/1/MyrvoldOxfordHandbookFinalVersion.pdf.

# Who Is Better, My Roommate or Me?

*Well, what do you think my answer could be?*

Suppose that a performance can be measured using only one metric or construct and we wish to compare two performers, for example, students from the same or different majors or athletes from the same or different sports. How do we go about it?

Let x present a performance measure and suppose that a sample $\{x_1, x_2, \ldots x_N\}$ of size N is available. First, we calculate the mean value "x-bar" or $x_{avg}$ and the standard deviation $s$. Then for each value $x_i$, we calculate the sample $z$-score by subtracting the mean and dividing by the standard deviation, that is $z_i = (x_i - x_{avg})/s$. By definition, the $z$-score of a value tells how many standard deviations that value is away from (either above or below) the mean value. Since standard deviation is positive, it follows that the $z$-score is positive if the value is above the mean, is negative if the value is below the mean, and is equal to zero if the value is exactly equal to the mean. We see that $z$-score provides some information regarding the relative standing of a measurement. If we changed the unit of measurements—that is, if we add or multiply the data values by a fixed number—the face values of x will change, but not their z-scores. This implies that z-scores are scale-invariant. Note also that the mean of the z-scores is always 0 and the standard deviation of the z-scores is always 1.

I'll demonstrate this with an example, to show the value of such analysis by the same professor. Consider a comparison of two students taking the same course, one in the morning and the other in the afternoon class, to determine who is the better student. Suppose that the following information is available.

| Description | Grade | Class Average | Class Standard Deviation | z-score |
|---|---|---|---|---|
| Student A in the morning class | 80 | 85 | 5 | $z = (80 - 85)/5 = -1$ |
| Student B in the afternoon class | 76 | 72 | 4 | $z = (76 - 72)/4 = 1$ |

It is clear that although student A has a higher grade, she has a lower z-score, which means that student B has a better relative standing. In other words, the grade of student B is one standard deviation above the average grade in her class, and the grade of student A is one standard deviation below the average in her class. This means that student B has relatively done much better in her class than student A in her class.

Since we don't know what the grades really represent, we try to compare each student with others in the same class. After all, they are all doing the same task. This is logical, noting that all performance measures are relative and we can only compare like with like. Also this method eliminates factors such as hard tests, bad teaching, inadequate textbooks, and so on. In other words, each student is judged based on his or her relative standing compared with other students who are doing the same work.

If distributions of grades in both classes were normal (bell shaped), we could, using the normal distribution table, find the percentile ranking of each student. For this example, they are 16 percent and 84 percent for A and B respectively. This shows that despite a better grade, A falls in the lower 20 percent of his or her class, and B in the upper 20 percent.

## Comparison of Baseball Players

In the 1910s, '40s, and '80s, the mean batting averages were 0.266, 0.267, and 0.261 respectively with standard deviations of 0.037, 0.0326, and 0.0317. Suppose that we want to compare three players, one from each period, to decide which player should be ranked highest. Obviously we can only compare like with like, since things have changed—better training, coaching, diet, equipment, and so on. So the best way would be to rank them in relationship to their contemporaries. The players' names and batting averages are Ty Cobb (0.420 in 1911), Ted Williams (0.4064 in 1941), and George Brett (0.390 in 1980). Their z-scores are 4.151, 4.264, and 4.07 respectively. Ted Williams was ranked as the best hitter, since he has a higher z-score—that is, a better relative standing.

It's interesting to note that $z$-scores can also be used to compare players from different sports. This is particularly useful when we want to rank the best athletes in the world. The same is true when comparing, for example, students from different majors or universities.

## Comparison of Soccer Teams

As an example involving teams, consider the English premiership data for 2001. The mean and standard deviation of the points (3 points for a win, 1 point for a tie, and 0 points for a loss) earned by twenty teams were respectively 52 and 14. The $z$-score for Manchester United, with 80 points, was 2. The nearest team, Arsenal, had a $z$-score of 1.29. This shows the strength of Manchester United and provides a reason for their popularity.

# The Stock Market: Deterministic or Random?

*The stock market cannot survive in a deterministic world.*

In recent years, picking stocks in an almost random fashion has become popular among some inventors on the grounds that it works as well as expert advice. People familiar with probability theory rely on the finding that what is known as random walk, Brownian motion and models of this type provide a reasonable description of stock market fluctuations. Although there is general agreement that such models are reasonable, why they work is not entirely understood. Following is an analysis of the general characteristics of these models, in an attempt to compare their behavior to the behavior of typical investors. Both deterministic and probabilistic analysis will be discussed, along with some comparison.

Paul Cootner was one of the first economists to recognize the importance of what was then largely statistical analyses of stock price movements and to begin to provide a theoretical foundation for the apparently random behavior of stock price changes. In his first paper on stock market prices in the sixties, he provided an operational definition of market efficiency and its relation to random walk. Cootner later discussed this in more detail in a collection of essays.

## Why Probabilistic Analysis?

Consider a single stock and the people who are interested in it. To study the stock's price changes, we'll pick a starting point and look at the situation as a system. A priori, the choice of initial conditions presents a considerable problem. Imagine just one popular stock and examine the possibility of representing the behavior of investors through some deterministic theory.

1. We would need to know the initial investment and initial direction (investment decisions, plan, motive, and so on) for every investor. This makes the initial data enormous.
2. To perform the calculation, we would need to solve a large system of equations featuring initial conditions. The result would consist of many numbers representing the state of the system at a later time.
3. Finally, we would need to calculate the readily measurable macroscopic performance variables as sums over these output values.

Given the present knowledge and technology, we can see that attempts to implement such a deterministic program must run into several insurmountable obstacles. First, there is the practical impossibility of knowing simultaneously the investment and the direction (plan) taken by individual investors. Next, even if we had this information, such calculations would require a large memory and would be so lengthy as to be impracticable. Finally, there is a methodological objection which one can formulate as follows: since the aim is to calculate macroscopically measurable quantities from microscopic data, might one not do this more easily in some other fashion than a deterministic analysis?

The story is similar to what happened in physics when Maxwell in 1859 could not but realize that in practice, deterministic calculation related to molecules of even one mole of gas is impossible. Here the initial investment and direction taken by an individual is similar to the initial position and velocity of a molecule. It was in this context that Maxwell made the conceptual leap of introducing into the theory the notion of unpredictability. His breathtaking intuition was developed further by Boltzmann and then confirmed half a century later by the work of Albert Einstein in 1905 and of Jean Perrin in 1908 on Brownian motion. It is important to note that Maxwell does not reject determinism as such, but he mitigates our ignorance of the initial conditions by introducing assumptions of probabilistic nature. His approach can be placed within a framework of the so-called "probabilities through ignorance." The introduction of this approach in 1872 led to the birth of statistical physics.

In a similar fashion, when modeling the stock market one can fruitfully exploit probabilities that represent our ignorance. Basically, we admit the deterministic nature of actions taken by investors, but try to find a way to treat them probabilistically. In other words, in order to construct the economic theory governing a deterministic system of a large number of investors, it is possible to exploit probabilities through ignorance with complete success. In sum, based on this discussion, the possible models may be described in the following way:

1.  Probabilistic models use randomness as a basic concept, so that market is governed, at least partially, by chance and associated laws of probability.
2.  Chaos offers the fascinating possibility of describing randomness as the result of a known deterministic market. Randomness may lie on the choice of initial conditions and the subsequent mechanism of the market change. Note that the term chaos is usually reserved for dynamical systems whose state can be described with differential equations in continuous time or difference equations in discrete time. This means that it is possible to represent the market using these models.

## References

Noubary, Reza. "The Stock Market: Deterministic or Random?" In *Applied Statistical Science*, edited by V. M. Ahsanullah, J. Kennyon, and S.K. Sarkar, 261–266. Nova Science, 2001.

# Imaginary Numbers

## Imaginary Numbers
### (Shorter and Simpler Version)

For human beings, imagination has always been a great toll, both for learning and creating. We have also learned a lot from reflections that are not real but very informative. An example includes mirrors and shadows. Just think about the car you are driving and the role your mirrors play. Mathematics has also benefited from the numbers known as imaginary numbers.

I look in a mirror, I see myself. Sometimes my image is even better looking than myself. So I try to shake his hand, but how can I? After all, he is simply imaginary. I realize that it is half a circle or 180 degrees away from me regardless of how far I stand away from the mirror.

Now imagine (imaginary again) a device that rotates any object 90 degrees counterclockwise. If one applies this action twice, the object would be rotated 180 degrees and its position will be a mirror image of its original position, like my image in the mirror. Mathematically relative to an origin, its position now is opposite or -1 times its original position. If we name the device $i$, then applying it twice is the same as $i$ times $i$ or $(i)(i) = i^2 = -1$. This means that $i = \sqrt{-1}$ which is not real but imaginary.

## Why Do We Need Imaginary Numbers?

Sometimes, if you want to describe the universe you live in accurately, you need to go beyond conventional thinking. In the early part of the 20th century, two revolutions in physics—Einstein's relativity and quantum mechanics—brought in the need for mathematics beyond what the real numbers could bring us alone. Ever since, complex mathematics, consisting of both *real* and *imaginary* parts, has been inextricably intertwined with our understanding of the Universe.

Mathematically, when we think about numbers, a few different categories come to mind.

- **Counting** numbers: 1, 2, 3, 4, etc.
- **Whole** numbers: 0, 1, 2, 3, etc., the counting numbers plus *zero*.
- **Integers**: ..., -3, -2, -1, 0, 1, 2, 3, etc. including the whole numbers and their negatives.
- **Rational numbers**: any number that can be expressed as a fraction of two integers. Note that any decimal representation of a rational number either has a finite length or, if infinite has repeating decimals or patterns. Conversely any infinitely repeating decimal can be expressed as a rational number.
- **Real numbers**: includes all of the rational as well as all of the irrational numbers, including the square roots of non-perfect squares such as √2 as well as π and a whole host of others. Note that irrational numbers cannot be written as a fraction of integers.

But, while the square root of a positive number is real, the square root of a negative number is not well defined, at least, it was not, until they were defined. An imaginary number is just like a real one, except that they have an *"i"* on the front of them as their unit. Numbers can also be complex, where they have both a real part (a) and an imaginary part (b), and are normally expressed as (a + b*i*).

## More on Imaginary Numbers

The introduction of imaginary numbers opened the door to many new ideas and concepts. Now negative numbers have square roots and all quadratic equations have solutions. As pointed out earlier when we look at a mirror, we see our picture. Our picture is obviously not real, but instead imaginary. Although imaginary, it is very useful and can give us lots of information and insight. Imaginary numbers are now a classical subject and, as with real numbers, information related to them a common knowledge. The sites medium.com and www.purplemath.com present a readable account of the role imaginary numbers play in science and technology. Here we plan to follow their presentation.

Recall that in school we have always been told that we cannot take the square root of a negative number. Well, by accepting the usefulness of imaginary numbers we can now take the square root of a negative number, but it involves using a new idea to do it. This new idea was invented (discovered?) around the time of the Reformation. At that time, nobody believed that any "real world" use would be found for this imaginary number, other than easing the computations involved in solving certain equations, so the new number was viewed as being a pretend number invented for convenience sake. But then, when you think about it, aren't all numbers inventions? It's not like numbers grow on trees! They live in our heads. We made them all up! Why not invent a new one, as long as it works okay with what we already have?

*Why imaginary I in the mirror is better looking than myself.*
*Is it my imaginary part that makes me attractive?*

Imagine a device that rotates an object 90 degrees counterclockwise. If you apply it twice, the object would be rotated 180 degrees and its position will be a mirror image of its original position. Mathematically relative to an origin, its position now is opposite or -1 times its original position. This means that if we name the device $i$, then applying that twice is the same as $i$ times $i = i^2 = -1$.

## Why Do We Need Imaginary Numbers?

Sometimes, if you want to accurately describe the universe, you need to go beyond conventional ways of thinking. In the early part of the twentieth century, two revolutions in physics—Einstein's relativity and quantum mechanics—brought in the need for mathematics beyond real numbers. Ever since, complex mathematics, consisting of both real and imaginary parts, has been inextricably intertwined with our understanding of the universe.

Mathematically, when we think about numbers, a several categories come to mind:

- Counting numbers: 1, 2, 3, 4, and so on.
- Whole numbers: 0, 1, 2, 3, and so on; counting numbers plus zero.
- Integers: …, -3, -2, -1, 0, 1, 2, 3, and so on, including whole numbers and their negatives.
- Rational numbers: any number that can be expressed as a fraction of two integers. Note that any decimal representation of rational numbers has either a finite length or, if infinite, repeating decimals or patterns. Conversely, any infinitely repeating decimal can be expressed as a rational number.

- Real numbers: all rational and irrational numbers, including the square roots of non-perfect squares such as $\sqrt{2}$, as well as $\pi$ and a whole host of others. Note that irrational numbers cannot be written as a fraction of integers.

While the square root of a positive number is real, the square root of a negative number is not well defined. At least, it wasn't until they were defined. An imaginary number is just like a real one, except it is multiplied by "$i$" or the square root of (-1). Numbers can also be complex, where they have both a real part (a) and an imaginary part (b), typically expressed as (a + b$i$).

## Imaginary Numbers

The introduction of imaginary numbers opened the door to many new ideas and concepts. Now negative numbers have square roots and all quadratic equations have solutions. When we look in a mirror, we see a reflection of ourselves—not real but imaginary, although that reflection can give us lots of information and insight. Imaginary numbers are now a classical subject, and as real numbers, information related to them is common knowledge. The websites medium.com and www.purplemath.com present a readable account of the role that imaginary numbers play in science and technology, and I will follow their presentation.

As mentioned earlier, we have always been told that we cannot take the square root of a negative number. Well, by accepting the usefulness of imaginary numbers, we can now take the square root of a negative number, but it involves using a new number to do it. This new number was invented (discovered?) around the time of the Reformation. At that time, nobody believed that any real-world use would be found for this new number, other than easing the computations involved in solving certain equations, so the new number was viewed as being a pretend number invented for the sake of convenience. But when you think about it, aren't all numbers inventions? It's not like numbers grow on trees. They live in our heads. We made them all up! Why not invent a new one, as long as it works okay with what we already have?

This new number (or scale or unit) was called "$i$", standing for "imaginary," because everybody knew that $i$ wasn't real. (That's why you couldn't take the square root of a negative number before. You had only real numbers without an "$i$" in them.) The imaginary is defined to be $i = \sqrt{-1}$. Then: $i^2 = (\text{sqr}(-1))^2 = -1$.

These are the top five fun facts about imaginary numbers!

1. The square root of *i* has both real and imaginary parts.
2. Any root of *i* has multiple unique solutions, and the N-th root has N unique solutions.
3. In an imaginary fraction, it actually matters whether the numerator or denominator has *"i"* in it.
4. 0, 1, e, π, and *i* appear in a beautiful identity (Euler's Identity):

$$e^{\pi i} + 1 = 0$$

   This is a simple and unexpected relationship between e, *i*, and π. These relations show up a lot in complex analysis. And yet, if you're willing to consider exponentials, this last one is a doozy …
5. *i* ^*i*, or *"i"* raised to the *"i"* power, is 100 percent real.

## References

Berry, Brett. "The Reality of Imaginary Numbers." Medium. July 26, 2017. https://medium.com/i-math/imaginary-numbers-explained-e5aa63bdb7ae.

Hom, Elaine J. "What Are Imaginary Numbers?" LiveScience. January 22, 2014. https://www.livescience.com/42748-imaginary-numbers.html.

# Inconsistent Runners Are More Likely to Set Records

*A consistently inconsistent runner may give the coach what he wants.*

Most coaches consider an athlete's consistency as a positive attribute, for obvious reasons. The performance of consistent players usually exhibits less variability (smaller standard deviation) and therefore is more predictable, something that coaches can use when working on a game plan. The following example, however, shows that in some sports, variability could be helpful for a different reason.

Think about the top two members of a college track team, A and B. Suppose that the coach has kept records and concluded that their times, in seconds, follow a normal distribution with means 10.4 and 10.6 and standard deviation 0.2 and 0.4 respectively ($N$ (10.4, 0.2) and $N$ (10.6, 0.4)). Note that the assumption of normality is not required here. Suppose also that the college competition's present record is 10 seconds. The coach thinks that on a good day, both runners have a chance to break the record, but he's not sure which runner has the better chance. His assistant prefers A, who has averaged 10.4 in the past.

The coach is wondering about another factor, B's inconsistency, because he has heard that athletes with larger mean value and greater irregular performance (larger standard deviation) can have a higher chance to drop below a chosen threshold. So he calculates the z-scores of each runner by subtracting the mean and dividing by standard deviation. Recall that z-score is a scale invariant measure for relative standing. The z-scores are respectively (10 − 10.4)/ 0.2 = -2 for A and (10 − 10.6)/ 0.4 = -1.5 for B. For normal distribution case, the probabilities of going below these values are 0.0228 and 0.0668 respectively. This shows that the athlete with larger mean value and greater irregular performances (larger standard deviation) have a better chance of breaking the 10-second record.

To better appreciate the difference, suppose that both runners can participate in ten tournaments during a season. Based on the above calculations, the probabilities that neither of them (during that season) would run under 10 seconds are respectively

$0.794 = (1 - 0.0228)^{10}$ and $0.501 = (1 - 0.0668)^{10}$. This implies that their probabilities of breaking the record are respectively 0.206 and 0.499.

We can analyze this situation differently by considering distribution of the minima of samples of sizes to 10 from a standard normal or any other parent population. This can be done through what is known as order statistics, which is the data ordered in ascending order.

It's interesting that the athlete with larger mean time and frequent irregular performance (larger standard deviation) can have a better chance to run below 10 seconds. In other words, the latter athlete, though more irregular and with smaller mean time, should be chosen for the competition if only one athlete must be chosen. This example illustrates how extreme values look and feel different from central value problems.

# Bell Curve, a Law of Nature

*Where the four most famous numbers of mathematics—0, 1, Pi, and Euler's e—meet.*

With its symmetrical shape, central peak, and gracefully sloping sides, the bell curve is one of the most important, well-studied, and best-known graphs for scientists, businesspeople, and the general public. It presents the distribution of any measurable attribute that has its more likely values around the center, less likely values to either side, and least likely values in the tails. It is used frequently partly because of the fact that distribution of many real-life variables follow its pattern, at least approximately. The standard normal curve N(0, 1), with mean 0 and standard deviation 1, has the four most amazing numbers—zero; one; Pi, the ratio of circle's circumference and radius; and the Euler number e, the base of the natural logarithm—in its representation. The area under the normal curve represents the probabilities of the variable falling in a certain range. The total area under the curve equals one.

## What Is Special?

As S. A. Frank explains in "The Common Patterns of Nature," we typically observe large-scale phenomena arising from the interactions of many hidden, small-scale processes. It's like looking down on earth from an aircraft flying far above. We see the big items and big green spaces without observing details and the movements. According to Frank, in all complex systems, our wish is to understand how large-scale patterns arise from the aggregation of small-scale processes. This is where the bell curve plays an important role.

## Why Is It Important?

Have you ever wondered why, to estimate our true blood pressure, doctors recommend measuring it several times a day and calculating the average? Like most of us, they know that the average provides a better estimate. A single measurement could be affected by excitement, fatigue, and other sources of variation. People have been aware of this problem for a long time, but they couldn't figure out how much improvement is achieved by adding one more measurement. Now the central limit theorem allows us to do inference about the sample average when inference cannot be done for a single measurement. The theorem states that under certain conditions, any observed variables in nature that arise from the summing up of many values will have a distribution close to a bell curve, and as we increase the sample size, the distribution will approach a complete bell curve.

## More on Central Limit Distribution

Why is the central limit theorem so important? Let's look at an example. Suppose that a fair di is rolled once and your job is to predict the observed number/outcome. Obviously, in this situation, any guess is as good as any other guess. Your chance of being right is 1/6 and of being wrong is 5/6, as there are six possible outcomes. Now suppose that two dice are rolled or one die is rolled twice, and your job is to guess the average of the two numbers/outcomes. Now there are thirty-six possible pairs. If you guess average 1, then the chance that you are right is only 1/36, because average of 1 only occurs if 1 and 1 or 1 is observed twice (1, 1). But if your guess is 3.5, then the chance that you are right is 6/36 because any of the following possible pairs—(1, 6), (2, 5), (3, 4), (4, 3), (5, 2), (6, 1)—will yield an average of 3.5. It's easy to show that 3.5 is the best guess. As the number of rolls is increased and averaged, the average 1 or 6 any numbers close to them become less likely, the center values (numbers close to 3.5) become more likely, and our guesses become better and better. Moreover, not only does the shape of the distribution tend to the bell curve, but the variability of the sample mean will also decrease and lead to a better inference.

Consider an example in medical science. Since the distribution of most measurements, such as blood pressure, are unknown, rather than inference about a single measurement, scientists use the central limit, do inference about the average of several measurements, and make a statement about the average. This makes sense since medical science is concerned with each individual person's average for the purpose of decision making.

## Final Word

According to Frank, there are two main reasons for the widespread use of normal distributions. First, many measurements fluctuate about a central location because of perturbing factors or errors in measurement. Second, when analyzing the measurement, an assumption of Gaussian fluctuations is the best (maximum entropy) choice when the only information available is about the precision or error in observations with regard to the average value of the population of measurements.

## References

Frank, S. A. "The Common Patterns of Nature." *Journal of Evolutionary Biology* 22 (2009): 1563–1585. https://stevefrank.org/reprints-pdf/09JEBmaxent.pdf.

# Flood Risks: Should I Buy Insurance?

*If a bus ticket costs $1 and the fine for fare dodging is $25, at what point is it rational to buy a ticket? Well, the key is how often someone comes around to check the tickets.*

After moving to Bloomsburg, Pennsylvania, and learning about past destructive floods, I wondered how residents close to the major rivers evaluated their risk associated with floods. To find out, I first talked to a few friends who live or have lived in a floodplain, both before and after significant floods. What I heard was interesting, but mostly personal, especially with regard to buying flood insurance. I realized that almost everybody did their best to find an answer to the following critical questions: At what point is it rational to take risk and not purchase insurance? At what point is it reasonable to purchase flood insurance? Some of them had realized that the key to an informed decision was to come up with a reliable estimate for the frequency of future destructive floods.

Next, I put myself in their situation and tried to approach the problem in a slightly more systematic way. Below is a summary of my calculations based on thirty-eight past floods, all greater than 19.8 feet, that occurred in Bloomsburg between 1850 and 2011 (water.weather.gov). These calculations predict the number of future floods and the probabilities related to them.

1. During the next ten years, two floods greater than 19.8 feet are expected.
2. The probability of a flood greater than 32.75 feet (2011 flood) during the next ten, twenty, thirty, and hundred years are respectively 5.81 percent, 11 percent, 15.6 percent, and 45 percent.
3. The probability of a flood greater than 33 feet at any time in the future is less than 10 percent. In other words, we are 90 percent confident that the largest possible flood in Bloomsburg will not exceed 33 feet.

Is any other helpful information available? To be honest, at best we can only assert that we live in an endangered area. This is because the subject is complicated, the earth is much too chaotic, and our knowledge is so limited. It is hard to develop any reliable risk prediction model for future floods. So for now, experts can only try to understand the processes better and develop guidelines for a more efficient management of natural disasters in general. Until then, a sensible approach would be to make a decision, as some of my friends did, based on cost benefit analysis using numbers such as the ones above (if useful), and purchase flood insurance (if affordable). Remember that although flood insurance has a long negative return, like any other insurance, but we're also purchasing peace of mind.

## References

"Historical Crests for Susquehanna River at Bloomsburg." National Weather Service. https://water.weather.gov/ahps2/crests.php?wfo=ctp&gage=bmbp1&crest_type=historic.

# Chaos, a Misunderstood Concept

*There is a higher order in chaos.*

Chaos is a subject that fascinates mathematicians and non-mathematicians alike, although what they understand of it may be quite different. People tend to think that chaos has no order or that it's all noise and no signal. This is unfortunate, since chaos actually refers to a high degree of order. In "Mathematics and Climate," Joseph Malkevitch says the following:

> We are used to noise of various kinds: static on the radio, conversations at other tables in a crowded restaurant, or the hums one hears from appliances around the house. In all of these situations, there is a 'randomness' or chance element in what we experience. The hum is not a single tone but is constantly changing. The static on the radio comes and goes in frequency and intensity. Thus, everybody was surprised when it became widely known that seemingly 'noisy' situations arose from systems that involved nothing random, but were completely deterministic. This phenomenon is now known as 'Chaos' or 'chaotic behavior.' The mathematical roots of insight into deterministic chaos go back to the great French mathematician Henri Poincaré. However, in more modern times, one early pioneer in noticing chaos was the meteorologist Edward Lorenz who lived from 1917 to 2008. Lorenz started his academic career by studying mathematics as an undergraduate at Dartmouth and earned a master's degree in mathematics from Harvard. Later, he received a doctorate from MIT in meteorology with a thesis entitled: 'A Method of Applying the Hydrodynamic and Thermodynamic Equations to Atmospheric Models,' where he put his mathematical training to work. Lorenz came across the phenomenon now known as chaos in

conjunction with the study of the behavior of the solution of differential equations.

## Chaos and Stocks

In physics, using James Clerk Maxwell's idea, we can show how chance could generate determinism. Here we look at a situation where determinism can generate chance and points out the way the resulting theory may be considered appropriate for stock market analysis. *Chaos* is a particularly unfortunate name, because unlike how we understand the word, it actually refers to a higher degree of order. To appreciate its importance, we can refer to the fact that the heart has to be largely regular or we die. But the brain has to be largely irregular—if not, we have epilepsy. This shows that irregularity, chaos, leads to complex systems. It is not all disorder. Chaos theory was pioneered near the end of the twentieth century, but only the advent of fast computers in the early 1960s made its development possible. Today chaos theory is an active field of research and has induced a far-reaching revolution in our concepts. To classify it, we make a semantic distinction between random and chaotic processes.

A dust particle suspended in water moves around randomly, executing what is called Brownian motion. This stems from molecular agitation through the impacts of water molecules on the dust particle. Every molecule, much like an investor, is a direct or indirect cause of the motion, and we can say that the Brownian motion of the dust particle is governed by many variables. In such cases, one speaks of a *random process;* to treat it mathematically we use the calculus of probabilities.

A compass needle acted on simultaneously by fixed and rotating fields constitutes a simple physical system pending on only three variables. However, we can choose experimental conditions under which the motion of the magnetized needle is so unsystematic that prediction seems totally impossible. In such simple cases whose evolution is nevertheless unpredictable, we speak of *chaos* and of *chaotic processes;* these are the terms we use whenever the variables characterizing the system are few.

Thus, when a system such as the one we based on behavior of individual investors is studied, we look at a large number of variables, so random process is more appropriate. However, when only a few variables, such as interest rate and currency rate, can characterize the system, chaos may be used.

The relevance of chaos to market behavior may also be explained by the following example. A pendulum swings with a regular back-and-forth motion, but if it is struck by the ball of a second pendulum before reaching its zenith, both pendulums may begin swinging in wildly erratic patters. In the financial market, a trend is enhanced or undermined by surprises in governmental announcements or economic actions by one or more influential nations.

## References

Malkevitch, Joseph. "Mathematics and Climate." American Mathematical Society. http://ams.org/publicoutreach/feature-column/fcarc-climate.

# No Lemon, No Melon

*There is a beauty in symmetry.*

Most humans find symmetrical patterns more attractive than asymmetrical ones. Our preference for symmetry might be a byproduct of our need to recognize objects irrespective of their position and orientation in the visual field. Much can be said about symmetry and its effects on human life. For example, many people find palindrome words and numbers interesting and memorable.

A palindrome is a word, phrase, or sentence that reads the same from left to right and right to left. Here are a few well-known palindromes:

DAD

MOM

RADAR

REVIVER

ROTATOR

I DID, DID I?

LEPERS REPEL

YO, BANANA BOY!

WAS IT A CAT I SAW?

MADAM, IN EDEN, I'M ADAM

A MAN, A PLAN, A CANAL, PANAMA

GO HANG A SALAMI! I'M A LASAGNA HOG!

The longest palindromic word in the *Oxford English Dictionary* is the onomato-poeic *tattarrattat*, coined by James Joyce in *Ulysses* (1922) for a knock on the door. The *Guinness Book of Records* gives the title to *detartrated*, the preterit and past participle of *detartrate*, a chemical term meaning "to remove tartrates."

## Palindrome Poems

As "Palindrome Poems" explains, "A line palindrome is when the individual lines of a text make a palindromic sequence." A good example is the poem "Doppelgänger," by James A. Lindon, which reads identically from the first line to the last, and from the last to the first. It's amazing how an identical line changes its meaning completely from one end of the poem to the other.

"Doppelgänger"

Entering the lonely house with my wife
I saw him for the first time
Peering furtively from behind a bush—
Blackness that moved,

…

Blackness that moved.
Peering furtively from behind a bush,
I saw him, for the first time
Entering the lonely house with my wife.

Susan Stewart has a terrific line palindrome poem in her recent book *Columbarium*, where the form mirrors the action of the poem (a journey into and out of hell). Here's an excerpt:

"Two Brief Views of Hell"

Leaving the fringe of light at the edge of the leaves, deeper, then deeper,
the rocking back and forth movement forward through the ever-narrowing circle
that never, in truth, narrowed beyond the bending going in,
not knowing whether a turn or impasse would lie at the place

…

not knowing whether a turn or impasse would lie at the place
that never, in truth, narrowed beyond the bending going in,
the rocking back and forth movement forward through the ever-narrowing circle.
Leaving the fringe of light at the edge of the leaves, deeper, then deeper.

If you have a half-written poem, try to rewrite it in reverse and sell it as a palindrome.

## Palindromic Number

Like palindromic words or lines, palindromic numbers are the same whether read from left to right or right to left. The first few palindromic numbers are 0, 1, 2, 3, 4, 5, 6, 7, 8, 9, 11, 22, 33, 44, 55, 66, 77, 88, 99, 101, 111, and 121.

A palindrome can be formed from a number that is not a palindrome by adding the original number to the number formed by reversing the digits and repeating the process if necessary. For example, $17 + 71 = 88$ and $123 + 321 = 444$.

## References

The Virtual World: Poetry, the Imagination, and the Creative Life. "Palindrome Poems," March 19, 2005. http://thevirtualworld.blogspot.com/2005/03/palindrome-poems.html.

# How Was Your Winter?

*Now I know why, when I was young, summers were warmer and winters were colder.*

Although some of my younger friends who have lived in Bloomsburg only a few years consider the winter of 2015 one of the coldest and snowiest, most of my older friends see 2015 as just a typical winter, and I wonder why. Could it be because my older friends are forgetful, or is there another reason? I hope you'll find my explanation convincing.

Allow me to simplify the problem and consider only the annual snowfall. Think of a group of babies who will be born on 1/1/2020 in different places where winters are similar to ours in Bloomsburg. I'd like to find a reasonable answer to the following question: How many personal (not historical) record snowfalls would children of this group experience during their lifetimes?

Obviously the first year's snowfall (2021) will be a record for all the babies, since they will have experienced only one winter. What about the second year (2022)? This will depend on whether 2021's snowfall was more or less than that of 2020. Since there is no significant trend in the amount of snowfall, the chances of having no (zero) new record and having one new record in 2021 are both 50 percent. By averaging the zeros and ones, we may count this as ½, which is the same as saying that half of the babies are expected to see a record. Using the same logic, the chance that the third year (2023) produces a new personal record is 1/3 and could be counted as 1/3 record. The same applies to years 4, 5, …, and we get the following formula:

Expected number of records = 1 + 1/2 + 1/3 + 1/4 + …

For example, for a baby or group of babies who live for one hundred years:

= 1 + 1/2 + 1/3 + 1/4 + … + 1/100 = 5.19

That is five records on average. We can also calculate the odds of experiencing a specific number of records, such as three or four. For example, for a hundred years the probability of experiencing five records is 21 percent—which is, in fact, the most likely scenario.

Using the above formula, by age one all babies will see one record. By age four, the expected or average number of records experienced is two ($1+1/2+1/3+1/4 = 2.083$). By age eleven, they should have seen three ($1+1/2+1/3+1/4+ \ldots 1/11 = 3.02$). By age thirty-one, they will have seen around four ($1+1/2+1/3+1/4+ \ldots +1/31 = 4.02$). Finally, by age eighty-three they may have seen around five record snowfalls ($1+1/2+1/3+1/4+ \ldots 1/83 = 5$). Of course, not all babies will experience the same number of personal records, but if we average the number of records each of them experience in their life, we get close to what the above formula predicts.

What does this have to do with our original question? Well, isn't this a key to the fact that in our youth, winters were colder with more snow? Just think about my friends, age thirty-two to eighty-two. Most of them remember the fourth record they have experienced around age thirty-one. As a result, for them all winters since then may feel just average or typical.

"Oh, the weather outside is frightful,
But the fire is so delightful.
And since we've no place to go,
Let it snow, let it snow, let it snow."

# Chapter 6
## Sports/Education

*Sports is something we all need and enjoy, I think*
*Something as necessary for living as food and drink*
*It is known to be beneficial for both body and mind*
*It cures many health problems, a treatment of own kind.*

# Baseball Rookie: Old-Timer Paradox

## Baseball Rookie's Paradox
### (Shorter and Simpler Version)

Even a curiosity glance at newspapers show the extent to which use of classical statistical methods has become a part of everyday life. This is particularly the case for popular sports such as baseball. Both experts and fans analyze the data to draw conclusions about players and teams. But, do application of popular classical statistical methods always lead to an appropriate conclusion? Here I want to present an instance in which different analyses of same data lead to apparently paradoxical results. Hopefully, it would not come up in the new season.

## Rookie vs Old-Timer

We describe an example of the so-called Simpson's paradox, named after a statistician who gave a careful discussion of it. Consider a scenario involving a rookie, R, who is trying to break into a baseball lineup by replacing an old-timer, O. He is told by the manager that the decision will be made on the basis of hitting ability, since he and O are equally proficient as fielders. The rookie feels assured that he will start because he is batting 0.224 and O is batting only 0.186 (both are good field, poor hit, players.) However, the rookie is dismayed to learn that O is designated to start the first game. He asks the manager why he is not starting, since his average is better than that of O. "Well," explains the manager, "the opponents are using a right-handed pitcher today, and O has a better average than you against right-handed pitches. His average is 0.179 and yours is 0.162."

Satisfied but chagrined by the explanation, R waits until the opponent's pitcher is left-handed, for then, surely, he will get to start. But, that day comes and O is once again the starting player. The manager points out that O has a better average than you against left-handed pitchers, too, batting 0.560 compared to yours 0.332.

The rookie is no longer satisfied with the explanation, and he asks how O can be better than me against both left- and right-handed pitchers but poorer overall.

The data shown in table below are persuasive. The arithmetic is correct, and careful analysis of the table may reveal the source of the paradox. The total batting percentage is determined by the percentages against the two types of pitchers but is determined differently for each of the two players. The overall percentage is a *weighted average* of the individual percentages, and the weights are determined by the number of times at bat against each of the types of pitchers. Although we expect the weighted average to preserve the order of the individual percentages, it does not.

|  |  | Times at Bat | Hit | Average |
|---|---|---|---|---|
| Totals | O | 4766 | 888 | 0.186 |
|  | R | 1276 | 186 | 0.224 |
| Against right- | O | 4675 | 837 | 0.179 |
| handed pitchers | R | 809 | 131 | 0.162 |
| Against left- | O | 91 | 51 | 0.560 |
| handed pitchers | R | 467 | 155 | 0.332 |

Although the story of the rookie is fictitious, the data is not. The lesson here is that we must be careful in reporting averages unless the groups under consideration are fairly homogeneous. In other words, one cannot always trust conclusions drawn from marginal tables and one way to avoid that is to consider all the dimensions of a table.

A different version of this counter-intuitive puzzler was adapted from a Car Talk radio show by David Lincoln the Catchup Math Account Manager:

Two baseball rookies had a bet about their first season: the one with the highest batting average would win. They both had the same number of at-bats. Player A bested player B in the first half of the season (0.300 vs 0.250) and also in the second half (0.400 vs 0.350). And yet, player B won the bet! How could this be possible!?

One answer: Player A was 30/100 (0.300) in the first half and 8/20 (0.400) in the second half. Player B was 5/20 (0.250) in the first half and 35/100 (0.350) in the second half. Thus, Player B's average of 40/120 (0.333) was higher than Player A's average of 38/120 (0.317).

As mentioned earlier, these are examples of what is known as Simpsons's paradox. The paradox occurs because collapsing the data can lead to an inappropriate weighting of the different populations. The lesson here is that one must be extremely careful in reporting averages unless the groups under consideration are fairly homogeneous. In general, the analysis based on details (higher dimensions) are preferred.

*I thought rookie was better for sure, but little did I know.*

Even a curious glance at a newspaper shows the extent to which the use of classical statistical methods has become a part of everyday life. This is particularly the case for popular sports such as baseball. Experts and fans analyze the data to draw conclusions about players and teams, and some people even apply well-known scientific methods or software. Here I want to present an instance in which different analyses of the same data lead to apparently paradoxical results. Although I know the answers, I leave it to the readers to decide which conclusion is more appropriate.

## Rookie Versus Old-Timer

Following is an example of Simpson's paradox, named for the statistician who first worked with it. Consider a scenario involving a rookie (R) who is trying to break into a baseball lineup by replacing an old-timer (O). R is told by the manager that the decision will be based on hitting ability, since he and O are equally proficient as fielders. The rookie feels assured that he will start, because he is batting 0.224 and O is batting only 0.186. (Both R and O are good field, poor hit, players.) However, R is dismayed to learn that O is designated to start the first game. He asks the manager why he is not starting, since his average is better than O's. "Well," explains the manager, "the opponents are using a right-handed pitcher today, and O has a better average than you against right-handed pitches. His average is 0.179, and yours is 0.162."

Satisfied but chagrined by the explanation, R waits until the opponent's pitcher is left-handed, for then, surely, he will get to start. However, when that day comes, O is once again the starting player. The manager points out that O has a better average against left-handed pitchers, too, batting 0.560 compared with R's 0.332.

No longer satisfied with the explanation, R asks how O can be better than him against both left- and right-handed pitchers, but poorer overall. The data shown in this table is persuasive.

|  |  | Times at Bat | Hit | Average |
|---|---|---|---|---|
| **Totals** | O | 4766 | 888 | 0.186 |
|  | R | 1276 | 186 | 0.224 |
| **Against right-** | O | 4675 | 837 | 0.179 |
| **handed pitchers** | R | 809 | 131 | 0.162 |
| **Against left-** | O | 91 | 51 | 0.560 |
| **handed pitchers** | R | 467 | 155 | 0.332 |

The arithmetic is correct, and careful analysis of the table may reveal the source of the paradox. The total batting percentage is determined by the percentages against the two types of pitchers, but it's determined differently for each of the two players. The overall percentage is a weighted average of the individual percentages, and the weights are determined by the number of times at bat against each of the types of pitchers. Although we expect the weighted average to preserve the order of the individual percentages, it does not.

The story of the rookie is fictitious, but the data is not. Here's another example adapted from a review of death rates for tuberculosis in 1910. The death rates from tuberculosis for both whites and nonwhites were greater in New York, New York than in Richmond, Virginia. Public health officials reached quite different conclusions, depending on which part of the table received their attention.

## Death Rates from Tuberculosis, 1910

| | Population | | Deaths from Tuberculosis | | Death Rate per 100,000 | |
|---|---|---|---|---|---|---|
| | New York | Richmond | New York | Richmond | New York | Richmond |
| White | 4,675,174 | 80,895 | 8,365 | 131 | 179 | 162 |
| Nonwhite | 91,709 | 46,733 | 513 | 155 | 560 | 332 |
| Total Population | 4,766,883 | 127,628 | 8,878 | 286 | 186 | 224 |

The lesson here is that we must be careful in reporting averages, unless the groups under consideration are fairly homogeneous. In other words, we cannot always trust conclusions drawn from marginal tables, and one way to avoid that is to consider all the dimensions of a table.

## References

Smith, Arthur. "At the Plate, a Statistical Puzzler: Understanding Simpson's Paradox." *The State of the USA | At the Plate, a Statistical Puzzler: Understanding Simpson's Paradox*, 20 Aug. 2010, www.stateoftheusa.org/content/at-the-plate-a-statistical-puz.php.

# Comparing Athletes: How Good Was Michael Jordan?

*Very good, but compared with whom? We can only compare like with like.*

People who follow sports compare their favorite athletes. This is not easy, especially if these athletes are from different sports or different years.

## Z-Score

Suppose that $x$ presents a performance measure in a specific sport. For a sample of size n, $\{x_1, x_2, ..., x_N\}$ of such measure we can calculate the sample mean $x_{avg}$ and the sample standard deviation $s$. Then for each measurement $x_i$, the sample $z$-score is calculated by subtracting the mean and dividing it by standard deviation, that is $z_i = (x_i - x_{avg})/s$. By definition, we see that the $z$-score of a value tells how many standard deviations that value is away from (either above or below) the mean. Since standard deviation is positive, it follows that if the $z$-score is positive, the value is above the mean; if the z-score is negative, the value is below the mean; and if the z-score is equal to zero, then the value is exactly equal to the mean. Thus, $z$-score provides some information regarding the relative standing of a given measurement. Note that if we change the unit of measurements by adding or multiplying the data values by a fixed number, the face values of $x$ will change but not their $z$-scores. In other words, $z$-scores are scale-invariant. The mean of the $z$-scores is always 0, and the standard deviation of the $z$-scores is always 1.

## Example

Suppose we wish to compare two students taking the same course at the same university, one in the morning and the other in the afternoon class, to determine who is the better student. Suppose that the following information is available.

| Description | Grade | Class Average | Class Standard Deviation | z-score |
|---|---|---|---|---|
| Student in the morning class | 80 | 85 | 5 | $z = (80 - 85)/5 = -1$ |
| Student in the afternoon class | 76 | 72 | 4 | $z = (76 - 72)/4 = 1$ |

From this table, it is clear that although the first student has a higher grade, she has a lower z-score, which means that the second student has a much better relative standing. In other words, the grade of the second student is one standard deviation above the average grade in her class, whereas the first student's grade is one standard deviation below the average grade in her class. This means that the second student has done better than many more students in her class than the first student in her class.

Since we don't know what the grades represent, a reasonable approach is to compare students using their z-score, which indicates their relative standing. This eliminates factors such as hard tests, bad teachers, and poor textbooks. In other words, each student is judged based on his or her relative standing in their own class. We can apply the same procedure when comparing athletes from different sports or students from different majors or universities.

## How Good Was Michael Jordan?

Data for basketball may be found in places such as the Pro Basketball Bible, nba.com, and espn.com. Data published includes number of games in which each player appeared, minutes per game (MPG), points per minute (PPM) played, field goal percentage (FGP), free throw percentage (FTP), assists per minute (APM), rebounds per minute (RPM), and so on. Suppose that performance is measured by points scored per minute played (PPM). Note that when comparing basketball players, we should consider the position they play, since their primary responsibility might be to distribute the ball rather than to score.

In *A Casebook for a First Course in Statistics and Data Analysis*, Chatterjee et al. analyzed data on 105 guards who played in the 1992–93 NBA season. Inspection of the data for guards showed that the distribution of PPM is close to a bell (normal) curve with mean and standard deviation of 0.4236 and 0.1159 points per minute respectively. So, we can calculate the z-score for Michael Jordan, whose PPM for that season was 0.8291, as

$$z = (0.8291 - 0.04236)/0.1159 = 3.5$$

Plotting the data reveals that the distribution of PPM is approximately normal. Using normal distribution table, we find that approximately 99.7 percent of guards had PPM to within three standard deviations of the mean. So a z-score of 3.5 is extremely unusual and quite impressive.

## Comparison of Baseball Players

In the 1910s, '40s, and '70s, batting averages were 0.266, 0.267, and 0.261 respectively with standard deviations of 0.037, 0.0326, and 0.0317. Suppose we want to compare three players and decide which should be ranked highest. Obviously we have to compare like with like, so the best way to rank them would be in relation to their contemporaries. The players' names and batting averages are Ty Cobb (0.420 in 1911), Ted Williams (0.4064 in 1941), and George Brett (0.390 in 1980). We calculate their z-scores as 4.151, 4.264, and 4.07 respectively. So Ted Williams was ranked as the best hitter, since he has a higher z-score, that is, a better relative standing.

## Comparison of Soccer Teams

As a different example, consider the English premiership data for the year 2001. The mean and standard deviation of the points (3 points for a win, 1 point for a tie, and 0 points for a loss) earned by twenty teams were respectively 52 and 14. The z-score for Manchester United, with 80 points, was 2. The nearest team, Arsenal, had a z-score of 1.29. This shows the strength of Manchester United in that season and provides a reason for their popularity.

## References

Barry, Rick. *Rick Barry's Pro Basketball Bible, 1995–96: Player Ratings and In-Depth Analysis of More Than 400 NBA Players and Draft Picks.* Marina Del Ray, CA: Basketball Books, 1995.

Chatterjee, Samprit, Mark S. Handcock, and Jeffrey S. Simonoff. *A Casebook for a First Course in Statistics and Data Analysis.* Hoboken, NJ: Wiley, 1995.

NBA Advanced Stats. https://stats.nba.com/.

"NBA Statistics." ESPN. http://www.espn.com/nba/statistics.

# Hot Hand

*Do I see patterns that do not even exist?*

Athletes, coaches, and fans of sports such as basketball and baseball overwhelmingly believe in the "hot hand," the idea that a player whose shooting percentage is higher than normal is likely to keep shooting better than normal—at least for a while. Indeed, coaches often rotate players based on a sense of who is hot or cold, even though academic scholars thought they had debunked this idea years ago. Starting with a famous 1985 study of basketball shooting, experts have argued in dozens of papers that hot hand is nothing more than a random occurrence of statistical noise. In "Investment Bankers Can Learn a Thing or Two From Athletes on a 'Hot Streak,'" Edmund Andrews argues that even though athletes seem to go on hot streaks, these are just random fluctuations without predictive value. People who believe in hot hands, the skeptics argue, are seeing patterns that do not exist.

In a major new study of baseball data, Jeffrey Zwiebel at Stanford and Brett Green at the University of California, Berkeley, concluded that hot hands are real and have predictive power. We may wonder why these business professors would jump into a sports debate, but the "hot-hand fallacy" is used by supporters of behavioral economics to argue that people can be irrational. For example, behaviorists have argued that investors often get lured into bad decisions by seeing patterns that are not real. According to behaviorists, investors make a wide range of cognitive mistakes that range from overconfidence in their own abilities to a tendency to overreact to the news.

According to Andrews, that critique gained a lot of traction in the wake of the mortgage bust and the great financial crisis. A 2009 publication lays out the theory and potential financial applications of the hot-hand fallacy. A 2012 paper argues that the hot-hand fallacy explains why people pay for useless investment advice. In a brand new publication, German scholars even cite evidence that people who believe in the hot-hand fallacy are more at risk of long-term unemployment.

Andrews says that the hot-hand fallacy has its roots at Stanford. Thomas Gilovich, a graduate student in the early 1980s, began comparing the widespread perception of hot streaks in basketball to the hard data. Gilovich led a study showing that the hot hand did not really exist; the shooting records of the Philadelphia 76ers provided no predictive value of subsequent shots. A player might be hot one minute but not the next. Fans and even sports professionals, they concluded, were making decisions based on myopic impressions.

Zwiebel and Green argue that the original finding failed to account for a key issue. In basketball, the opposing team quickly adjusts to a hot player, devoting extra coverage and forcing that player to attempt more difficult shots. As a result, it's inevitable that a hot player's shooting percentage will decline—not because the hot streak was an illusion, but rather that the hot player attracted more opposition.

They also points out that baseball is different because pitchers and coaches have limited ability to redeploy resources against a hitter on a hot streak. Pitchers and coaches play to a hitter's particular weaknesses, but they cannot put more people in the hitter's way.

To test their ideas, Zwiebel and Green amassed data on two million Major League Baseball at-bats over twelve years. They looked at ten categories of performance, from batting averages and home-run percentages to strike-out rates. For pitchers, they looked at data such as the average number of hits allowed. They also controlled for the fundamental ability of both pitchers and hitters in order to isolate the actual "streakiness" of a player's performance.

A player's most recent twenty-five times at bat were a significant predictor of how that player would do at his next time up—good enough to justify an adaptive reaction by coaches. When a player is hot, the researchers calculated, his expected on-base percentage will be twenty-five to thirty points higher than it would be if he has been cold. Similarly, a player on a hot streak will be 30 percent more likely to hit a home run than if he has been on a cold streak.

## Further Analysis

As mentioned earlier, several publications have demonstrated that statistically hot hand phenomenon may not even exist. Amos Tversky, a psychologist who studied every basket made by the Philadelphia 76ers for more than a season, has concluded the following:

1. The probability of making a second basket (hit) did not rise after a successful shot (success did not breed success).
2. The number of runs or baskets in succession was no greater than what a coin-tossing model would predict.

To clarify, consider a good player who makes half of his shots. For such a player, four hits in a row (HHHH) is expected to occur once in sixteen sequences of four shots, as this is one of the sixteen equally likely outcomes. The chance that this player hits at least three shots in a row (HHHH, HHHM, MHHH) is 3/16, assuming that trials are independent. Does this mean that the player has a hot hand? Suppose I flip a coin four times and get four heads in a row. Could I claim that I have a hot hand for heads?

Clearly, a great player will have more sequences of five hits than an average player, but not because he has greater will or gets into a magic rhythm more often. He has longer runs because his average success rate is so much higher, and he has a much better chance of having more frequent and longer sequences. Suppose we simulate the game of a great basketball player whose chance of making a field goal is 0.6. Such a player will get five in a row about once in every thirteen sequences, since the chance of this event is 1/13 or $1/(0.6)^5$. If another player's chance of making a field goals is 0.3, he will get his five hits in a row only about once in 412 times. In other words, we need no special explanation for the apparent pattern of long runs, except perhaps when the performance is far beyond what is expected from a player based on his past statistics.

Similar studies in baseball indicate that nothing ever happened in baseball above and beyond the frequency predicted by fair or loaded coin-tossing models. The longest run of wins or losses are as long as they should be and occur about as often as they ought to. Again, this can be demonstrated using computer simulation. However, this rule has one exception that should never have occurred—DiMaggio's fifty-six-game hitting streak in 1941. Purcell calculated that to make it likely (probability greater than 50 percent) that a run of even fifty games will occur once in the history of baseball up to now (and fifty-six is a lot more than fifty in this kind of league), baseball's rosters would have to include either four lifetime 0.400 batters or fifty-two lifetime 0.350 batters over careers of a thousand games. In actuality, only three men have lifetime batting averages in excess of 0.350, and no one is anywhere near 0.400. He then concluded that DiMaggio's streak is the most extraordinary thing that ever happened in American sports.

The questions still remain: How do people define hot hand, and are their definitions based on patterns, reality, or perceptions? A 1989 study by Larkey, Smith, and Kadane reveals that different measures for hot hand lead us to consider different players hot. It is interesting that although the precise meaning of *hot hand* is unclear, its common use implies a shooting record that departs from coin tossing with the probability of success greater than expected. An equally interesting point is that fans who talk about hot hand usually refer to patterns of streak shooting—something that is noticeable, memorable, or unlikely. Examples are observations such as HHHHHM or MHHHHH. But then why is an outcome like HMHMHM, which presents a sequence of hits followed by misses and vice versa, not considered a notable or extraordinary pattern, and why it is nameless? As is pointed out in the Skeptic's Dictionary, the clustering illusion is the intuition that random events that occur in clusters are not really random events. The illusion is due to selective thinking based on a false assumption. A good example occurs in the lottery. People think that a number like 2,145,362 is more random than 2,222,222, but if I'm randomly choosing a seven-digit number, they have the same chance of being selected.

Here's another example of the fact that people recognize certain patterns and ignore many others. Let's replace hit by 1 and miss by 0. Then we have a sequence of ones and zeros (a number in binary system). Consider, for example,

$$0\ 0\ 0\ 0\ 0\ 0\ 1\ 1\ 1\ 1\ 1 \text{ and } 1\ 1\ 1\ 1\ 0\ 0\ 1\ 1\ 0\ 1\ 0.$$

The first sequence may be recognized as having a pattern, but what about the second sequence? In fact, this is a famous pattern—the binary presentation of the number 1946, my birth year. To me, this is a recognizable pattern, but to other people it is not. A similar thing happens in poker. Getting a royal flush is surprising, even though the chance of any specific hand in poker is extremely low. It is also possible to argue in favor of hot hand. In "Simpson's Paradox and the Hot Hand in Basketball," Robert Wardrop presents many discussions concerning an inherent weakness in the methods used by Gilovich et al. (1985) and Tversky and Gilovich (1989). Hooke (1989) discusses the inherent difficulty of using statistical methods to study complete phenomenon, such as a game of basketball. Hale (1999) has discussed this issue and raised several questions, arguing that hot hand is an internal phenomenon and that the sense of being hot does not predict hits or misses. When a player realizes he is hot, he tends to push the envelope and attempt more difficult shots, which leads predictably to a failure. He might also raise the question: Precisely how unlikely does a streak of success need to be before we are prepared to count it as a legitimate instance of hot hand?

According to Hale, there are three prominent arguments that conclude there are no hot hands in sports. The first argument of the hot hands critics creates a tradition in the very act of destroying it. By making "Success breeds success" a necessary condition of having hot hands, the critics have established a previously undefended and barely articulated account of hot hands, only to demolish it. Instead Hale has argued that there are good reasons to reject "Success breeds success" as a requirement for having hot hands. While it is true that many players believe that future success is more likely when they are already hot, is this only a belief that their current state has causal efficacy into the future, or is it inductive reasoning that their current high rate of success is evidence of future success? Yet neither disjunction makes "Success breeds success" part of the concept of having hot hands.

The next two arguments offered by the critics of hot-hand theory are of a well-known, skeptical pattern: Set the standards for knowledge of something extremely high, then show that no one meets those standards. The canonical reply to this strategy, of which Hale availed himself, is to reject those standards in favor of more modest ones that charitably preserve our claims of knowledge. The skeptical insistence upon exceedingly rare streaks or statistically remote numbers of streaks as being the only legitimate instances of hot hands is arbitrary and severe. Hale has then argued that "being hot" denotes a continuum, one that is nothing other than deviation from the mean itself. This obviously comes in degrees.

To summarize the arguments against the hot hand, Tversky and Gilovich, using several data sets, conclude that existing data does not support hot hand. They devised a clever experiment to obtain convincing evidence that knowledgeable basketball fans are much too ready to detect occurrences of streak shooting and hot hand in sequences that are actually the outcome of Bernoulli trials. To further clarify this argument, they have considered the data on free throws for nine regular players of the Boston Celtics from 1980 to 1982. Then they asked the following question: When shooting free throws, does a player have a better chance of making the second shot after making the first shot than after missing the first shot? To answer this, they randomly chose a hundred Cornell and Stanford students. The responses were 68 percent yes, implying hot hand, and 32 percent no, implying independence or negative association.

After analyzing the data, Tversky and Gilovich concluded that it provided no evidence that the outcome of the second shot depends on the outcome of the first.

Adams (1992), using data on eighty-three players, showed that the mean interval from making a field goal (n − 372) to making a field goal in nineteen NBA games did not differ from the mean interval from making to missing (n = 394), which further challenges assumptions regarding hot hand.

In a more recent study, Koehler and Conley offered further evidence against hot hand in a unique setting, the NBA Long Distance Shootout. They concluded that declarations of hotness in basketball are best viewed as historical commentary rather than as a prophecy about future performance.

Having discussed opposing views, the final and perhaps more important question is why arguments for and against hot hand seem convincing. To answer this question, Wardrop (1995) performs an interesting analysis of data for Boston Celtics players, based on the fact that the data available to laypeople may be quite different from that available to professional researchers. In addition, laypeople unfamiliar with a counterintuitive result, such as Simpson's Paradox, may give the wrong interpretation to the pattern in their data and their analysis. There are many problems of this type in probability theory in which the right answer is counterintuitive. For demonstration, we will borrow Wardrop's data on observed frequencies for pairs of free throws by Larry Bird and Rick Robey and the collapsed table.

| Larry Bird | | | |
|---|---|---|---|
| | Second | | |
| First | Hit | Miss | Total |
| Hit | 251 | 34 | 285 |
| Miss | 48 | 5 | 53 |
| Total | 299 | 39 | 338 |
| Rick Robey | | | |
| | Second | | |
| First | Hit | Miss | Total |
| Hit | 54 | 37 | 91 |
| Miss | 49 | 31 | 80 |
| Total | 103 | 68 | 171 |

| Collapsed Table | | | |
|---|---|---|---|
| | Second | | |
| First | Hit | Miss | Total |
| Hit | 305 | 71 | 376 |
| Miss | 97 | 36 | 133 |
| Total | 402 | 107 | 509 |

(Wardrop 1995, Table 1)

Let Ph = the proportion of first-shot hits followed by a hit, and Pm = the proportion of first shot misses followed by a hit.

Ph = 251/285 = 0.881 and pm = 48/53 = 0.996 for Larry Bird, and
Ph = 54/91 = 0.593 and pm = 49/80 = 0.612 for Rick Robey.

But for collapsed data we have

Ph = 305/376 = 0.811 (= (285/376)(251/285) + (91/376)(54/91)), and
Pm = 97/133 = 0.729

Note that, contrary to hot hand theory in the sense of success breeds success, each player's shot is slightly better after a miss than after a hit, even though, as demonstrated by Wardrop, the differences are not statistically significant.

It is possible, of course, to ignore the identity of the player attempting the shots and examine the collapsed data. For example, on 509 occasions, either Bird or Robey attempted two free throws, on 305 of those occasions both shots were hit, and so on. For the collapsed data, ph = 0.811 and pm = 0.729. These values support the hot hand theory, that is, a hit was much more likely than a miss to be followed by a hit.

The data from Bird and Robey illustrate Simpson's paradox, namely, ph < pm in each component table, but ph > pm in the collapsed table. It is easy to verify algebraically that the proportion of successes for a collapsed table proportions equals the weighted average of individual player's proportions, with weights equal to the proportion of data in the collapsed table that comes from the player. For the after-a-hit condition, for example, the weight for Bird is 285/376 = 0.758, the weight for Robey is 91/376 = 0.242, and the proportion of successes for the collapsed table, 305/376 = 0.811, is $(285/376)(251/285)=(91/376)(54/91)$. As a result, even though both Bird and Robey shot better after a miss than after a hit, the collapsed values show the reverse pattern due to the huge variation in weights associated with each player. In short, Wardrop has concluded that Simpson's paradox has occurred because the after-a-miss condition, when compared with the aftera-hit condition, has a disproportionately large share of its data originating from Robey, the much inferior shooter.

## References

Adams, Robert M. "The 'Hot Hand' Revisited: Successful Basketball Shooting as a Function of Intershot Interval." *Perceptual and Motor Skills* 74, no. 3 (June 1992): 934. http://journals.sagepub.com/doi/abs/10.2466/pms.1992.74.3.934.

Andrews, Edmund. "Investment Bankers Can Learn a Thing or Two from Athletes on a 'Hot Streak.'" *Quartz*, March 30, 2014. https://qz.com/193256/investment-bankers-can-learn-a-thing-or-two-from-athletes-on-a-hot-streak/.

Gilovich, Thomas, Robert Vallone, and Amos Tversky. "The Hot Hand in Basketball: On the Misperception of Random Sequences." *Cognitive Psychology* 17 (1985): 295–314. http://wexler.free.fr/library/files/gilovich%20(1985)%20the%20hot%20hand%20in%20basketball.%20on%20the%20misperception%20of%20random%20sequences.pdf.

Hale, Steven D. "An Epistemologist Looks at the Hot Hand in Sports." *Journal of the Philosophy of Sport* 26, no. 1 (1999): 79–87. Published online March 30, 2012. https://www.tandfonline.com/doi/abs/10.1080/00948705.1999.9714580.

Hooke, Robert. "Basketball, Baseball, and the Null Hypothesis." *Chance* 2, no. 4 (1989): 35–37. Published online September 20, 2012. https://www.tandfonline.com/doi/abs/10.1080/09332480.1989.10554952?journalCode=ucha20.

Koehler, Jonathan J., and Caryn Conley. "The 'Hot Hand' Myth in Professional Basketball." *Journal of Sport & Exercise Psychology* 25 (2003): 253–260. https://papers.ssrn.com/sol3/papers.cfm?abstract_id=1469609.

Larkey, Patrick D., Richard A. Smith, and Joseph B. Kadane. "It's Okay to Believe in the 'Hot Hand.'" *Chance* 2, no. 4 (1989): 22–30. Published online September 20, 2012. https://amstat.tandfonline.com/doi/abs/10.1080/09332480.1989.10554950#.WseI0C7waCg.

Tversky, Amos, and Thomas Gilovich. "The Cold Facts About the 'Hot Hand' in Basketball." *Chance* 2, no. 1 (1989): 16–21. http://www.medicine.mcgill.ca/epidemiology/hanley/c323/hothand.pdf.

Tversky, Amos, and Thomas Gilovich. "The 'Hot Hand': Statistical Reality or Cognitive Illusion?" *Chance* 2, no. 4 (1989): 31–34. Published online September 20, 2012. https://www.tandfonline.com/doi/abs/10.1080/09332480.1989.10554951.

Wardrop, Robert L. "Basketball." In *Statistics in Sport*, edited by Jay Bennett. London: Hodder Education Group, 1998.

Wardrop, Robert L. "Simpson's Paradox and the Hot Hand in Basketball." *American Statistician* 49, no. 1 (1995): 24–28. Published online February 27, 2012. https://amstat.tandfonline.com/doi/abs/10.1080/00031305.1995.10476107#.WseIcS7waCg.

Zwiebel, Jeffery, and Brett Green. "The Hot Hand Fallacy: Cognitive Mistakes or Equilibrium Adjustments? Evidence from Baseball." *Stanford Graduate School of Business*, Nov. 2013, www.gsb.stanford.edu/faculty-research/working-papers/hot-hand-fallacy-cognitive-mistakes-or-equilibrium-adjustments.

# Table Tennis: A Teaching Tool

*Surprisingly, table tennis lends itself to mathematics better than most popular sports.*

Table tennis, also known as ping-pong, is a popular sport, especially in the Far East. The rules are easy to understand, and it's a game for all ages. Here we present a brief analysis of a game of table tennis. The picture below illustrates a game to 11 (new rules) played by two players, A and B.

                    0-0
                  1-0 0-1
                2-0 1-1 0-2
              3-0 2-1 1-2 0-3
            4-0 3-1 2-2 1-3 0-4
          5-0 4-1 3-2 2-3 1-4 0-5
        6-0 5-1 4-2 3-3 2-4 1-5 0-6
      7-0 6-1 5-2 4-3 3-4 2-5 1-6 0-7
    8-0 7-1 6-2 5-3 4-4 3-5 2-6 1-7 0-8
  9-0 8-1 7-2 6-3 5-4 4-5 3-6 2-7 1-8 0-9
10-0 9-1 8-2 7-3 6-4 5-5 4-6 3-7 2-8 1-9 0-10
11-0 10-1 9-2 8-3 7-4 6-5 5-6 4-7 3-8 2-9 1-10 0-11
  11-1 10-2 9-3 8-4 7-5 6-6 5-7 4-8 3-9 2-10 1-11
    11-2 10-3 9-4 8-5 7-6 6-7 5-8 4-9 3-10 2-11
      11-3 10-4 9-5 8-6 7-7 6-8 5-9 4-10 3-11
        11-4 10-5 9-6 8-7 7-8 6-9 5-10 4-11
          11-5 10-6 9-7 8-8 7-9 6-10 5-11
            11-6 10-7 9-8 8-9 7-10 6-11
              11-7 10-8 9-9 8-10 7-11
                11-8 10-9 9-10 8-11
                  11-9 10-10 9-11

A's game, Advantage A                  Tie                  Advantage B, B's game

A game is won by player A, who either

Case 1: reaches 11 points by a margin of two, or
Case 2: gains a lead of 2 points after reaching the score of 10:10 (tie).
Combining Cases 1 and 2, the probability that A wins the game is

$$P(A \text{ wins a game}) = P(\text{Case 1}) + P(\text{Case 2})$$

For case 1 to occur, A must win 10 out of the respective 10, 11, …,19 points played, plus the last point.
For case 2 to occur, A and B must first reach the score of 10:10 (tie). Then A should either win the next two points, or A and B split the first two points, get back to tie, and start over.

Let x be the probability of winning a point and g(x) be the probability of winning a game for A, that is P(A wins the game). Looking at the graph of g(x), it's easy to see that for x = 0.50, g(x) = 0.50 and for x > 0.80, g(x) is almost 1, as expected.

## An Alternative Analysis

Suppose that g(i, j) = the probability of A winning a game starting from a score of i:j. Since either A wins the next point and starts from score of i+1:j or loses the next point and starts from score of i:j+1, we have the following relationship:

$$g(i, j) = xg(i + 1, j) + (1 - x) g(i, j + 1)$$

For example:

$$g(10,10) = xg(11,10) + (1 - x) g(10,11),$$
$$g(11,10) = xg(12,10) + (1 - x) g(11,11),$$

Here g(12,10) =1 and g(10,12) = 0. Also g(10,10) = g(11, 11). Using these, we can calculate and plot all values of g(i, j).

Details and further analysis can be found in "Analysis of a Table Tennis Game: A Teaching Tool," by Reza Noubary.

# References

Noubary, Reza. "Analysis of a Table Tennis Game: A Teaching Tool." *IMA Sport*, edited by Percy et al., 147–151. 2007.

Noubary, Reza. "Probabilistic Analysis of a Table Tennis Game." *Journal of Quantitative Analysis in Sports* 3, no. 1 (January 2007): 1–18. https://doi.org/10.2202/1559-0410.1053.

# Records of the 100-Meter Race

*Is there any speed limit for the 100-meter dash? And if so, what could it possibly be?*

In the 2016 Olympics in Brazil, two thousand athletes from more than two hundred nations were set to compete for forty-seven titles. According to the experts, some athletes and countries were on the brink of rewriting Olympic history.

Looking back to some extraordinary events at previous Olympics, I remember Michael Phelps's eight gold medals at Beijing in 2008. That was also the year that Usain Bolt, a Jamaican, won the men's 100-meter sprint in a world record time of 9.69 seconds. In 2009, Bolt put on another amazing performance at the world championships, shattering his own record in the 100 meters by 0.11 seconds to an almost inhuman 9.58 seconds. Also in 2009, he lowered the 200-meters record by the same amount to set the current record of 19.19 seconds. Bolt became the first man to win back-to-back Olympic sprint doubles when he successfully defended his 100m and 200m titles in the 2012 London Olympics. In 2016 at Rio de Janeiro, the Jamaican sprinter could have won an unprecedented third sprint double. If he had won the 4 x 100m at Rio, as he did in Beijing and London, Bolt's Olympic gold medal tally would stand at nine. Only one man has ever won more Olympic gold medals in track and field—American Ray Ewry won ten, including two at the Intercalated Games in Athens.

The 100m run defines the fastest man on earth. In well over one hundred years, only twenty-five men have been named "the fastest man on earth." Bolt is the most recent, and his performance has forced experts to alter their predictions related to the 100-meter run.

In 2016, Justin Gatlin, an American, ran the 100m in 9.45 seconds to slip under Bolt's record time of 9.58. However, Gatlin had plenty of help for his audacious stunt, which was done on a Japanese TV game show. Gatlin had a giant fan placed behind him at the starting line and four other fans strategically placed alongside his lane farther down the track. He was literally blown to the finish line by the wind, running at an estimated 32 km/h—four times the legal limit.

For most people, the most interesting element of these predictions is what they reveal about human strength and limits. For teachers like me, such problems are even more interesting because of their educational value. I have done a lot of research on the 100-meter run, as evidenced in the references at the end of this article. My own prediction for the ultimate record is 9.40 seconds with 90 percent confidence, and this prediction drew a great deal of attention from the sports community and media during the 2012 and 2016 Olympics. I obtained this number by applying several newly developed statistical methods and their modifications. Independent of my calculations, Bolt, too, thinks that world records will stop at 9.40.

Of course, it's hard to predict the magnitude of athletic talent at the extreme margins of humanity with certainty. Bolt, as it turns out, is a perfect example. He combines the mechanical advantages of taller men's bodies with the fast-twitch fibers of smaller men.

As the 2016 Olympics approached, people wondered if Bolt or some other runner could break the record of 9.58 seconds. This seemed possible, since the data from the 2009 World Championship showed that, among the top five runners, Bolt had the fastest run time (9.434 seconds) but the slowest reaction time (0.146 seconds). There was room for improvement, as everybody knew.

Is there a runner who could set a new record? I think this is unlikely, but possible. In addition to experienced runners, several young talents in the top ten fastest men could do it on a good day and with plenty of luck.

## References

Brigstock-Barron, Rory. "Justin Gatlin Breaks Usain Bolt's 100m Record with 9.45 Second Dash on Japanese Television Show … But It Wouldn't Count." *Mail Online*, February 29, 2016. https://www.dailymail.co.uk/sport/othersports/article-3470075/Justin-Gatlin-breaks-Usain-Bolt-s-100m-record-9-45-second-dash-Japanese-television-wouldn-t-count.html.

International Association of Athletics Federations. "Usain Bolt Athlete Profile." https://www.iaaf.org/athletes/jamaica/usain-bolt-184599.

Noubary, Reza. "What Is the Speed Limit for Men's 100 Meter Dash." www.mathaware.org/mam/2010/essays/NoubaryRun.pdf.

Noubary, Reza. "Tail Modeling and Prediction of Track and Field Records." *Journal of Applied Statistical Science* 16, no. 3 (2009): 287–292.

Noubary, Reza. "Tail Modeling, Track and Field Records, and Bolt's Effect." *Journal of Quantitative Analysis in Sports* 6, no. 3 (January 2010): Article 9. http://www.bepress.com/jqas/vol6/iss3/9.

Noubary, Reza. "What Is the Speed Limit for Men's 100 Meter Run?" In *Mathematics and Sports*, edited by Joseph A. Gallian, 287–294. Washington, DC: Mathematical Association of America, 2010.

Noubary, Reza, and Farzad Noubary. "Survival Analysis of the Men's 100 Meter Dash Record." *Applications and Applied Mathematics* 11, no. 1 (2016): 115–126.

Olympics Statistics. https://www.olympic.org/olympic-results.

# Sports Psychology and Culture

*Popular sports are reflections of our culture.*

Sports are a popular pastime around the world, and every country has its own favorites. In Europe, soccer is the most popular sport by a long shot, but other favorites include tennis, table tennis, golf, and cricket. This is in sharp contrast to the United States, where football, basketball, and baseball are the big three. Some experts think this is because Americans having shorter attention spans and prefer to watch higher-scoring games, and apparently we even need cheerleaders to help hold our attention.

In European football/soccer, the highest scoring league is the German Bundesliga, according to *Mirror*, the British sports magazine. Bundesliga matches average 2.93 goals per game, or about 1 goal per thirty minutes. Ice hockey also has a presence in Europe, with the most prevalent European leagues being Sweden's SHL and Russia's KHL, whose websites provide information on scores of their respective games. In the first round of the 2010 KHL playoffs, the number of goals per game was 3.2, while goals per game in the SHL was 5.8. Although this scoring average is higher than that of soccer, it's nothing in comparison to sports such as basketball.

The lowest scoring American sport is baseball. During the first four months of 2018, MLB runs per game sat at 4.26, but the Yankees lead the league with 6.05. In the 2017 NFL season, points per game sat around 43, and average points per game in the NBA's regular season was 213.2. To put that in perspective, 213. 2 points in sixty minutes is over 3.5 points per minute. The MLB and NFL websites have detailed scoring on their respective sports.

As mentioned above, some people attribute this to European attention spans being longer than those of Americans. The average attention span of an adult in Britain is fourteen minutes, according to Emma Elsworthy. Because basketball and football lead to more scoring, they may be more appealing to Americans.

In the United States, football is the favorite sport. According to Andrew Both, 160 million viewers worldwide watched Super Bowl 48 in 2014, and CBS News reports that 111.5 million of those views came from the United States. That leaves 48.5 million viewers from other countries around the world (30.31%). Although that sounds like a large number, it's nothing compared with what the FIFA World Cup tournament brings in. The 2014 FIFA World Cup Finals brought in a global audience of a billion people, including 18.2 million Americans, who watched the game live, according to Reuters Sports News.

Another difference is the competitive balance in sports. Since 2006, only three soccer teams out of twenty have won the La Liga Division in Spain. Realistically, if all twenty teams were evenly matched, there would be a 15 percent chance that one of those three teams would win each year. Over the course of eleven years, that would be an inconceivably small percent of what is actually happening. A similar phenomenon applies to the most popular league in the world, the English Football League, which includes teams from England and Wales. Since some teams, such as FC Barcelona and Real Madrid, are so rich and dominant, they practically take over the sport.

Over the same eleven-year period from 2006 to 2017, nine different NFL teams have won. In the MLB, eight different teams have won Only 2 teams had multiple championships in both of these instances. That is another huge difference between American and European sports.

## References

Both, Andrew. "Super Bowl Has Ways to Go in Captivating Global Audience." *Reuters Sports News*, January 24, 2015. https://www.reuters.com/article/us-nfl-international/super-bowl-has-ways-to-go-in-captivating-global-audience-idUSKBN0KX0KK20150124.

Cox, Kevin. "Super Bowl 2014 Ratings Set New Record." *CBS News*, February 3, 2014. https://www.cbsnews.com/news/super-bowl-2014-ratings-set-new-record/.

Dubas-Fisher, David. "Is the Premier League REALLY the most entertaining league in the world?" *Mirror*, May 9, 2014. https://www.mirror.co.uk/sport/football/news/european-big-four-leagues-goals-3513388.

Elsworthy, Emma. "Average British Attention Span Is 14 Minutes, Research Finds." *Independent*, December 28, 2017. https://www.independent.co.uk/news/uk/home-news/attention-span-average-british-person-tuned-in-concentration-mobile-phone-a8131156.html.

Kontinental Hockey League. https://en.khl.ru/.

"The Most Popular Sports in America." *Ranker*. https://www.ranker.com/crowdranked-list/most-popular-american-sports.

Official Site of Major League Baseball. https://www.mlb.com/.

Official Site of the National Football League. https://www.nfl.com/.

"One Billion Watched 2014 World Cup Final on TV." *Reuters Sports News*, December 16, 2015. https://uk.reuters.com/article/uk-soccer-world-television/one-billion-watched-2014-world-cup-final-on-tv-idUKKBN0TZ21Y20151216.

"Popular Sports in Europe." 7 Continents List, December 8, 2015. https://www.7continentslist.com/europe/popular-sports-in-europe.php.

Swedish Hockey League. https://www.shl.se/.

# Sports in America and Great Britain

*Two countries where sport is like a religion.*

The importance of sports in today's world is evident to everyone. Sports are one of the greatest unifying factors, and events such as the Olympics and the World Cup are indications of that. This article explores the difference between sports in the two major sporting countries, the United States and Great Britain. The game most specifically associated with Great Britain is cricket. Although many other British games have been enthusiastically adopted by other cultures, cricket has found a home only inside the British Commonwealth. A fondness for cricket appears to mesh well with the British attitude. If so, however, the British may be losing some of their natural spirit, because a great majority of Brits have become much more enthusiastic about the eight months of the football (soccer) season than the four months of the cricket season. There are plenty of amateur football clubs, and professional clubs are a big business. Next to football, the chief spectator sports in England are horse racing and polo. Betting is common in all these sports.

The most popular sports in the United States are baseball, American football, and basketball. Not quite as popular, but still widely watched, is ice hockey. Baseball is an American pastime, and every year millions of people attend games and watch it on television. American football is quite different from football in the rest of the world. British football, called soccer in America, is not yet as popular as the three main sports—football, baseball, and basketball.

Most American professional football games are played on Sundays, though recent years have seen some games move to Monday and Thursday nights, and college football games are played on Saturdays. All three sports have teams associated with major cities or states, and teams will sometimes move to another city or state that offers them more attractive terms. One hundred percent American in origin, basketball is popular at colleges and high schools, just like football and baseball. Statewide basketball tournaments are held annually. US professional basketball teams are among the world's best, and the winner of the NBA championship is recognized as the champion of the world.

Obviously there are many differences between British and American culture, even though the United States began as an English colony. A study of the divergence of cultures is also a study of how people with similar ancestry can develop different cultures even when separated for only a relatively short time. Such studies can provide insight into how cultures develop and provide insight into cultures different from our own.

In the United States, sports have gradually turned into entertainment, complete with cheerleaders, marching bands, and other associated activities. In both countries, where many people watch games on television, sports are a big business as well.

In the United States education system, sports are sometimes considered more important than academics. Often a large percentage of a school's budget, in both high schools and postsecondary institutions, goes toward building sports facilities. Students on athletic teams and cheerleaders are often more popular than students who excel at academics. Many parents attend all of their children's sports events, though they may rarely or never request to observe their classes. This is not the case in Great Britain, where sports are more similar to religious and family traditions.

## References

Ranker. "The Most Popular Sports in America."
    https://www.ranker.com/crowdranked-list/most-popular-american-sports.

# Chapter 7
## Global/Social

*Do global issues cause social issues?*

*There is a war going on, not in the Middle East, but right here.*
*You see it on our streets and in our schools, almost everywhere.*
*Kids have no good role models, only some wrong crowd.*
*They talk about crack and dope with no shame or fear.*
*The media is full of fake news, hate, and many things unreal.*
*Indifference has become normal everywhere, far and near.*

# Are Human Beings Rational?

*In November 2018, Payless shoes were displayed in a "classy" store in an upscale neighborhood. Although the shoes were priced in hundreds of dollars, they were sold easily. The buyers were later refunded and invited to keep the shoes.*

To most of us, the universe seems complex, confusing, and sometimes meaningless. As observers, we can shape the meaning of reality only through our own logic or wishes, so we often view even the most obvious coincidences as evidence or guidance. Fortunately, time usually leads us to the realization that the likelihood of uncovering the secrets of this world is almost zero.

> God had imprisoned our minds in space.
> Those puny things have remained prisoners.
> Thought, the hungry bird of prey fought the curse,
> but never breached its diamond bars' embrace.
> —Mihály Babits

Does this line of thought apply to man-made ideas and systems too? It might, but perhaps not to the same degree. For example, as with most other conceptual things, it takes time and effort to understand mathematics for what it is. Time also changes what we see and appreciate in mathematics. When we're young, we notice its power to explain; in our middle years, we see its applications and details; and in old age, we appreciate its beauty and depth. But at any level, this requires intellectual acumen, and some people never develop any sense for mathematics beyond dislike and confusion.

According to some research, people who deeply understand mathematics are rare, especially in our technology-dominated era. In fact, most of us manage only to somehow get used to the mathematical terminology we have learned. Consider, for example, the numbers we use on a daily basis. Most people don't realize that rational numbers, including integers and fractions, though unlimited, are nothing compared with irrational numbers. In fact, if we drop all integers and fractions from the number line, nothing happens to it. Nevertheless, we hardly use irrational numbers because as humans, we do only what we know how to do. In other words, people in general have a weak grasp of irrational numbers, and when we use numbers, we want them to be positive numbers and integers. This is characteristic of our somewhat selfish and self-centered views toward life.

A classic example is the birthday match problem. We all know people who share a birthday, yet birthday matches surprise us because we think they are unlikely events. In fact, with only forty people in a room, the likelihood of at least one birthday match is over 90 percent.

Of course, this is not only about mathematics. It also applies to the fact that we define *humanity* in the way that best serves people. For example, is it our right to kill and eat billions of animals, especially when they're defenseless? To justify this, we convince ourselves that animals don't experience pain, loss, and death. We classify other creatures as good or bad, depending on whether they serve us or give us pleasure. A similar and even more revealing example is discrimination. We frequently rail against discrimination, except in situations where we actually benefit from it or when criticizing it makes us uncomfortable. Discrimination against people who are ugly, fat, or old is rampant in our culture, for example, but we never discuss it, let alone do anything about it.

Now let's turn back to the question in the title of this article, with an example about rational choice. Students at the University of Oregon, recruited by an ad in the student newspaper, were randomly given Form I or Form II of a questionnaire about vaccination. Form I described a disease expected to affect 20 percent of the population and asked people whether they would volunteer to receive a vaccine that protects half the people receiving it. Form II described two mutually exclusive and equi-probable strains of the disease, each likely to affect 10 percent of the population. The vaccine would provide complete protection against one strain of the disease but no protection against the other. Even though both vaccination forms proposed no risk to the volunteers and offered a reduction of the probability of the disease from 20 percent to 10 percent, the framing of the situation led to a "yes" response of 57 percent for Form II but only 40 percent for Form I.

Another study, published in *Scientific American*, explored at length the role that the framing of a choice plays in the resulting decision. Compare, for example, the following pairs of choices:

First pair  (A) Either collect $50 for sure, or
           (B) gamble with a 25 percent chance of winning $200 and a 75 percent chance of winning nothing.
Second pair (C) Either lose $150 for sure, or
           (D) gamble with a 75 percent chance of losing $200 and a 25 percent chance of losing nothing.

Most people prefer A to B and D to C, even though the expected outcomes of A and C are identical and the expected outcomes of B and D are identical.

Here's another interesting example. The winning ticket in a lottery was 865304. Three people compare the ticket they hold with the winning number. John holds 361204, Mary holds 965304, and Bill holds 865305. None of them win, since the chance of winning was only one in a million. Why was Bill the most upset, whereas John was only mildly disappointed?

We are neither as rational as we think nor as rational as we would like to be. Here's a final example.

## Lottery

Participants in a study were offered an option of paying one dollar for a one-in-one-million chance of winning a million dollars. Nearly half of the respondents accepted the offer, including a large number of risk-averse people. When the offer changed to a one-in-ten-million chance of winning ten million dollars, nearly 75 percent of participants, including those who were risk averse, accepted it. This explains why some recent lotteries have attracted so many people whose real reward was, in fact, picturing or dreaming of being rich for a few days.

## References

Slovic, Paul, Baruch Fischhoff, and Sarah Lichtenstein. "Behavioral Decision Theory Perspectives on Protective Behavior." In *Taking Care: Understanding and Encouraging Self-Protective Behavior*, edited by N. D. Weinstein, 14–41. New York: Cambridge University Press, 1987. https://scholarsbank.uoregon.edu/xmlui/bitstream/handle/1794/22331/slovic_250.pdf?isAllowed=y&sequence=1.

Amos Tversky; Daniel Kahneman. The Journal of Business, Vol. 59, No. 4, Part 2: The Behavioral Foundations of Economic Theory. (Oct., 1986), pp. S251-S278.

# Is There Such a Thing As Human Rights?

*Is human rights defined by human fair?*

According to some experts, human rights are rights inherent to all people independent of their birthplace, nationality, gender, sex, ethnicity, skin color, religion, language, or any other status. Everybody is entitled to human rights by virtue of being human. Based on the principle of respect for the individual, human rights include life, liberty, equality, a fair trial, and freedom. The Universal Declaration of Human Rights (UDHR), adopted by the United Nations General Assembly in 1948, is a milestone document in the history of human rights.

Cyrus the Great, the first king of Persia, freed the slaves when he conquered the city of Babylon in 539 B.C. His next actions marked a major advance for humankind when he declared that all people have the right to choose their own religion and established the rule of racial equality. Cyrus's decrees regarding human rights were inscribed in the Akkadian language on a baked-clay cylinder known today as the Cyrus Cylinder. Recognized as the world's first charter of human rights, the Cyrus Cylinder has been translated into all six official languages of the United Nations, and its provisions parallel the first four articles of the UDHR.

## The Spread of Human Rights

According to several websites, such as peacecharter.org from Babylon, the idea of human rights spread quickly to India, Greece, and eventually Rome. There the concept of "natural law" arose from the observation that people tend to follow certain conventions in the course of life, and Roman law was based on rational ideas derived from the nature of things. Documents asserting individual rights, such as the Magna Carta (1215), the Petition of Right (1628), the US Constitution (1787), the French Declaration of the Rights of Man and of the Citizen (1789), and the US Bill of Rights (1791) are the written precursors to many of today's human rights documents.

## What Rights Are Human Rights?

Each person is a moral and rational being who deserves to be treated with dignity. This is the fundamental assumption of human rights, but is it applied in the real world? Yes, to some extent. Do humans think that other creatures should have rights too? Yes, but only those who give us pleasure, such as our pets, and are not harmful to us.

Consider this statement by Heather Moore of People for the Ethical Treatment of Animals: "Chickens feel pain, fear, love and happiness, just as we do. They, too, have complex social structures, adept communication skills, and distinct personalities. They form strong family ties and mourn when they lose a loved one. When they are not confined to factory farms, hens lovingly tend to their eggs and 'talk' to their un-born chicks, who chirp back. Chickens have at least 24 distinct vocalizations, so other birds know when they are warning them about a predator or just saying 'hey.' Studies show that these smart birds can anticipate the future and demonstrate self-control."

Since childhood I have always wondered about animals and their rights. According to Heather Moore, chickens—and by implication, other animals—understand feelings of loss, pain, and death, and are capable of many simple and complex emotions. Anyone who has ever had a pet could tell you more about this. Nevertheless, people kill billions of animals every day, and we hardly ask whether we have such a right. We do this simply because most of us consider it natural and even our right to do so.

If I kill a cat or a dog, I will be classified a cruel person, and I may even be charged with a crime. However, the same is not applied to most other animals. In fact, we simply classify animals according to whether we find them tasty, useful, or pretty, and then we treat them accordingly. We do this realizing that animals do not know if they are pretty or ugly, useful or else. They just act instinctively. We even assume that animals exist for our benefit and that it is our right to decide their fate. Yet there are billions of animals deep in the ocean of whose existence we are not even aware, and their lives are governed by the environment and evolution.

## Recent Changes

In "The Case Against Human Rights," Eric Posner says that although major human rights treaties—there are nine core treaties—have been ratified by a large majority of countries, the human rights agenda is going through hard times. In much of the Islamic world, women lack equal rights, religious dissenters are persecuted, and political freedoms are absent. The Chinese model of development, which combines political repression and economic liberalism, has attracted numerous admirers in the developing world. Political authoritarianism has gained ground in Russia, Turkey, Hungary, and Venezuela. Backlashes against LGBT rights have taken place in countries as diverse as Russia and Nigeria. The traditional champions of human rights—Europe and the United States—have floundered.

According to Posner, Europe has turned inward as it has struggled with a sovereign debt crisis, xenophobia toward its Muslim communities, and disillusionment with Brussels. The United States, which used torture in the years after 9/11 and continues to kill civilians with drone strikes, has lost much of its moral authority. Even age-old scourges such as slavery continue to exist; a recent report estimates that nearly thirty million people are forced against their will to work. It's not supposed to be like this.

## Freedom of Speech

Consider the right to freedom of expression discussed in tokyoroseinlalaland.blogspot.com. From a global perspective, the right to freedom of expression is contested. The United States takes this right particularly seriously, though it excludes fraud, defamation, and obscenity. In Europe, most governments believe that freedom of expression does not extend to hate speech. In many Islamic countries, defamation of Islam is not protected by freedom of speech. Human rights laws blandly acknowledge that the right to freedom of expression may be limited by considerations of public order and morals. However, a government trying to comply with the international human right to freedom of expression is given no specific guidance whatsoever.

## Effect of Globalization

Globalization, which has intensified social relations, encourages the shaping of local affairs by events occurring in faraway places. Some communities feel they are gradually losing their livelihood, identity, and freedom of action in the process of reacting and adjusting to rapid changes occurring around the world. Some developed countries are now trying to get out of global agreements, protocols, supply chains, and exchanges they have built with others; negotiate new agreements; and establish new borders. On the other hand, other countries are trying to make their present entanglements work.

Support for disentanglement is evident from the popularity of ideas presented by

Trump's camp, the British vote for Brexit, and the electoral successes of nationalist and protectionist politicians in democracies worldwide. In fact, what is happening in the United States, England, Germany, France, Turkey, Greece, Brazil, Austria, the Philippines, and other countries reminds us that our new openness and connectedness cannot be taken for granted. Aside from its economic effects, globalization has become a test of human character by creating hope, opportunity, and prosperity for some people, but conflict, anxiety, pessimism, anger, despair, and even violence for others. Some groups have even started using their shared beliefs and identities to specify targets of hostility, legitimize aggression, and coordinate action.

## Human Rights and Culture

Human rights as defined by Westerners may be at odds with other cultures. According to Michael Ignatieff, "The West now masks its own will to power in the impartial, universalizing language of human rights and seeks to impose its own narrow agenda on a plethora of world cultures that do not actually share the West's conception of individuality, selfhood, agency, or freedom." An example is the education of children, which we see as a human right and wish to enforce globally. However, many poor countries depend on children working in order for the family to eat and survive. Most of the world population lives in rural areas and depends on agriculture for its livelihood. When children are forced to go to school, their families lose breadwinners, and parents can be forced to cease work to attend to children who no longer work at home. Also, schooling in poor and developing countries is costly, especially for big families. This results in deepening impoverishment before the fruits of the child's education kick in many years later. Is education still an easily recognizable human right? It is not always so simple.

## Final Words

In *Human Rights as Battlefields*, we read that the language of human rights is the only universally available moral vernacular that validates the claims of women and children against the oppression they experience in patriarchal and tribal societies. It is the only vernacular that enables dependent people to perceive themselves as moral agents and to act against practices—arranged marriages, purdah, civic disenfranchisement, genital mutilation, domestic slavery, and so on—that are ratified by the weight and authority of their cultures. These agents seek out human rights protection precisely because it legitimizes their protests against oppression.

# References

Blouin-Genest, Gabriel, Marie-Christine Doran, and Sylvie Paquerot. *Human Rights as Battlefields: Changing Practices and Contestations.* Palgrave Macmillan, London 2019.

Ignatieff, Michael. "The Attack on Human Rights." *Foreign Affairs*, November/December 2001. https://www.foreignaffairs.com/articles/2001-11-01/attack-human-rights.

Posner, Eric. "The Case Against Human Rights." *The Guardian*, December 4, 2014. https://www.theguardian.com/news/2014/dec/04/-sp-case-against-human-rights#img-1.

# Indifference, a Tragedy of the Modern Era

*The opposite of love is not hate, it is indifference.*
—Elie Wiesel

Indifference is everywhere. Like a cancer, it has grown slowly but steadily, reaching a point where it has become a norm. Some people have become indifferent to indifference itself. Some of us do not care about our neighbors, our communities, or even our personal and family issues. We no longer care about things that are backed by history or logic.

Indifference can be defined as a lack of interest or concern, the quality of having an indifferent attitude or feeling toward other people and current affairs. Among all the seemingly intractable crises we face today, none in the long run is as serious as our unfamiliarity with the rest of the world. Indifference to the rest of the world puts us at a great disadvantage, and this is particularly true since we are still a relatively new country. It also partly explains why some countries have a negative view toward the United States, even those whom we help financially. Our indifference makes it hard for our politicians to deal with international conflicts confidently and competently.

According to Sanford Ungar in "American Ignorance," whether motivated by exceptionalism, isolationism, triumphalism, Trumpisim, or sheer indifference—probably some of each over time—our government and the popular media have failed to equip a significant percentage of US citizenry with the basic information necessary to be part of the global community, let alone participate in formulating and executing foreign policy. This condition also reflects the basic inadequacy of our educational system at every level. Compared with other countries, we score lower on geography, current-events awareness tests, and even locating major countries on a map. Our students do not develop an appreciation for their history, cultures, or roles in global affairs. As a result, most of us do not appreciate what we have or how lucky we are.

Ungar argues that young Americans do not appreciate the importance of learning foreign languages, and that indifference is only increasing. According to a recent report from the Modern Language Association, college students in the United States are studying languages 6.7 percent less now than they did five years ago (2014). Even enrollments in Spanish, America's second language, declined 8.2 percent during that period, Arabic 7.5 percent, and Russian 17.9 percent. Admittedly, English is in ascendance as the international language of science, business, and trade, but we will not get away with waiting for the entire world to learn it.

Today the situation seems even worse. Unger says that almost twenty years after the shock of September 11, a complex international environment feels ever more distant, unknowable, and strange. Only a third of Americans are thought to hold passports—compared with about 50 percent in Australia, more than 60 percent in Canada, and some 80 percent in the United Kingdom. Study-abroad rates at American colleges and universities are, on average, stuck in the low single digits.

With the world moving toward globalization, a broader familiarity with other countries and cultures is essential. Unger says it will take decades—a generation or two—for the United States to develop a deeper appreciation of the complex forces at work around the world such that popular attitudes are no longer subject to crass manipulation.

## Final Words

The cruelty and non-emotional detachment of people who are indifferent is reflected in their indifference to pain, suffering, torture, starvation, displacement, dictatorial rule, homelessness, and even murder. Indifference is a continuing theme of human tragedy. It is humanity's inhumanity to humanity. It has existed since the beginning of humankind, and it continues in full force today.

Think of the poor, the hungry, and the homeless right here in America. It is comforting to see people helping people. Then think of the politics and the blame game of why some people are poor, homeless, and hungry. Politicians spend money and time pretending to address the issues, yet literally end up creating more of what they are trying to reduce. Some of the richest Americans claim to be on the side of poor and needy people, and yet they grow richer every year. People who do not practice what they preach exhibit another form of indifference. Finally, think about the mass shootings that leave our minds immediately afterward.

## References

Modern Language Association. "Enrollments in Languages Other Than English in United States Institutions of Higher Education." http://www.mla.org/ enrollments_surveys.

Ungar, Sanford J. "American Ignorance." *Inside Higher Ed*, March 23, 2015. https://www. insidehighered.com/views/2015/03/23/essay-problems-american-ignorance- world.

# Owning Guns: Pros and Cons

*Guns could be beneficial and could be harmful. The question is which we weigh more.*

Gun control is presently a highly controversial topic in the United States. From protests at the White House to discussions around our dinner tables, the debate over whether we should own guns continues. Ownership of guns dates back to the Second Amendment to the Constitution: "A well-regulated Militia, being necessary to the security of a free State, the right of the people to keep and bear Arms, shall not be infringed." Following recent mass shootings, especially in schools, there have been many proposals and protests about needing stricter gun laws. People are entitled to their own opinions, but there are pro's and con's to owning guns and gun control.

For a scientific study of this issue, we need to design and implement an experiment lasting several years and with participants from several locations to make sure that all types of gun owners are represented. The study should have a clear objective, such as to determine what the country will gain or lose by passing new laws, how many lives will be saved or lost as a result of gun ownership, and what the effects on related issues will be.

People who oppose gun control assert that it is our constitutional right to own a gun, while many people in favor of stricter gun control laws argue that the Second Amendment does not constitute the right to own any type of gun, but only guns necessary for basic protection. Although this controversy is discussed in nearly every home, more research is needed to provide sufficient information to resolve the issue.

Supporters of gun control argue for stricter gun control laws or regulations, and some people want to get rid of all guns. Gun control supporters believe the Second Amendment gives our military the right to own guns, but not individual citizens. They argue that high-capacity magazines should be banned because they turn murder into *mass* murder. Follman, Aronsen, and Pan, in "U.S. Mass Shootings, 1982–2012," found that high-capacity magazines were used in 50 percent of mass shootings between 1982 and 2012. In "Analysis of Recent Mass Shootings," we read that when high-capacity magazines are used, the death rate increases 63 percent and the injury rate rises 156 percent. Some people argue that legally owned guns may be stolen and used by criminals. "Firearm Use by Offenders," a Bureau of Justice Statistics report, says that 1.4 million guns were stolen from US homes during property crimes between 2005 and 2010. According to the CDC's "Data & Statistics," there were 464,033 total gun deaths between 1999 and 2013: 270,237 suicides (58.2 percent of total deaths); 174,773 homicides (37.7 percent); and 9,983 unintentional deaths (2.2 percent).

Some people claim that stricter gun control laws would reduce gun deaths, but opponents argue that crime is deterred not by gun control laws, but by gun owners, according to "Should More Gun Control Laws Be Enacted?" on ProCon.org. This website includes a statement from journalist John Stossel, who asserts that "Without the fear of retaliation from victims who might be packing heat, criminals in possession of these [illegal] weapons now have a much easier job." Although this is a strong argument, fighting fire with fire may not be the best solution. As the number of people who own guns rises, the number of mass shooting victims has declined by over 80 percent in the US. These claims are promising, but nearly seventy US mass shootings took place in the first half of 2018, which is frightening itself.

Opponents of gun control believe stricter gun control laws will not prevent criminals from breaking the law and obtaining guns. According to the Bureau of Justice, in 1997, 40 percent of inmates who had gun-related charges obtained the gun from a family member or friend. Procon.org refers to statistics that show that in 2014, Chicago had 2,089 shooting victims, including 390 murders—even with their strict gun laws. Mexico has strict gun control laws compared with most other countries, but statistics show no improvement. "In 2012, Mexico had 11,309 gun murders compared to the United States that had 9,146 gun homicides ... Between 2006 and 2010, Mexico's one gun shop sold 6,490 guns, yet in 2012, Mexicans own 15,000,000 guns, or about 13.5 guns per 100 people."

Proponents of gun control laws argue that more laws would reduce gun deaths. In nearly fourteen years, guns were responsible for more than 460,000 deaths, according to the Procon website. Such varied statistics make this issue even more debatable in the United States than in other countries, such as Mexico.

## Statistical View

One study on gun restriction from the University of Washington focuses on the hypothesis that lower rates of gun ownership positively correlate with lower incident rates of gun-related homicides. The study was conducted based on six different percentiles of statewide gun ownership of a population size of 100,000 people. The six percentiles were respectively 10, 20, 30, 40, 50, and 60 percent gun ownership per 100,000 people. The study was conducted within one standard deviation and no level of significance was included. Since such a wide range of data was collected from different areas, each consisting of significant variations in gun ownership, it is safe to conclude that the margin of error that this study allowed was very generous.

Operating on the data supplied at 1 standard deviation, the homicide incident rate from a gun at 10 percent gun ownership per 100,000 individuals was roughly two people. At 20 percent gun ownership per 100,000 people, the incident rate was still roughly two people per 100,000 individuals. The correlation between gun ownership and gun homicides can finally be seen at 30 and 40 percent gun ownership per 100,000 people, where the homicide rate increased to roughly five people per 100,000 people. The study also included information on the 50 and 60 percentiles for gun ownership per 100,000 people, but the amount of evidence was not definitive enough to make a conclusion about the correlation between gun homicide rates and gun ownership.

It is apparent that gun-related homicide rates tend to increase when gun ownership rates increase, which strongly suggests that stronger gun control laws might actually be our government's best option for reducing gun-related crime and making the lives of American citizens safer.

## Summary and More Statistics

Data from SmallArmsSurvey.org and William Krouse's "Gun Control Legislation" report give us an idea of which countries have the most guns. In "Mapped: The Countries with the Most Guns," Hugh Morris analyzes this data: As of October 22, 2016, the top ten countries with the most guns were the United States (112.6 guns per hundred residents), Serbia (75.6), Yemen (54.8), Switzerland (45.7), Cyprus (36.4), Saudi Arabia (35), Iraq (34.2), Uruguay (31.8), Sweden (31.6), and Norway (31.3).

Firearms legislation in Switzerland is comparatively liberal, more similar to gun politics in the United States than to that in most European Union countries. The reason is a long tradition of shooting (tirs) as a formative element of national identity in the post-Napoleonic Restoration of the Confederacy. In fact, Switzerland has one of the highest rates of gun ownership in the world, but little gun-related street crime. Some opponents of gun control hail it as a place where firearms play a positive role in society. However, Swiss gun culture is unique, and guns are more tightly regulated than many people assume.

## Final Words

Maybe we need to go a little deeper to find the root problem. Why don't other countries with high rates of gun ownership have school shootings? Maybe it's a cultural issue. Some people think that popular activities reflect what people value in a society. For example, football's popularity in the United States may reflect an appreciation for aggression.

## References

Ali, Tanveer. "Though Chicago Murders Are Down, 'Gang Culture' Remains an Issue: Top Cop." DNAinfo, December 29, 2014. www.dnainfo.com.

Bureau of Justice Statistics. "About 1.4 Million Guns Stolen During Household Burglaries and Other Property Crimes From 2005 Through 2010." November 8, 2012. https://www.bjs.gov/content/pub/press/fshbopc0510pr.cfm.

Bureau of Justice Statistics. "Firearm Use by Offenders." https://bjs.gov/content/pub/pdf/fuo.pdf.

Centers for Disease Control and Prevention. "Data & Statistics (Web-based Injury Statistics Query and Reporting System)." wisqars.cdc.gov.

"Chicago Shooting Victims." *Chicago Tribune*, February 10, 2015. www.crime.chicagotribune.com.

"Chicago Shooting Victims." *Chicago Tribune*, March 22, 2015. crime.chicagotribune.com/chicago/shootings.

Defilippis, Evan, and Devin Hughes. "New Study Is Latest to Find That Higher Rates of Gun Ownership Lead to Higher Rates of Violent Crime." *The Trace*, June 24, 2015. https://www.thetrace.org/2015/06/new-study-is-latest-to-find-that-higher-rates-of-gun-ownership-lead-to-higher-rates-of-violent-crime/

Everytown for Gun Safety. "Analysis of Recent Mass Shootings." August 2015. https://everytownresearch.org/documents/2015/04/analysis-of-recent-mass-shootings.pdf.

Follman, Mark, Gavin Aronsen, and Deanna Pan. "A Guide to Mass Shootings in America." *Mother Jones*. https://www.motherjones.com/politics/2012/07/mass-shootings-map/.

Follman, Mark, Gavin Aronsen, and Deanna Pan. "US Mass Shootings, 1982–2012: Data From *Mother Jones'* Investigation." *Mother Jones.* https://www.motherjones.com/politics/2012/12/mass-shootings-mother-jones-full-data/.

Krouse, William J. "Gun Control Legislation." Congressional Research Service. https://fas.org/sgp/crs/misc/RL32842.pdf.

Morris, Hugh. "Mapped: The Countries With the Most Guns (No Prizes for Guessing #1)." *The Telegraph*, October 22, 2016. https://www.telegraph.co.uk/travel/maps-and-graphics/mapped-the-countries-with-the-most-guns/.

ProCon.org. "Should More Gun Control Laws Be Enacted?" https://gun-control.procon.org/?print=true.

Simon Rogers. "Gun Homicides and Gun Ownership Listed by Country." *The Guardian*, July 22, 2012. www.theguardian.com.

Small Arms Survey. http://www.smallarmssurvey.org/home.html.

United Nations Office on Drugs and Crime (UNODC). "Global Study on Homicide." Access date October 30, 2014. www.unodc.org.

# A Tale of Two Worlds: Rich and Poor

*Extremely rich and increasingly poor, a defining narrative of many modern societies.*

The disparity between rich and poor people, along with related problems, is not new. Oxfam recently called for action to tackle the growing gap between the rich and the poor. According to their "Research and Publications," just 42 of the richest people have wealth equal to the poorest half of the world's 7.4 billion population. That 42 people was 61 last year, and 380 in 2009. In this country Bill Gates, Jeff Bezos, and Warren Buffett sit on a combined $248.5 billion fortune, which is as much wealth as the 160 million making up the bottom half of the US population.

## Analysis of Wealth

According to "Billionaire Bonanza 2017," by Chuck Collins and Josh Hoxie, the growing gap between rich and poor is now critical because it has created a moral crisis. In 2017, the four hundred richest people in the United States were worth a combined $2.68 trillion. To see what this means, we refer to the Oxfam reports indicating that 82 percent of the global wealth generated in 2017 went to the wealthiest 1 percent. Also, as mentioned as above, forty-two people hold the same wealth as the world's 3.7 billion poorest. The booming global stock markets have been the main reason for increase in wealth of people holding financial assets during 2017. The founder of Amazon, Jeff Bezos, saw his wealth rise by $6 billion in the first ten days of 2017 because of a bull market on Wall Street, making him the world's richest man. The charity (Oxfam) also points out that, on average, the wealth of billionaires had risen by 13 percent a year in the decade 2006 to 2015, with the increase of $762 billion in 2017 enough to end extreme poverty seven times over. Incidentally, 90 percent of the world's billionaires are men.

## Wealth and Life Expectancy

Here's another effect of poverty: According to Richard Luscombe, the average life expectancy now varies by more than twenty years depending on where a person lives in the United States. In "Inequalities in Life Expectancy Among US Counties, 1980 to 2014," we read that America's life expectancy gap is predicted to grow even wider in the future, with 11.5 percent of counties having experienced an increase in the risk of death for residents aged 25 to 45 over the period studied (1980–2014). No previous study has put the disparity at even close to twenty years. While residents of certain affluent counties in central Colorado had the highest life expectancy at eighty-seven years, people in several counties of North and South Dakota, typically those living on Native American reservations, could expect to die far younger, at only sixty-six. Overall, average life expectancy in the United States is 79.1 years, an increase of 5.3 years from 1980.

## Social Differences

According to "Same City, Different Worlds," by Gabe Rosenberg, not only has the income divide in the United States grown wider, but rich and poor people now effectively occupy different worlds, even when they live in the same cities and states. Rosenberg notes that cities and their residents are now shaped by poverty and wealth, but very unevenly. In places such as Columbus, Ohio, the outcomes can be alarming. In "Segregated City: The Geography of Economic Segregation in America's Metros," Richard Florida and Charlotta Mellander conclude that Columbus has the second-highest level of economic segregation among our nation's cities, second only to Austin, Texas.

## Final Words

Fortunately, there is no real difference between rich and poor after basic needs are met. The poor have fewer choices, but many valuable things can't be bought with money, such as character, principles, honesty, trustworthiness, morals, politeness, respect, thoughtfulness, and family. These are lifestyle choices available to all people. After all, a $5,000 watch and a $50 watch both tell the same time. The same loneliness lives in $100,000 houses and $4,000,000 houses. Fortunately, true happiness is not found in material things. It comes from health, love, family, and the things we value. We all end up in holes of the same size.

Nonetheless, poverty has many negative effects on people's well-being. Americans are tolerant of wealth difference but intolerant of inequality in opportunity, unlike people in most other countries. Maybe instead of leaving it to the government, rich people need to help more—and some of them need to practice what they preach.

## References

Collins, Chuck, and Josh Hoxie. "Billionaire Bonanza 2017: The Forbes 400 and the Rest Of Us." Institute for Policy Studies. https://inequality.org/wp-content/uploads/2017/11/BILLIONAIRE-BONANZA-2017-Embargoed.pdf.

Dwyer-Lindgren, Laura, Amelia Bertozzi-Villa, Rebecca W. Stubbs, Chloe Morozoff, Johan P. Mackenbach, Frank J. van Lenthe, Ali H. Mokdad, and Christopher J. L. Murray. "Inequalities in Life Expectancy Among US Counties, 1980 to 2014: Temporal Trends and Key Drivers." *JAMA Internal Medicine* 177 (2017): 1003–1011. https://jamanetwork.com/journals/jamainternalmedicine/fullarticle/2626194.

Florida, Richard, and Charlotta Mellander. "Segregated City: The Geography of Economic Segregation in America's Metros." Martin Prosperity Institute, University of Toronto, Rotman School of Management. http://martinprosperity.org/media/Segregated%20City.pdf.

Luscombe, Richard. "Inequality Gap Widens as 42 People Hold Same Wealth as 3.7bn Poorest." http://www.iran-daily.com/News/208550.html.

Luscombe, Richard. "Life Expectancy Gap Between Rich and Poor US Regions Is 'More Than 20 Years.'" *The Guardian*, May 8, 2017. https://www.theguardian.com/inequality/2017/may/08/life-expectancy-gap-rich-poor-us-regions-more-than-20-years.

Oxfam. "Research and Publications." https://www.oxfamamerica.org/explore/research-publications/.

Rosenberg, Gabe. "Same City, Different Worlds." *Chasing the Dream*, WOSU Public Media, November 6, 2017. http://www.pbs.org/wnet/chasing-the-dream/stories/city-different-worlds/.

# East-West Confusion

*It is hard to judge others with one's own cultural logic.*

I am an immigrant who loves America dearly. I came to the United States in 1988 at the age of forty-three, and except for a year in Illinois, I've lived in a small rural town in Pennsylvania. Through hard work and determination, my family and I realized our dream and have a successful and comfortable life. Like most educated people around the world, before moving to the United States I had great respect and admiration for this country, especially for its contributions to science, technology, and human development.

Since I've experienced life in other countries, I naturally compare the lifestyles, beliefs, outlooks, views, and perceptions of the people in the places I lived. I expected that as time passed, I would do less of this, but I was wrong—mainly because of the worldwide growth of Islam and its effect on people's everyday lives. Twenty years ago, most Americans weren't concerned about Islam, but now it has become a huge concern for many people. Some of my friends who know my background ask me questions that indicate their concern and confusion.

Unfortunately the American press, whose job is to inform people in an unbiased way, perpetuates misinformation. Most actions of Muslims are judged by American values and logic, which often leads to unhelpful conclusions. The same is true in how other countries view America, but to a lesser extent, since the rest of the world knows significantly more about the United States through movies and news media. American news media bundles Muslim countries together as one, despite significant differences between them.

Therefore I thought it might be useful to present my thoughts and observations, and to analyze them from two different angles or views. Both interesting and educational, this process can help us learn more about ourselves and other people.

## Example

Recently there was an article in our local newspaper regarding prayer before a football game. The author was obviously a considerate person with good intentions, and I understood the general idea and reason behind the article. However, it's unreasonable to argue that prayer might make a Muslim student uncomfortable, and this example illustrates my point. People with even a little knowledge about Islam know that no prayer to either God or Jesus will make a Muslim uncomfortable. A Muslim will be much more uncomfortable sitting in a classroom with liberally dressed female students, which happens every day, rather than listening to a prayer before a football game.

## Summary of My Observations

According to "A Comparison of Eastern and Western Culture," the East values spiritualism and the West values materialism. People of the East care more for the development of the soul and life after death than for the life and physical comforts of this world. Westerners, on the other hand, are more worldly minded. Unconcerned with eternal life, they want to enjoy their present life. In the West we see more of the race for wealth, luxury, and comfort. Maybe because the East has been the birthplace of religious teachers—Christ, Buddha, Mohammad, and Gandhi—the trend is set. The West is the home of the Renaissance and modern science and technology, and wonderful inventions have allowed for a great deal of power over nature.

The temperaments of Easterners and Westerners are also different. Easterners learn tolerance and self-sacrifice, and they expect little from their government, partly because they have never been given much. They can bear the greatest hardships for other people and sacrifice their own good for their family and friends. Because of their political insecurity, they stick to each other like family on rainy days. They make friends with whom they have much in common, knowing the importance of such relationships. They try to view someone in a governmental organization as a customer who is always in a weak position. Most Westerners, on the other hand, trust their government and authority more and let them handle the problems. There is also less corruption in the West.

Finally, different philosophies are prominent in these cultures. In the East are Buddhist, Confucian, Hindu, Integral Yoga, Islamic, Taoist, and Zen modes of thought. In the West, Christianity, rationality, scientific, and logical philosophies are common.

## References

Study Mode. "A Comparison of Eastern and Western Culture," October 20, 2011. https://www.studymode.com/essays/a-Comparison-Of-Eastern-And-Western-812135.html

# Globalization: A Problem or a Solution?

## A Critical Poem

*Globalization is the process of interactions and integrations*
*It takes place between people and governments of different nations*
*It is driven by international trade, investment, and cultural relations*
*Its popularity and speed is aided by technology and access to information*
*The process has effects on environment, culture and on communication*
*And more so on economic development, prosperity, and human condition.*

## Some Pros and Cons

*Globalization has potential to make the world better and solve some deep-seeded problems*
*But could also lead to fear, abuse, human trafficking, and labor exploitation*
*It could result in disappearance of physical borders between the nations*
*But may help creation of virtual borders inside countries resulting in polarization*
*Losing borders could mean losing one's identity leading to tension and discrimination*
*Many countries interfere with free trade practice through new form of manipulation*
*That kills what globalization hopes to achieve namely lower prices through competition*
*It provides richer countries with an opportunity to get right through incursion*
*It also creates tax havens in some countries for large multi-national corporations.*

## Globalization

The world is constantly changing—expanding, shrinking, moving apart, and getting closer, all at the same time. Some analysts believe this is a result of globalization, a process that intensifies social relations and shapes local affairs by events occurring in faraway places. They also believe that globalization makes some communities feel they are gradually losing their livelihoods, identities, and freedom to act, while trying to adjust to rapid changes occurring around the world. Moreover, the massive shift of populations, capital, and production systems has made many people feel vulnerable and anxious, resulting in an environment of frustration, conflict, and social unrest.

Thanks to globalization, borders between large communities and countries have disappeared and reappeared in different places within these countries. In the United States we see evidence of this phenomenon under a variety of names and titles.

So the major question is which of the two following choices is better for countries such as the United States?

1. Try to get out of the global agreements, protocols, supply chains, and exchanges they have built with others, and try to negotiate new agreements and establish new borders.
2. Seek to make their present entanglements work.

Support for choice 1 is evident from the popularity of the ideas partially presented by Trump's camp, the British vote for Brexit, and the electoral successes of nationalist and protectionist politicians in democracies worldwide. In "There's Never Been a Better Time to Be Alive," we read that what is happening in the United States, England, Germany, France, Greece, Brazil, Austria, the Philippines, and other countries reminds us that our new openness and connectedness cannot be taken for granted. Beyond economic effects, globalization has really become a test of the human character. It has created hope, opportunity, and prosperity for some people, but conflict, anxiety, pessimism, anger, despair, and even violence for others. Some groups have even started using their shared beliefs and identities to specify targets of hostility, legitimize aggression, and coordinate action.

According to Charles Lerche in "The Conflicts of Globalization," while globalization seeks to homogenize, it also increases awareness of social heterogeneity. Groups whose identity and solidarity is based on race, ethnicity, religion, or language have become increasingly vocal and use the global media to make their discontent known. Some people have developed strategies to defend their values and identities. In some cases, the same has happened to internal groups who believe that the state in which they live no longer promotes and protects their domestic interests, but instead is collaborating with outside forces.

Lerche mentions prominent political analysts who have argued variations of the same theme. Samuel Huntington, for instance, considers inter-civilizational conflict as the new danger to the dominant powers in world affairs. According to Huntington,

"The efforts of the West to promote its values of democracy and liberalism as universal values, to maintain its military predominance and to advance its economic interests engender countering responses from other civilizations." He also thinks that any future world war will be fought not between countries, but between civilizations.

## References

Lerche, Charles O. "The Conflicts of Globalization." *International Journal of Peace Studies* 3, no. 1 (January 1998). http://www.gmu.edu/programs/icar/ijps/vol3_1/learch.htm.

Plus Company Updates. "There's Never Been a Better Time To Be Alive. So Why the Globalization Backlash?" July 13, 2016.

# Gender Equality

*Let us wish that one day we find great minds sexier than great bodies.*

Gender equality has been a topic of interest throughout history. Today in the United States, men and women are considered equal in the sense that they have the opportunity to do the same things if they wish. Legally, both women and men can vote, own land, and have high-paying jobs, but we need to realize that men and women have some natural differences.

According to the Bureau of Labor Statistics, 57 percent of the world's working-age women are in the labor force, compared with 70 percent for men. Based on this statistic, some people might argue that men are still getting picked for jobs over women, but this is not true. We have to think about how men and women are different in this instance. Women are more likely than men to leave their jobs, for reasons such as pregnancy or the desire to have a big family. Although some men voluntarily leave their jobs, it is far more common for women to do so. This gap in percentages is not caused by men holding more jobs than women, but because men and women have different mind-sets and priorities.

Another hot topic in the United States today is women in the military. Because of a relatively new law, all positions in the US military are open to either sex, including combat positions. Some people argue that the bar for women should be lower than for men, but that's not fair to anyone. It is a proven fact that men are physically stronger than women. On average, men have twenty-six pounds more of skeletal muscle than women, which makes it easier for men to pass combat training tests than women. Women should definitely have the same opportunities as men, but men and women are different, so it's no surprise that combat is easier for men. Similarly, women have an advantage when it comes to jobs that involve caregiving, simply because they have more talent or patience with nursing.

In many countries, people value what each gender contributes to the society. Being a mother, for example, is highly valued in many countries, but not in Western countries. This forces many women to seek jobs and build careers outside the home. Though this is helpful to a society in one way, it may be harmful in other ways. Both genders are important, and societies should think more about equity than equality.

Men and women should have the same opportunities, but that doesn't mean they should be forced into equality. The two genders have different strengths and weaknesses, and we cannot ignore the value and necessity of both. Although men and women are different, it's only fair that they be given the same opportunities. These days people live longer and need more care, so women are in more demand for caregiving jobs, whereas men do more of the risky jobs such as working in mines, driving trucks, and construction.

## References

Bureau of Labor Statistics. "Civilian Labor Force Participation Rate, by Age, Sex, Race, and Ethnicity." https://www.bls.gov/emp/tables/civilian-labor-force-participation-rate.htm.

# Pay Discrimination

*It could be a fact, but then it could be a paradox too.*

Consider a business with one hundred employees, fifty Type A and fifty Type B, with comparable duties and average pay of $16,000 (total payroll = $800,000) and $14,000 (total payroll = $700,000) per person per year respectively. Type A employees earn more than Type B employees, suggesting a pay discrimination in favor of Type A. But when we consider the details, we find that the data contains other relevant information. Length of employment also factors into pay rates.

Suppose that ten Type A employees have been working for the company for fewer than five years with an average pay of $10,000 (total payroll = $100,000), and forty Type A employees for more than five years with an average pay of $17,500 (total payroll = $700,000). $100,000 + $700,000 = $800,000.

In the Type B group, forty employees have been working there for fewer than five years with average pay of $12,500 (total payroll = $500,000) and ten employees for more than five years with average pay of $20,000 (total payroll – $200,000). $500,000 + $200,000 = $700,000.

This analysis suggests that the average pay of Type B employees is higher than that of Type A employees in both categories, suggesting a pay discrimination in favor of Type B employees—which contradicts our earlier conclusion.

## Final Words

This example demonstrates how different analyses of the same data may lead to apparently conflicting results and sometimes incorrect decisions. The lesson is that making decisions based on averages is not a straightforward process. We must be careful in reporting averages unless the groups under consideration are homogeneous. The problem gets even more complicated (and interesting) if we consider more than one classifier, such as education or experience.

# Pollution

*A problem of the industrialized world.*

The *American Heritage Science Dictionary* defines pollution as the "contamination of air, water, or soil by substances that are harmful to living organisms. Pollution can occur naturally, through volcanic eruptions, for example, or as the result of human activities, such as the spilling of oil or disposal of industrial waste." Some people believe that our planet is being destroyed at an alarming rate because of the way the human race has treated it over the past few centuries. They point out that with advancement has come a high rate of pollution. As a result, millions of people do not have access to clean drinking water, often because of industrial run-off invading bodies of water. In addition, animal species are going extinct and chronic illnesses are rising.

Air pollution has damaging effects on human cognitive ability, a conclusion arrived at by Zhang, Chen, and Zhang in "The Impact of Exposure to Air Pollution on Cognitive Performance." According to "State of Global Air 2018," a report from the Health Effects Institute, nearly 95 percent of the world's population currently live in areas with air pollution exceeding global air quality guidelines. Zhang et al. cite data from nationwide cognitive tests in China, including scores of verbal and mathematics questions for over 31,000 individuals, which were compared with air quality data from 2010 to 2014. They concluded that polluted air impairs cognitive ability as people age.

In the past five years, air pollution has increased by 8 percent, according to "Air Pollution Levels Rising in Many of the World's Poorest Cities," a World Health Organization publication. This alarming statistic is based on data compiled from three thousand cities. China is no longer the country with the most polluted air, not because the Chinese government has taken steps to clean their air, but because other countries are becoming more polluted. The most polluted countries include Bahrain, India, Iran, and Egypt. According to "The State of Consumption Today," Americans make up about 5 percent of the global population but consume 25 percent of the world's natural resources. Every year, people use more of the world's natural resources than can be produced. Soon there will be no fuel to burn, water to drink, or food to eat. Between pollution, which has caused an exponential rise in chronic illnesses such as lung cancer, and the high yearly depletion of natural resources, the future of our world looks dismal.

According to "Top 10 Most Polluted Countries in the World," living in one of the cleanest countries in the world ensures a happy and healthy life. Young children who need special care especially benefit from growing up in a clean environment. Countries that are the most polluted have dirty air—containing dirt, smoke, pollen, mold, and other particulates—that can destroy respiratory systems. When pollution is inhaled, it accumulates in the respiratory system and causes chronic disease. According to the World Health Organization, estimates indicate that approximately seven million deaths can be attributed to air pollution each year. The best indicator used for assessing health impacts that result from air pollution is PM2.5, measuring the concentration of air pollution in micrograms per cubic meter of air.

"Top 10 Most Polluted Countries in the World" gives us a quick glance at the countries with the dirtiest air and highest levels of air pollution, based on their average PM2.5 pollution.

1. Pakistan
2. Qatar
3. Afghanistan
4. Bangladesh
5. Iran
6. Egypt
7. Mongolia
8. United Arab Emirates
9. India
10. Bahrain

These ten countries have the least polluted urban areas:

1. Australia
2. Brunei
3. New Zealand
4. Estonia
5. Finland

6. Canada
7. Iceland
8. Sweden
9. Ireland
10. Liberia

## References

BioFriendly Planet. "Countries with the Highest and Lowest Levels of Air Pollution," February 1, 2018. https://biofriendlyplanet.com/eco-awareness/air-quality/air-pollution/countries-least-polluted-urban-areas/.

Health Effects Institute. "State of Global Air 2018." https://www.stateofglobalair.org/.

TopTeny. "Top 10 Most Polluted Countries in the World." https://www.topteny.com/top-10-most-polluted-countries-in-the-world/.

World Health Organization. "7 Million Premature Deaths Annually Linked to Air Pollution." https://www.who.int/mediacentre/news/releases/2014/air-pollution/en/.

World Health Organization. "Air Pollution Levels Rising in Many of the World's Poorest Cities." http://www.who.int/news-room/detail/12-05-2016-air-pollution-levels-rising-in-many-of-the-world-s-poorest-cities.

Worldwatch Institute. "The State of Consumption Today." http://www.worldwatch.org/node/810.

Zhang, Xin, Xi Chen, and Xiaobo Zhang. "The Impact of Exposure to Air Pollution on Cognitive Performance." *Proceedings of the National Academy of Sciences* 115, no. 37 (September 2018): 9193–9197. http://www.pnas.org/content/115/37/9193.

# Prostitution

*A problem and yet a solution.*

Prostitution is a complex issue that has been the subject of intense debate in some countries for many years. To a large extent, the focus of these debates has been on legalization of what people refer to as the world's oldest profession. Since the mid-1980s, prostitution has been a subject of legislative action in the United States. According to Janice Raymond in "Legalization of Prostitution Is a Gift to Traffickers," some European countries, most notably the Netherlands and Germany, have legalized and/or decriminalized systems of prostitution, which includes decriminalizing pimps, brothels, and buyers. Some countries—Thailand, for instance—legally prohibit prostitution activities and enterprises, but in reality tolerate brothels and the buying of women for commercial sexual exploitation, especially in its sex tourism industry. Sweden has taken a different legal approach, penalizing the buyers while at the same time decriminalizing the women in prostitution.

In "Top 10 Reasons Why Prostitution Should Be Legalized," Dave Anderson says that African and Asian countries legally prohibit prostitution and any activities associated with it, including running of brothels and pimping. Prostitution is also illegal in the United States, except in some parts of Nevada. The spread of sexually transmitted diseases, such as HIV/AIDS, and increased risk of sexual exploitation, violence, and trafficking are the most disconcerting issues why some countries choose to keep it illegal. However, countries such as the Netherlands, Germany, Indonesia, New Zealand, and Canada legally accept the exchange of money for sex. Mexico, Argentina, Austria, France, and Italy also allow prostitution, but do not allow pimping and running of brothels. Some people believe that legalizing prostitution brings lots of benefits, not only for the workers but also for the economy as well.

Business Insider's Dylan Love had his expectations shattered when he reported on a Nevada brothel and observed that legalized, well-regulated prostitution can be both safe and profitable. Nevada allows prostitution only in licensed brothels that test workers routinely for sexually transmitted infections. Although Love is not the first to observe that legal prostitution can be relatively safe, Nevada's rural counties are the only place in America where the world's oldest profession is officially allowed.

## Should Prostitution Be Legalized?

Many prominent politicians have suggested the legalization of prostitution so that American citizens may consider it a legitimate occupational option. Countries around the world have legalized prostitution because if regulated, it reduces crime and the spread of STDs. Three things make the legalization of prostitution sensible: liberty, safety, and taxed income.

First and foremost, people should have the liberty to choose what they want to do with their bodies. But when we look at countries such as Germany or France, we see that legalizing and regulating prostitution can create a safer environment. Germany has a €14.5 billion sex trade industry, as well as being the largest market for prostitution in the European Union. Also, a law enacted in 2016 makes it illegal to have sex without a condom when engaging in relations with prostitutes.

Along with legalization of prostitution and brothels, regulations regarding hygiene and safety can be put into place. Brothels are legal in Germany, but a license is required to own one. Anyone found in violation of any of these laws—whether pimps or buyers of prostitutes—could be fined between 1,000 and 50,000 Euros. All of these regulations promote the safety of sex workers.

The sex trade in America is also unusually large, representing a lot of income that is not being taxed. Atlanta's sex trade earned almost $300 million just in 2007, according to Erin Fuchs in "Atlanta's Underground Sex Trade Is Booming."

High rates of prostitution can point to underlying structural problems in the United States. Many people who seek out prostitutes do so because of a sex addiction, and a high percentage of people are intoxicated when they purchase sex in the United States.

Also, it's not the case that people necessarily want to work as prostitutes; most of the sex trade is provided by people who can't find other opportunities. As Carina Kolodny says, "The researchers found people largely stay in or come back to the sex trade because they can't find work that makes as much elsewhere."

But this raises other questions. What would be the legal age to register as a prostitute? Should legalization happen at the state or federal level? If prostitutes have insufficient health care (or none at all), would they have access to free STD screenings, birth control, and other care? These are all important questions to be addressed if prostitution were to be legalized in the United States.

## Summary

There are some evidence that legal prostitution reduces violence and sex crimes. It would also protect minors, give employment rights to sex workers, guarantee sex workers' rights to their own bodies, and make the sex trade healthier. In addition, legal prostitution could help in the fight against human trafficking, save the country a lot of money, and benefit the country through taxes.

## References

Anderson, Dave. "Top 10 Reasons Why Prostitution Should Be Legalized." List Land, December 8, 2014. https://www.listland.com/top-10-reasons-prostitution-legalized/.

Fuchs, Erin. "7 Reasons Why America Should Legalize Prostitution." Business Insider, November 13, 2013. https://www.businessinsider.com/why-america-should-legalize-prostitution-2013-11?IR=T.

Fuchs, Erin. "Atlanta's Underground Sex Trade Is Booming." Business Insider, March 12, 2014. https://www.businessinsider.com/atlantas-sex-economy-is-booming-2014-3.

Kolodny, Carina. "9 Things You Didn't Know About American Prostitution." Huff Post, March 14, 2014. https://www.huffingtonpost.com/2014/03/12/sex-trade-study_n_4951891.html.

Raymond, Janice G. "Legalisation of Prostitution Is a Gift to Traffickers." Eye on Human Trafficking 15 (2007). http://southafrica.iom.int/system/files/drupal-private/EYE_2007.pdf.

# Bullying, A Universal Epidemic

*A burning desire for feeling superior.*

We are approaching the end of summer and the time to complain about something other than heat. It is also the time for tens of millions of kids to return to school, some happy and excited and some not so happy. Bullying is a major reason for some students to be anxious about returning to school.

## Bullying

Bullying can be defined as the use of superior strength or influence to intimidate or force someone to do what one wants. In 2014, according to "Facts About Bullying," the Centers for Disease Control and Prevention and the Department of Education jointly released the first federal uniform definition of bullying for research and surveillance. The core elements of the definition include unwanted aggressive behavior, observed or perceived power imbalance, and high likelihood of repetition.

## Modes and Types of Bullying

Bullying is divided into two modes and four types. The modes are (1) direct, such as bullying that occurs in the presence of a targeted youth, and (2) indirect, such as bullying not directly communicated to a targeted youth, such as spreading rumors. The four types include broad categories of (1) physical, (2) verbal, (3) relational (e.g., efforts to harm the reputation or relationships of the targeted youth), and (4) damage to property.

Electronic bullying or cyberbullying involves primarily verbal aggression (e.g., threatening or harassing electronic communications) and relational aggression (e.g., spreading rumors electronically). Cyberbullying can also involve property damage resulting from electronic attacks that lead to the modification, dissemination, damage, or destruction of ones' privately stored electronic information.

Various sources try to quantify the total amount of bullying that occurs. Among these sources are the National Education Association, the PACER Center, and StopBullying.gov.

An estimated 160,000 US children miss school every day because they're afraid of attack or intimidation by other students. One out of every ten students who drop out of school does so because of repeated incidents of bullying.

Almost 50 percent of children in grades four through twelve have reported being bullied and about 31 percent admit to bullying others. The most common types of bullying are verbal, social, physical, and cyberbullying. Middle-school students experience bullying in various ways. For instance, 44.2 percent are called names, 43.3 percent are teased, 29.2 percent are hit, 32.4 percent are pushed or shoved, 28.5 percent are left out, and 27.4 percent are threatened. Rumors or lies affect 36.3 percent, sexual comments and gestures affect 23.7 percent, and email and blogging affect 9.9 percent. These are just a few examples of various types of bullying that affect middle-school students.

Bullying can occur in any age group. It also occurs within the workplace and in the adult world. Adults bully each other in different ways. They may be sneakier or perhaps just childish about it. Many people are bullied or singled out for things such as religion, beliefs, race, ethnic background, and sexuality.

Some types of bullying—harassment, hazing, or assault, for example—fall into criminal categories. Twenty-eight percent of US students in grades six–twelve and 20 percent of US students in grades nine–twelve have experienced these types of bullying.

Of young people, 70.6 percent say they have seen bullying in their schools. Bullying has been seen by 70.4 percent of school staff, with 62 percent witnessing it two or more times in the last month, and 41 percent witnessing it once a week or more. When bystanders intervene, bullying stops within ten seconds 57 percent of the time.

Nine percent of students in grades six–twelve and 15 percent of students in grades nine–twelve experience cyberbullying, but a staggering 55.2 percent of LGBTQ students experience cyberbullying. "Facts About Bullying" also says that 40.6 percent of students report some type of frequent involvement in bullying, with 23.2 percent being frequently bullied, 8 percent who frequently bullied others, and 9.4 percent playing both roles frequently.

According to www.martialyou.com, the most common types of bullying are verbal and social. Physical bullying happens less often, and cyberbullying happens the least frequently. Most bullying takes place in school, outside on school grounds, and on the school bus, but bullying also happens wherever kids gather in the community. Of course, cyberbullying occurs on cell phones and online.

According to one large study (StopBullying.gov) the following percentages of middle school students have experienced bullying in these various places at school: classroom (29.3 percent), hallway or locker (29.0 percent), cafeteria (23.4 percent), gym or PE class (19.5 percent), bathroom (12.2 percent), and playground or recess (6.2 percent). Only 20 to 30 percent of students who are bullied notify adults about the bullying.

The United States has an average amount of bullying compared with other countries, according to a World Health Organization survey.

## Bullying and Suicide

"Facts About Bullying" points out that the relationship between bullying and suicide is complex. Many media reports oversimplify this relationship, either insinuating or directly stating that bullying can cause suicide, but the facts tell a different story. In particular, it is not accurate and potentially dangerous to present bullying as the cause or reason for a suicide, or to suggest that suicide is a natural response to bullying. It is recommended that the news media avoid using the word "bullycide."

Research indicates that persistent bullying can lead to or worsen feelings of isolation, rejection, exclusion, and despair, as well as depression and anxiety, which can contribute to suicidal behavior, according to "Facts About Bullying." Most young people who are bullied do not become suicidal, and most young people who die by suicide have multiple risk factors. Some, such as LGBTQ youth, are at increased risk for suicide even when bullying is not a factor.

## References

National Education Association. http://www.nea.org/.

"Facts About Bullying." StopBullying.gov. December 27, 2018. National Law Enforcement Officers Memorial Fund https://www.stopbullying.gov/media/facts/index.html.

"Bullying Facts." National Bullying Prevention Center. https://www.pacer.org/bullying/resources/facts.asp.

# Natural Disasters: A Real Global Problem

*Natural disasters do not discriminate.*

Natural disasters have a profound impact on the environment and the socio-economic system. They do not recognize gender, race, or religion, and they claim the lives of many innocent people, especially those who are most vulnerable. Although natural disasters occur frequently and cause a great deal of destruction and suffering, they do not receive the attention they deserve—unless they happen close to home. Natural disasters are hardly a subject of lobbying. One look at the budget allocated to events affecting celebrities versus those effecting underrepresented people makes it clear how such decisions are made.

All of this happens despite the fact that in recent years, the world, including the United States, has witnessed many catastrophic natural disasters. The residential and commercial development along coastlines and areas that are prone to disasters suggests that future losses will only grow—a trend that emphasizes, as never before, the need for further research, investigation, and education. In "Normalized Hurricane Damage in the United States," by Rogers et. al., the team of scientists found that the increase in economic damage from hurricanes, for example, in the United States, has been caused by greater population, infrastructure, and wealth along coastlines—*not* a spike in the number or intensity of hurricanes. According to that investigation, the economic cost of hurricane damage in the United States has doubled every ten to fifteen years.

## Consequences of Natural Disaster

Natural disasters are a potential threat to the world community, and to reduce their impact, complete international cooperation is essential. EM-DAT data discussed in "The Human Cost of Natural Disasters" tells us that between 1994 and 2013, 1.35 million lives have been claimed on average per year. "Cost of Natural Disasters," published by the Weather Channel, says that the economic damage from natural disasters has quadrupled in recent decades.

Disasters degrade the social and economic conditions of the most vulnerable people, resulting in deteriorating health and a decline in education and other social services. For some nations, the political economy of disasters results in negative effects on balance of payments, increased food import needs, and opportunity costs caused by the diversion of development resources to relief activities. Ensuing economic consequences also lead to a degradation of the social structures that uphold human rights, resulting in a further marginalization of those people already discriminated against because of such factors as class, gender, race, or religion. It is therefore important to situate disasters in a larger perspective and to view relief, disaster preparedness, and development as part of the same continuum. The world can no longer afford to take a pay-as-you-go approach to natural disasters and the consequences.

The United Nations designated October 11 as the International Day for Natural Disaster Reduction, to remind us of the great human suffering and losses. The experience of recent years shows that improved public education is essential to the success of natural disaster reduction, which aims to reduce, through appropriate action, loss of life and property damage. While activity at the local or national level is necessary, the world also needs active and informed citizens furthering safe societies on a global scale. Such a global citizenry may be promoted through school curricula, as well as within the overall pre-college curriculum, social studies, and especially geographical education. The emphasis must be on the study of disaster rather than on a list of behaviors to be adopted in the event of impending disaster.

It is important to note that disasters result from people's vulnerability to natural events and their inability to cope with these natural forces. Vulnerability itself is a result of social, cultural, and economic processes. While schools can and should promote appropriate behavior in the face of potential hazards, they also have a responsibility to help young people understand the physical and human systems that, in certain combinations, lead to disasters.

Education in a larger scale is, of course, the responsibility of the news media. After all, natural disasters do not respect borders, race, or religion. They are really everybody's problem and nobody's fault, and those usually most affected are the socially disadvantaged groups who are least equipped to cope with them. Making disaster reduction a priority in public policy is essential if we want a safer, healthier, and more productive world in the twenty-first century.

## Summary

Natural disasters continue to claim the lives of many innocent people, especially those who are most vulnerable. The impact of natural disasters, in terms of human and economic losses, has risen in recent years and society has become more vulnerable to natural disasters. While the number of lives lost has declined in the past twenty years, the number of people affected has risen in the past decade. As the world's population increases and areas previously almost uninhabited become more heavily settled, the propensity for natural disasters to cause damage also increases. In addition to physical effects, disasters degrade the social and economic conditions of people most vulnerable, resulting in deteriorating health and a decline in education and other social services.

It is important to situate disasters in a wider perspective and view relief, disaster preparedness, and development as part of the same continuum. The world can no longer afford to take a pay-as-you-go approach to natural disasters and their consequences. While activity at the local or national level is necessary, the world needs active and informed citizens furthering safe societies on a global scale as well. Such a global citizenry may be promoted through school curricula, and within the overall pre-college curriculum, social studies, and especially geographical education. Within this curriculum, the emphasis must be on the study of disaster rather than on a list of behaviors to be adopted in the event of impending disaster.

## References

Weather Channel. "Cost of Natural Disasters Has Quadrupled in Recent Decades, Official Says," June 6, 2014. https://weather.com/science/environment/news/cost-natural-disasters-has-quadrupled-recent-decades-official-20140606/.

Wallemacq, Pascaline, Debarati Guha-Sapir, and Denis McClean. "The Human Cost of Natural Disasters: A Global Perspective." Centre for Research on the Epidemiology of Disasters, March 2015. https://www.researchgate.net/publication/317645955_The_Human_Cost_of_Natural_Disasters_-_A_global_perspective.

Weinkle, Jessica & Landsea, Chris & Collins, Douglas & Musulin, Rade & Crompton, Ryan & Klotzbach, Philip & Pielke, Roger. (2018). "Normalized hurricane damage in the continental United States 1900–2017. Nature Sustainability." 10.1038/s41893-018-0165-2.

# Are We Sensible About Risks?

*I thought we are, but then I realized that we are not.*

A driver who refuses to pass over a bridge until he has personally tested the soundness of every part of it is not likely to go far. Some things have to be risked in life. Risk pervades virtually all areas of human endeavor, whether these endeavors be for personal, social, commercial, or national purposes. It is important to know how to evaluate risk if choices are to be made meaningfully.

## The Media Effect

Studies have found that people's attitudes toward risk are often formed based on the coverage of these risky events in popular media and their local newspapers. For example, some people think that traveling by plane is inherently more dangerous than driving, because plane crashes are often headline news. One study examined the coverage by newspapers in New Bedford, Massachusetts, and Eugene, Oregon, and found the following patterns:

- Although diseases take about sixteen times as many lives as accidents, the newspapers contained more than three times as many articles about accidents.
- Although diseases claim almost one hundred times as many lives as do homicides, there were about three times as many articles about homicides than disease-related deaths.
- Furthermore, homicide articles tended to be more than twice as long as articles reporting disease and accidental deaths.

People who read these newspapers assessed the risk of death by homicide as much greater than the risk of death by accident—which, in turn, was much greater than the risk of death by disease. Although this assessment was incorrect, nevertheless, it was a correct interpretation of the deaths about which they read. In other words, the readers' number sense was working correctly with bad information.

Another study investigated the ordering of perceived risk by two groups of ordinary citizens and experts regarding certain risky activities and technologies. Out of twenty such activities, ordinary citizens ranked nuclear power as the riskiest, but experts ranked it the least risky. The deviation from the expert's ordering is believed to be partly a result of the news coverage and the group membership.

## Risk Perceptions

Students at the University of Oregon, recruited by an ad in the student newspaper, were randomly given Form I or Form II of a questionnaire about vaccination. Form I described a disease expected to affect 20 percent of the population and asked people whether they would volunteer to receive a vaccine that protects half of the people receiving it. Form II described two mutually exclusive and equi-probable strains of the disease, each likely to affect 10 percent of the population. The vaccine would provide complete protection against one strain of the disease but no protection against the other. Even though both vaccination forms proposed no risk to the volunteers and offered a reduction of the probability of the disease from 20 to 10 percent, the framing of the situation led to a "yes" response of 57 percent for Form II, but only 40 percent for Form I.

A different study published in *Scientific American* explores, at length, the role that the framing of a choice plays in the resulting decision. Compare, for example, the following pair of choices:

- Choice A: Collect $50 for sure, or gamble with a 25 percent chance of winning $200 and a 75 percent chance of winning nothing.
- Choice B: Losing $150 for sure, or gamble with a 75 percent chance of losing $200 and a 25 percent chance of losing nothing.

For A, most people preferred not to gamble, whereas for B, most preferred to gamble even though the expected outcomes are identical.

Finally, here is an interesting example of how we think about risk-related situations. The winning ticket in a lottery was 865304. Three people compare the tickets they hold to the winning number. John holds 361204, Mary holds 965304, and Bill holds 865305. All three lost since the chance of losing was only 999,999 in a million.

Why was Bill quite upset, compared with Mary and John, who were only mildly disappointed?

## References

Slovic, Paul, Baruch Fischhoff, and Sarah Lichtenstein. "Behavioral Decision Theory Perspectives on Protective Behavior." In *Taking Care: Understanding and Encouraging Self-Protective Behavior*, edited by N. D. Weinstein, 14–41. New York: Cambridge University Press, 1987. https://scholarsbank.uoregon.edu/xmlui/bitstream/handle/1794/22331/slovic_250.pdf?isAllowed=y&sequence=1.

Amos Tversky; Daniel Kahneman The Journal of Business, Vol. 59, No. 4, Part 2: The Behavioral Foundations of Economic Theory. (Oct., 1986), pp. S251-S278.

# Chapter 8
## Expository/Miscellaneous

*Knowledge is a tree with unlimited branches.*

*I am miscellaneous and do not fit in any category*
*But I am happy to have my own individual territory*
*I do not need to say things that are customary*
*I cover anything I wish, nothing is force or mandatory.*

# Why a Police Officer?

*To judge what police officers do and why, put yourself in their shoes for just a day.*

In the past few years, the death rate of police officers has skyrocketed, according to a report from the National Law Enforcement Officers Fund. The report shows that from 2017 to 2018, the total fatality rate of officers increased by 14 percent. In 2017, approximately 43 out of 122 law enforcement deaths were firearms related. Between January 1 and November 28, 2018, those numbers increased to forty-nine out of 128 deaths being firearms related. These statistics have completely erased my thoughts of becoming a police officer. I respect police officers a lot, because an average person cannot endure the stress and pressure on those officers.

For as long as cops have been in service to this great nation, they have always been members of a highly respected profession. This is one of the many reasons some people want to become police officers. They believe that when a person puts on that badge, they are given the power to make a difference in the lives of other people. They have the power to protect and save lives, which is a noble thing. Being a police officer means helping those in your community, whether that means saving someone's life or getting a drug user the help they need.

Another reason some people want to be a cop is for the salary. According to the Bureau of Labor Statistics, in 2017 the median salary for cops was $62,960, and there are usually annual salary increases for cops who continue to serve in the same precinct. Most precincts offer overtime pay as well, and officers get great retirement and insurance packages that make it possible to enjoy an early retirement. Officers usually retire after twenty to twenty-five years in the force. Another reason to be a police officer is because it's easy to advance in rank.

There are also a number of career options once a person becomes a police officer. They can advance to sergeant or sheriff, or go down a different path and become a detective. To obtain these jobs, they need a bit of extra studying and a lot of experience on the job. The unpredictability is also intriguing. Every day is different and there will always be something new to do, so it is difficult to become bored. But one of the biggest reasons to become a police officer is to make a difference in the community. Police officers are ready to commit to the people of their township and put their lives on the line so that other people can live better lives.

According to the BLS, between 2016 and 2026 the number of people who want to become cops will increase by about 53,000, and the job outlook will improve by about 7 percent. The fear of not being able to get a job after college terrorizes many of today's youth, and competition is fierce for a lot of occupations. However, there will always be a need for public safety, so becoming a police officer may be a wise choice.

## References

Bureau of Labor Statistics, US Dept. of Labor. "Police and Detectives." *Occupational Outlook Handbook.* https://www.bls.gov/ooh/protective-service/police-and-detectives.htm.

National Law Enforcement Officers Fund. "Preliminary 2018 Law Enforcement Officer Fatalities." https://nleomf.org/preliminary-2018-law-enforcement-officer-fatalities.

National Law Enforcement Officers Memorial Fund. "144 Law Enforcement Officer Fatalities Nationwide in 2018." GlobeNewswire News Room. December 27, 2018. https://www.globenewswire.com/news-release/2018/12/27/1678383/0/en/144-Law-Enforcement-Officer-Fatalities-Nationwide-in-2018.html.

# Are Americans Happy?

*The United States does not shine on the happiness map, but it is certainly visible enough.*

In the United States, recent changes caused by advances in technology and globalization have called into question whether the resulting lifestyle changes are truly beneficial. The things that make us happiest in life are simplicity, human relationships, peace, and serendipity, but young people are obsessed with texting, tweeting, and posting the details of their lives. Although technology connects us in ways that we could never have imagined a few years ago, it sometimes adds to our insecurities and worries. Another factor in this equation is the state of affairs in this country. According to some studies, America is facing an all-time high corruption rate in government and regarding social issues. How have these changes affected our happiness?

A recent 2017 online Harris Poll surveyed 2,345 adults through a number of multiple-choice questions. The results are as follows:

- Overall about 774 out of 2,345 Americans surveyed were "very happy."
- There was a 2 percent drop in happiness in the last five years (now 33 percent).
- There appears to be a direct correlation between levels of stress and declining economic conditions and happiness.
- Stress levels decrease as individuals grow older. When stress levels decrease, happiness levels increase.
- The "happiest" age group are individuals 65+ (41 percent happy), and the unhappiest are 30 to 39 (28 percent happy). This confirms the theory that older people are happier.
    - 18 to 24 years old (31 percent of age group is happy)
    - 25 to 29 (30 percent of age group is happy)
    - 30 to 39 (28 percent of age group is happy)
    - 50 to 64 (36 percent of age group is happy)
    - 65+ (41 percent of age group is happy)

Of course, this survey provides no substantial evidence supporting or rejecting any meaningful theory about happiness. Here are issues with this article.

- The poll used only an online survey, which means that people who do not use technology avidly were excluded from the poll. This includes the poor and individuals who not have access to technology. Because of the idea that technology could lead to unhappiness, excluding those participants from the survey leads to a skewed result.
- The population of the United States is around 325.7 million. Using less than 1 percent, a small sample lacks reliable representation of American happiness.
- These results do not say how many individuals were interviewed in each age category. Obviously a survey based on ten adults is not equivalent to one based on ten thousand.

Americans may be declining in happiness because of our increased stress and fast-paced lives. To improve our happiness as a society, we need to learn where and how to look for happiness—to be content with what we have and value what is important.

# Democrat-Republican Statistics

*A never-ending dispute, a never-ending conflict.*

The early twenty-first-century American political landscape is littered with extreme partisan ideologies, politicians out of touch with their constituents, and public policies that favor polarizing partisan values instead of legislation that actually has the power to make lasting positive effects on American citizens. The landscape is dominated by politicians willing to sacrifice their moral values for political expediency, and collaboration and bipartisanship are extremely rare. One of the most divisive issues has been the 2016 presidential election between Republican nominee Donald Trump and Democratic nominee Hillary Clinton, which pitted these two political ideologies against each other. The three factors that most strongly influence political affiliation in the United States are education, age, and gender. It is believed that more education and a younger age correlate with being more likely Democratic, and less education and an older age correlate with being more likely Republican.

Most of the statistics used here are retrieved from a *New York Times* article covering the statistics of voters during the 2016 presidential election. The polling was conducted by Edison Research, and the sample size was 28,935. The polling was done randomly and 24,537 of the 28,935 were polled from 350 voting places across the country. The remaining 4,398 were randomly polled via telephone interviews.

Of the 28,935 individuals polled, 18 percent (roughly 5,208) held a high school diploma or less, and another 18 percent held an associate's degree. Of the remaining 64 percent, 32 percent (roughly 9,259) held a bachelor's degree, and 32 percent held a postgraduate degree. Of the 18 percent who held high school diplomas or less, 51 percent voted Republican compared with 45 percent who voted Democrat. Of the 18 percent who held an associate's degree, 52 percent voted Republican and only 43 percent voted Democrat. Of the 32 percent who held a bachelor's degree, 49 percent voted Democrat compared with 43 percent who voted Republican, while the remaining 32 percent who held postgraduate degrees overwhelmingly voted Democrat at 58 percent compared with only 37 percent who voted Republican.

Next, 48 percent (13,889) polled were male and the remaining 52 percent (15,046) were females. Of the males polled, 53 percent voted Republican and 41 percent voted Democrat. Of the females polled, 54 percent voted Democrat and 42 percent voted Republican.

The last category evaluated was age. This poll was divided into four age groups: 18–29, 30–44, 45–64, and 65 and older. Of those surveyed, 5,498 were 18–29; 7,234 were 30–44; 11,574 were 45–64; and 4,340 were 65 or older. Of the two youngest age groups, 18–29 and 30–44, a little over 50 percent voted Democrat (55 percent and 50 percent respectively), compared with only about 40 percent who voted Republican (37 percent and 42 percent respectively). Of the two lower age groups, the average who voted Democrat was roughly 52.5 percent, and approximately 39.5 percent voted Republican. Of the two older age groups, 53 percent ages 45–64 voted Republican and 53 percent 65 and older voted Republican, compared with the 44 percent ages 45–64 who voted Democrat and 45 percent ages 65 and older who voted Democrat. The average who voted Republican for both older age groups was 53 percent, whereas only 44.5 percent voted Democrat.

Based on these statistics, it is reasonable to hypothesize that younger, more-educated voters are more likely to align with the Democratic Party, while older, less-educated voters are more inclined to align with the Republican Party. Another factor that affects party alignment is gender, and the data suggests that women are far more likely to align with the Democratic Party, while men are more inclined to align with the Republicans.

In conclusion, younger, more-educated women are more likely to identify with the Democratic Party, and older men who lack a higher education degree are more inclined to identify with the Republican Party. Of course, more education does not necessarily correlate with better judgment, but being older and more experienced might.

## References

Huang, Jon, Samuel Jacoby, Michael Strickland, and K. K. Rebecca Lai. "Election 2016: Exit Polls." *New York Times*, November 8, 2016. https://www.nytimes.com/interactive/2016/11/08/us/politics/election-exit-polls.html.

Webster, Tom. "Behind the Numbers: The 2016 National Election Exit Poll." Edison Research, November 10, 2016. http://www.edisonresearch.com/behind-numbers-2016-national-election-exit-poll/.

# Why Do Some Young Muslims Become Extreme?

*Not only could pain from our strongest needs and desires override their joy
and pleasure, but they could lead to extreme frustration and anger.*

Many Westerners must wonder why some Muslims do the things we hear about these days. I personally can think of two reasons, one applicable to individual Muslims and the other to groups representing Islam as a political tool or ideology. It's well known that most Islamic laws restrict expression and manifestation of some of the strongest human needs and desires. For example, the need for relationships with the opposite sex and romance, in particular, is strongest in most healthy young adults. Nevertheless, Islamic law and Muslim society allow only legal marriage and forbid any relationship, including socialization, prior to marriage. This is not helpful to young adults, because they cannot get married until they have a stable source of income, place to live, and so on. Most people living in urban areas can't get to this level until they reach their mid-twenties, and that's if they're lucky.

Meanwhile, this forced suppression of their natural needs and urges dictates, to a large extent, their views and outlook on the world. Many young, unmarried Muslims become depressed, angry, emotional, irritable, and short tempered. These feelings manifest in their extreme behaviors, which are often hard to rationalize. Watching Western movies often adds to their frustration and anxiety, because they conflate Hollywood culture with the typical Western lifestyle. Byproducts of this phenomena are jealousy and hate for Westerners, especially Americans, because they are the major producers and promoters of this fantasy life.

At a group level, Muslims see themselves as victims of unfair treatment. They feel that they are left behind to watch others in the West make progress, enjoy life, and go beyond their basic needs. They see themselves as a society with practically no contribution to modern life and recent advances. As a result, they feel unsatisfied and believe they are not respected. They notice that being Muslim is associated only with negative terms such as *terrorism* and *suicide bomber*. They find themselves having no choice but to follow the West in almost all aspects of life, and they develop a dislike for their own lives. As a result, they believe most conspiracy theories, including the theory that the West plans to take advantage of their countries and natural resources. Additionally, they see that stand-out Muslims leave their countries for more freedom and a better life and settle in the West. This process is exacerbated by governments in Muslim countries who force Islamic laws on them by any means necessary, and Western news that constantly criticizes their own government and amplifies even minor wrongdoings.

So where do all these frustrations go? Well, partly toward other Muslims, especially the leaders who practically act as dictators. Another part, possibly bigger, is toward Westerners and their system. They blame the West for every little problem, since they cannot take on their own government which has a zero tolerance for opposition. Some make up stories and accept extreme conspiracy theories that are often untrue and unreal. All these factors eventually lead to extreme views, lack of trust, and negativities that are hard to change or correct. With a little attention, encouragement, or the promise of a better life (especially the romantic part), young Muslims are easily absorbed into extreme groups.

## Why Muslims Hate America

Most people in other countries think that Americans are self-serving and self-centered with almost no regard for other countries' affairs and cultures. This is evident to them as they watch American news media and read American newspapers. While millions of people face serious problems such as war, internal conflicts, and crooked elections, American media hardly covers or even mentions such events. Instead, they cover every detail of the lives of actors, singers, athletes, and politicians, or they focus on sex scandals.

When a typical Muslim watches a gay marriage, romance between two men, or Hollywood celebrities proudly announcing the details of their relationships with several people, they get extremely angry and look at Americans as people who proudly celebrate values that Muslims consider wrong. They believe that Americans don't care about moral issues. They notice how American athletes with tattoos and strange hair are worshiped by millions of fans, while deserving people are ignored. They don't understand why a group of half-naked young girls need to dance in the middle of a football game. In short, they see America as a society where anything of this nature has become normal and everyday. Although most of these thoughts are incorrect, they are understandable when we consider that American media is their only source of information.

# Alcoholism Is More Prevalent Than We Think

*Many individuals are normal until they introduced to alcohol.*

Drinking has been an accepted part of Western culture for generations, associated with everything from weddings to wakes. Studies show that moderate consumption of alcohol decreases the risk of heart disease, ischemic stroke, and diabetes. However, excessive misuse of alcohol creates many problems and takes an extremely heavy toll on families and society.

## Global Alcohol Statistics

Alcohol, a semi-luxury beverage, is also a drug that acts on the central nervous system. Intemperate indulgence had always been regarded as either a bad habit or a sin, but we didn't realize that alcoholism is a disease until the turn of the 21$^{st}$ century. According to the World Health Organization, alcohol misuse causes 3.3 million deaths annually and contributes to more than two hundred diseases and injuries. Globally, it is the fifth-leading risk factor for premature death and disability among people aged 15–49 and the first risk factor for people 20–39.

## US Alcohol Statistics

The National Institute on Alcohol Abuse and Alcoholism reports a variety of statistics, some gathered from the National Survey on Drug Use and Health. In the United States, alcohol misuse costs approximately $250 billion annually. It is responsible for approximately 88,000 deaths (62,000 men and 26,000 women) per year, making it the fourth-leading preventable cause of death. In 2013, of the 72,559 liver disease deaths in age group twelve and older, 45.8 percent were alcohol related. It was also the primary cause of almost one in three liver transplants. Drinking alcohol increases the risk of cancers of the mouth, esophagus, pharynx, larynx, liver, and breast. The article "Statistics on Alcoholics" contains additional data on alcohol in the United States.

- Alcohol is the number one drug problem.
- There are more than twelve million alcoholics in the United States.
- Eighteen thousand people are killed in an alcohol-related car accident every year.
- In 2000, nearly seven million people between twelve and twenty years old were binge drinkers. Binge drinking is defined as having five or more alcoholic drinks on one occasion for men and four or more for women.
- Of all high school seniors, 75 percent report being drunk at least once.
- Young people who begin drinking before their fifteenth birthday are four times more likely to become alcoholics than those who do not begin drinking until the age of twenty-one.
- Surprisingly, people with a higher education are more likely to drink.
- People with higher incomes are more likely to drink.
- Excessive drinking is responsible for more than 4,300 deaths among underage youth each year.
- People ages twelve to twenty drink 11 percent of all alcohol consumed.

A variety of studies seek to quantify alcohol's effect on crime. For example, see the National Council on Alcoholism and Drug Dependence. The statistics on alcoholics listed above do not include additional victims of alcohol consumption who may not drink at all. Some studies say that alcohol contributes to 73 percent of all felonies, 73 percent of child beatings, 41 percent of rapes, 81 percent of wife beatings, 72 percent of stabbings, and 83 percent of homicides. Other studies estimate that while there are twelve million alcoholics, forty to fifty million additional people, such as family members, suffer the consequences of alcoholism.

## College Students

The following findings come from the 2015 National Survey on Drug Use and Health:

- 58 percent of full-time students ages eighteen–twenty-two drank alcohol in the previous month, compared with 48.2 percent of other people of the same age.

- 37.9 percent reported binge drinking in the past month, compared with 32.6 percent of other people of the same age.
- 1,825 students between eighteen and twenty-four die from alcohol-related unintentional injuries, including motor-vehicle crashes.
- 696,000 were assaulted by other students who had been drinking.
- 97,000 reported experiencing alcohol-related sexual assault or date rape.
- Roughly 20 percent meet the criteria for alcohol use disorder.
- About 25 percent report academic consequences for drinking, including missing class, falling behind in class, doing poorly on exams or papers, and receiving lower grades overall.

## Everything Has a Price

The excessive use or abuse of alcohol creates many problems and takes an extremely heavy toll on families and society. It is an example of the price societies pay for what is referred to as freedom of choice. The main drawback of such freedom is the price others have to pay for the choices we make. Alcoholism is one of the world's greatest health problems. Apart from environmental, sociocultural, and psychological influences, recent epidemiological studies have provided clear evidence of a genetically conditioned predisposition toward alcoholism.

## Is There Any Safe Level of Alcohol?

Although some medical studies—and a great deal of media attention—have focused on possible health benefits of drinking alcohol in moderation, a report published in *The Lancet* in August 2018 warns that the harm of alcohol greatly outweighs any potential beneficial effects. The study looked at data on twenty-eight million people worldwide and determined that considering the risks, there is no safe level of alcohol: "The conclusions of the study are clear and unambiguous: alcohol is a colossal global health issue and small reductions in health-related harms at low levels of alcohol intake are outweighed by the increased risk of other health-related harms, including cancer."

## References

Learn-About-Alcoholism.com. "Statistics on Alcoholics." https://www.learn-about-alcoholism.com/statistics-on-alcoholics.html.

National Council on Alcoholism and Drug Dependence. "Alcohol, Drugs and Crime."
   https://www.ncadd.org/about-addiction/alcohol-drugs-and-crime.

National Institute on Alcohol Abuse and Alcoholism. "Alcohol Facts and Statistics."
   https://www.niaaa.nih.gov/alcohol-health/overview-alcohol-consumption/
   alcohol-facts-and-statistics.

# Smoking: The Largest Preventable Cause of Death and Diseases

*Smoking, a global issue.*

The Centers for Disease Control and Prevention is one of many sources that attempts to quantify the prevalence of smoking in the United States. In 2015, an estimated 36.5 million US adults were cigarette smokers, of whom 27.6 million smoked every day and 8.9 million smoked some days. A smoker is a person who reports smoking at least one hundred cigarettes during his or her lifetime and who, at the time when they participated in a survey, reported smoking every day or some days. Fortunately, the percentage of the US population who smokes declined from nearly 21 percent in 2005 to about 15 percent in 2015.

## Risks

According to sites such as www.cancer.org, tobacco use remains the single largest preventable cause of death and disease in the United States. It kills more than 480,000 Americans each year, including more than 41,000 deaths from exposure to secondhand smoke. This accounts for 272,000 men and 208,000 women. Smoking kills more Americans than alcohol, car accidents, HIV, guns, and illegal drugs combined. It shortens male smokers' lives by about twelve years and female smokers' lives by about eleven years. Today, more than sixteen million Americans live with a smoking-related disease. The costs exceed $300 billion a year, including nearly $170 billion in direct medical care and $156 billion in lost productivity. About half of all Americans who keep smoking will die because of the habit, about fifteen of every hundred adults (2015).

According to the American Cancer Society, many experts believe that smoking causes cancer and can damage nearly every organ in the body, including the lungs, heart, blood vessels, reproductive organs, mouth, skin, eyes, and bones. It accounts for about 30 percent of all cancer deaths in the United States, including about 80 percent of all lung cancer deaths. Lung cancer is the leading cause of cancer death in both men and women, and it's one of the hardest types of cancer to treat. Smoking is also a risk factor for cancers of the mouth, larynx, pharynx, esophagus, kidney, cervix, liver, bladder, pancreas, stomach, colon/rectum, and blood cells. "Health Risks of Smoking Tobacco" says that smoking is by far the most common cause of chronic obstructive pulmonary disease (COPD), a condition with no cure classified as the third-leading cause of death in the United States. More women than men die from COPD. Smoking also causes chronic bronchitis and emphysema, which are the other types of COPD.

Smoking tobacco is also a major cause of coronary heart disease, as it damages heart and blood vessels. It also causes high blood pressure, lowers the ability to exercise, makes blood more likely to clot, and decreases HDL (good) cholesterol levels in the blood, which can cause or worsen poor blood flow to the arms and legs.

According to "Health Risks of Smoking Tobacco," women who smoke are more likely to have trouble getting pregnant and tend to be younger at the start of menopause than nonsmokers. Smoking also damages the arteries and blood flow, a key factor in male erections, resulting in a higher risk of sexual impotence. Smoking also leads to an increased risk of gum disease and tooth loss, and a smoker's wounds take longer to heal. Smoking also weakens the immune system and increases the risk of developing type 2 diabetes. Other effects include decreased sense of smell and taste, premature aging of the skin, bad breath, stained teeth, increased risk for cataracts, lower bone density, higher risk of developing rheumatoid arthritis, increased risk for age-related macular degeneration, and increased risk of peptic ulcers.

## Concluding Remarks

Many of the health problems linked to smoking can steal a person's quality of life long before death. Smoking-related illness can make it harder to breathe, move, work, or play. Quitting, especially at younger ages, can reduce smoking-related disability.

Teen tobacco users are more likely to use alcohol and illegal drugs. Cigarette smokers are also more likely to get into fights, carry weapons, attempt suicide, suffer from mental health problems such as depression, and engage in high-risk sexual behaviors. This does not necessarily mean that tobacco use causes these behaviors, but they are more common in teens who use tobacco.

Finally, smokers may also be responsible for many accidental fires and wildfires. According to *National Geographic*, on average, more than 100,000 wildfires clear four to five million acres of land in the United States every year. In recent years, wildfires have burned up to nine million acres of land. Home fires can also present an issue, as addressed in the article "Seven People Die Each Day in Reported U.S. Home Fires," which says that one in every 320 households per year had a reported home fire during a specific five-year period. These home fires caused an estimated average of 2,570 civilian deaths, 13,210 civilian injuries, and $7.2 billion in direct property damage per year.

## References

American Cancer Society. "Health Risks of Smoking Tobacco." https://www.cancer.org/cancer/cancer-causes/tobacco-and-cancer/health-risks-of-smoking-tobacco.html.

Centers for Disease Control and Prevention. "Burden of Tobacco Use in the U.S." https://www.cdc.gov/tobacco/campaign/tips/resources/data/cigarette-smoking-in-united-states.html.

Connecticut State Commission on Fire Prevention and Control. "Seven People Die Each Day in Reported U.S. Home Fires." https://portal.ct.gov/CFPC/_old/State-Fire-Administrator/General/Seven-People-Die-Each-Day-in-Reported-US-Home-Fires.

Creamer, MeLisa R., Gabriela V. Portillo, Stephanie L. Clendennen, and Cheryl L. Perry. "Is Adolescent Poly-tobacco Use Associated with Alcohol and Other Drug Use?" *American Journal of Health Behavior* 40, no. 1 (January 2016): 117–122. https://www.ncbi.nlm.nih.gov/pmc/articles/PMC4869866/.

"Learn More About Wildfires." *National Geographic.* https://www.nationalgeographic.com/environment/natural-disasters/wildfires/.

# Drug Overdose: A New Epidemic

*In 2017, more Americans died from opioids than in the Vietnam War.*

Drug overdose has become a serious problem in the United States and around the world. According to the Centers for Disease Control and Prevention (CDC), on average, ninety-one Americans die every day from an overdose of opioids such as heroin, the synthetic opioid fentanyl, prescription painkillers such as OxyContin, and now the elephant tranquilizer, Carfentanil. Drug use is now the leading cause of accidental death in America. In 2016, more Americans (around 60,000) died from drug overdoses than from AIDS, guns, or car crashes. In 2015, Pennsylvania, with 3,264 deaths, was ranked second only to California, with 4,659 deaths. This is significant, because the population of Pennsylvania is less than one-third the population of California.

Some studies, such as the "National Survey on Drug Use and Health," attempt to quantify substance abuse. According to some estimates, in the United States alone, more than twenty million people aged twelve and older struggle with a substance abuse disorder. Of that number, two million struggle with addiction to prescription painkillers and 600,000 suffer from heroin addiction. The Centers for Disease Control and Prevention reports that since 1999, the amount of prescription opioids sold on the market has quadrupled.

## Overdose

An overdose is defined as the intentional or accidental ingestion of a drug over the normal or recommended amount. The body's response to an overdose is often characterized by severe symptoms, because it's overwhelmed and unable to metabolize the drug quickly enough. An overdose can cause a person to fall into unconsciousness, enter a state of psychosis, or experience painful symptoms. Each type of overdose poses significant health risks, including contributing to a person's death.

Most people believe the opioid epidemic involves illegal drugs only, but it actually started with legal drugs. Back in the 1990s, doctors were persuaded to treat pain as a serious medical issue, and pharmaceutical companies took advantage of this. Through a big marketing campaign, they got physicians to heavily prescribe products such as OxyContin and Percocet—even though the evidence for opioids treating long-term chronic pain was very weak, and the evidence that opioids cause harm in the long term was very strong.

These painkillers proliferated, landing not only in the hands of patients, but also in the hands of teens rummaging through their parents' medicine cabinets, as well as family members and friends of patients, resulting in their easy availability on the black market. Subsequently, opioid overdose deaths trended up—sometimes involving opioids alone, at other times involving drugs such as alcohol or benzodiazepines typically prescribed to relieve anxiety.

According to German Lopez, having noticed the rise in opioid misuse and deaths, officials cracked down on prescription painkillers. Law enforcement, for instance, threatened doctors with incarceration and the loss of their medical licenses if they prescribed these drugs unscrupulously. These strategies were helpful, but many people who lost their access to painkillers remained addicted. Since they could no longer obtain prescribed painkillers, many addicts turned to cheaper, more potent opioids—heroin and fentanyl, a synthetic opioid manufactured illegally for nonmedical uses. This pushed the number of victims to a new high. In addition, according to a 2016 report by the surgeon general, only 10 percent of Americans with a drug use disorder obtain specialty treatment, partly because of the shortage of treatment options.

## Worldwide Statistics

Efforts have been made to quantify the number of drug-related deaths around the world, such as the information compiled by International Overdose Awareness Day. According to some international bodies, in 2014 there were about 207,000 drug-related deaths, with overdose accounting for up to half and with opioids involved in most cases. China accounted for 49,000 and Oceania, including Australia and New Zealand, had around 2,000. In European Union countries, more than 70,000 lives were lost to drug overdoses in the first decade of the twenty-first century.

## Final Words

Overdosing has replaced moderation in our culture. Every day, people are dying from overdose, and the numbers are growing at alarming rates. According to the Centers for Disease Control and Prevention, for opioid overdoses, the three-year period between 2014 and 2016 has been the deadliest, for several possible reasons:

1. The cost of heroin is roughly five times less than the cost of prescription opioids on the streets.
2. People who abuse or depend on prescription painkillers are forty times more likely to abuse heroin.
3. Treatment options are few or nonexistent.

Considering this situation, we need to take the following steps:

- Look at the problem more deeply, especially the social and behavioral side of it.
- Investigate why about 100 million Americans suffer from chronic pain despite the fact that we spend more money for health care than the next ten big spenders combined. (See "Institute of Medicine of the National Academies Report.")
- Seriously pursue policies that would curb this growing problem.

## References

"Behavioral Health Trends in the United States: Results from the 2014 National Survey on Drug Use and Health." https://www.samhsa.gov/data/sites/default/files/NSDUH-FRR1-2014/NSDUH-FRR1-2014.pdf.

Centers for Disease Control and Prevention. "Understanding the Epidemic." https://www.cdc.gov/drugoverdose/epidemic/.

Centers for Disease Control and Prevention. "Increases in Drug and Opioid Overdose Deaths." https://www.cdc.gov/mmwr/preview/mmwrhtml/mm6450a3.htm.

DARA: Drug and Alcohol Rehab in Thailand. "Overdose Facts, Myths and Symptoms." https://alcoholrehab.com/drug-addiction/overdose-facts-myths-and-symptoms/.

Lopez, German. "In One Year, Drug Overdoses Killed More Americans Than the Entire Vietnam War Did." *Vox,* June 8, 2017. https://www.vox.com/policy-and-politics/2017/6/6/15743986/opioid-epidemic-overdose-deaths-2016.

Institute of Medicine of the National Academies Report. "Relieving Pain in America: A Blueprint for Transforming Prevention, Care, Education, and Research." http://books.nap.edu/openbook.php?record_id=13172&page=5.

International Overdose Awareness Day. "Facts & Stats." https://www.overdoseday.com/resources/facts-stats/.

# Poems about Pi

*I love to say hi, I love to eat pie, I could eat it with coffee, but I really prefer chai.*

The ubiquity of pi (π) makes it one of the most widely known numbers, both inside and outside the scientific community. Pi is the ratio of a circle's circumference to its diameter. A circle is a corner-less geometric object—or as many mathematicians claim, a geometric object with an infinite number of corners.

> There once was a girl who loved pi
> I never could quite fathom why
> To her it's a wonder
> To me just a number
> Its beauty revealed by and by.
> —Eve Anderson

Pi day is celebrated on March 14. The official celebration begins at 1:59 p.m. to make an appropriate 3.14159 when combined with the date.

> Three point one four one five nine
> Makes the lazy student whine,
> But give this ratio a try—
> You'll find that it's as easy as pi!
> —Fred Russcol

People around the world celebrate the day by participating in a variety of activities. Some gather and tell jokes about pi, and others read poems with interesting connections to pi.

## Never Talk to Pi. He'll Go On Forever.

Consider humble pi. It is a number never ending.
It never repeats itself as its value keeps ascending.
Based upon a circle, many men have tried,
to calculate the ratio of its width to its outside.
It is called irrational because it cannot be made a fraction.
The challenge of its nature has been a call to action.
If you cannot appreciate why I hold this number high,
then shame! It is you that should be eating humble pie.
—Ken Johnson

## Pi Is Patternless

Ancient civilizations needed the value of pi to be computed accurately for practical reasons. In the twentieth and twenty-first centuries, mathematicians and computer scientists have extended the decimal representation of pi to—as of 2015—over 13.3 trillion ($10^{13}$) digits. Why? It is believed that the primary motivation for these computations is the human desire to break records—and in this case, to find out if digits of pi follow a random distribution.

It is a habit of mine,
A new value of pi to assign
It's simple you see,
Just to use three
Instead of three point one four one five nine.
—Clifford Morse

## References

Andersson, Eve. "Pi Poetry." http://www.eveandersson.com/pi/poetry/.
Nifty Ideas. "Thorsday Tonic: It's Pi Day!" March 14, 2013. www.niftyatheist.com.

# Pi in Pop Culture

*How did I become so famous? I guess my close-friend circle had something to do with it.*

The concept of pi ($\pi = 3.14 \ldots$) is deceptively simple. Pi is the ratio between a circle's circumference and its diameter. Although pi is never ending, the record for finding its consecutive digits from 3.14 onward has been broken several times in recent years. Attempting to recite, for example, only the first twelve billion digits of pi without stopping requires approximately 250 years. If typed in a normal-size font, it will reach from Kansas to New York City.

Number enthusiasts enjoy memorizing the digits of pi. Many use mnemonic techniques, known as piphilology, to help them remember. Akira Haraguchi from Japan is able to recite the digits from memory to 83,431 places and holds the world record. March 14, Pi Day, is also Albert Einstein's birthday.

## Pi in Pop Culture

Many references to pi can be found in pop culture. "All About Pi: Everything You Need to Know & Then Some" shares some of the following examples:

- Literary nerds invented a dialect known as Pilish, in which the numbers of letters in successive words match the successive digits of pi, as in these examples: "May I have a large container of coffee (3.1415926)" and "How I want a drink, alcoholic of course, after the heavy lectures involving quantum mechanics." Mike Keith wrote *Not a Wake* (Vinculum Press, 2010) entirely in Pilish.
- A Love like Pi is an electronic rock band with two pi-related albums.
- The 1998 movie *Pi*, directed by Darren Aronofsky, is about a lonely, paranoid mathematician named Max who believes that everything in life is governed by numbers.

- In a 1995 movie, Sandra Bullock is a computer software expert who stumbles across a nefarious online plot. She solves it by clicking on a pi symbol that appears on her computer screen.
- Pi plays a part in the season two *Star Trek* episode "Wolf in the Fold." Captain Kirk and Mr. Spock are able to conquer an evil being by using their computer to calculate all decimal places of pi.
- There's a music video about pi that has wizards, robots, and a graffiti artist.
- The song "Bye-Bye Miss American Pi" is a parody of Don Mclean's "American Pie," rewritten as "American Pi."
- The pi-related song "Lose Yourself (In the Digits)" by "Pi Diddy" is a parody of Eminem's rap song "Lose Yourself."
- The lyrics of the song "Pi" by Kate Bush include the decimal places (or maybe numbers) that make up pi.
- Givenchy makes a cologne for men called pi that smells like citrus and forests.
- The TV show that discusses what people search for on Google each day has a segment all about Pi Day.
- There is a website that allows one to download up to 50 million digits of pi. Its different sections include Pi Records, Pi People, Pi Literature, Pi News, and Pi Aesthetics.
- There is a website that includes all advanced mathematical properties of pi.
- The Pi Trivia Game allows someone to test his or her knowledge about pi. It includes twenty-five questions ranging from pi's history to its mathematical properties.
- There are several funny cartoons about pi, videos that use colored shapes, and pieces of music that teach the basic mathematical properties of pi.
- The clearly nerdy company Pi-Dye T-Shirts carries several kinds of T-shirts.

## Remarks

Let's celebrate Pi Day, but remember that

1. too much pi gives us a large circumference, and
2. our opinion without pi is just an onion.

Here are three different ways to approximate the value of $\pi$:

1. $\pi/2 \sim= (2x2x4x4x6x6x8x8x \ldots) / (1x3x3x5x5x7x7x9x \ldots)$
2. $\pi/4 \sim= 1 - 1/3 + 1/5 - 1/7 + 1/9 - 1/11 + \ldots$
3. $\pi \sim= 3 + 1/10 + 4/10^2 + 1/10^3 + 5/10^4 + 9/10^5 + \ldots$

The symbol "$\sim=$" means "approximately." They are not equalities but can be very close. Try them out in your calculator. It's fun!

## References

Lewis, Tanya. "Happy Pi Day! Fun Facts about Our Favorite Irrational Number." *Live Science*, March 14, 2014. https://www.livescience.com/44091-facts-about-pi-for-pi-day.html.

Student Guide. "All About Pi: Everything You Need to Know & Then Some." http://www.studentguide.org/all-about-pi-everything-you-need-to-know-then-some/.

# Coincidences: A Motivating Theme

*Coincidences are good teachers, and that itself is a coincidence.*

Like most of us, young people are fascinated by coincidences and analyses of them. Because of that, it is possible to develop lessons on mathematics and probability to grab their attention and get them excited about these subjects. I suggest the following, which is how I did it. Details may be found in "Coincidences—a Motivating Theme for an Introductory Probability Course" by Reza Noubary and Behzad Noubary.

1. Sample students attitudes toward coincidences and involve them in their analysis.
2. Provide a context for the instructor to develop technical concepts of mathematics and probability.

At this point, the students' responses have given a clear picture of the high degree of their naiveté about the concepts of mathematics and probability. More importantly, they have provided us with information that can be used for teaching these concepts. Here are details of what we did.

## Introduction

Teaching the basic concept of probability presents a challenge to instructors of introductory courses on mathematics, probability, and statistics. Most students approach these courses reluctantly and are suspicious of results obtained by the methods discussed in the class. Additionally, many are easily befuddled by complex formulas. Helping them overcome these obstacles—and like these subjects—is thus a difficult task.

To introduce students to these subjects, coincidence is a very good course theme. This is true whether or not they have any prior experience with probability or statistics.

As their teachers, we can relate the concepts to any experiences they might have had and thereby help them become more comfortable with the material. When students see a connection between what they study and a familiar subject that fascinates them, they usually show more interest and pay more attention. Additionally, students, like others, are intrinsically interested in the analysis of information about their own views and those of others.

Based on our experience, in addition to laying the groundwork and easing the difficulties of learning basic concepts, the questionnaire described below helps students develop a better attitude toward probability and statistics. Discussions stemming from the questionnaire increase class participation. We have noticed that students feel pride in seeing how their own experiences contribute to the development of the course. Many have mentioned that their participation helped them see firsthand that probability and statistics are disciplines with relevant applications and deep meanings. We think this approach is adaptable to all levels at which probability and statistics are taught.

The coincidence-centered teaching begins with a questionnaire, a version of which is shown below. On the first day of class, we give each student the assignment of completing the questionnaire for the next class period. To assure that students will participate carefully in this activity, we promise to count it as a quiz. When handing out the questionnaire, we ask students to read it over and make sure they understand each question. We speak with students individually and offer clarifications. Some questions may seem a little vague and confusing. However, every time we've used them, they've led to good class discussion—including discussion of the need for precise, agreed-upon definitions. The same questionnaire may be given to the students in the end of semester to see whether their responses remain the same or change.

## Opening Day Questionnaire

1. What is a coincidence? Explain.
2. Can you name a popular coincidence?
3. Why do people consider the event in question 2 a coincidence?
4. Could you name a coincidence that happened to you?
5. Why do you consider the event in question 4 a coincidence?
6. What makes a coincidence interesting?
7. Do you think coincidences are events with a very low probability of occurrence? If your answer is yes, how low?

8. What does the word *random* remind you of? Do you think we all perceive randomness the same way?

9. Do you think our intuition about coincidences is closely related to our understanding of randomness?

10. People react to coincidences according to whether they are willing to accept most of them as insignificant or insist on always finding a meaning behind them. Do you agree?

11. Did you know that a woman named Evelyn Marie Adams won the New Jersey Lottery twice, in 1985 and in 1986?

12. Did you know that of the first five presidents of the United States, three died on July 4? Would you classify this as a coincidence?

13. Suppose you are sitting in a class with thirty students. If you find that one or more students have the same birthday as you, will you be surprised? Will you consider this a coincidence?

14. Could you come up with an estimate for the probability of the event in question 12? Explain how you arrived at your estimate. Also, if you used words like *low* or *very low*, could you convert that to a numerical value?

15. Do you think other students would come up with the same estimate for the probability in question 12?

16. What kind of background information does a person need to make reasonable numerical estimates of the probability in question 12?

17. What branches of science are involved in the process of estimating or calculating the probability in question 12?

18. Two important elements of coincidences are (a) their probability of occurrence and (b) the degree of surprise if they occur. Do you agree?

19. If you flip a coin five times and observe heads every time, would you think that tails is due next?

20. If your answer to question 18 is no, would you conclude that the coin is not fair?

21. * What do you think about the following definition? "A coincidence is a surprising concurrence of events, perceived as meaningfully related, with no apparent casual connection."

22. According to *Webster's New Collegiate Dictionary (11ᵗʰ Edition)*, coincidences are the occurrences of events that happen at the same time by accident but seem to have some connections. What do you think about this definition?

23. ** Which of the following do you consider a reasonable statement?

A. Religious faith is based on the idea that almost nothing is coincidence.

B. Science is an exercise in eliminating the taint of coincidence.

C. Police work is often a feint and parry between those trying to prove co-incidence and those trying to prove complicity.

D. Without coincidence, there would be few movies worth watching, and literary plots would come grinding to a disappointing halt.

E. Coincidences feel like a loss of control. Believing in fate, or even conspir-acy, can sometimes be more comforting than facing the fact that some-times things just happen.

F. The really unusual day would be one in which nothing unusual happens.

* Definition suggested by Diaconis and Mosteller, *Journal of the American Statistical Association* 84, 1989.
** Discussions presented in article by Lisa Belkin, "The Odds of That", *New York Times*, August 11, 2002.

## Examples of Coincidences and Their Analysis

This section includes the discussion we present after collecting students' responses to the questionnaire. Referring to question 1 and students' general view toward coinci-dences, we usually start by mentioning that people often relate coincidences to the un-expected or unusual occurrence of an event or series of events. We ask students if they think this is the case. We then let them express their opinions and discuss opposing views. We continue by pointing out that people also think that coincidences are events with a very low probability of occurrence. We ask if they consider this line of thought reasonable. Usually a large number of students consider this reasonable. We ask what they consider a very low probability. The answer varies from 1 in 100 to 1 in 1,000,000. We then ask them to express their opinion about the following argument: Suppose that a coincidence is defined as an event with a one-in-a-million chance of happening to someone in the United States today. Given that there are 330 million people in the United States, this means that at least 330 times a day (more than 100,000 times in a year), that one-in-a-million event is going to occur. That is, it will occur to one person out of a million. Also, because people do many different things in a given day, some occurrences are even less likely to happen than others. We usually let students express and discuss their views. We encourage them to think about examples of this type. In response to this, one student mentioned that while driving to the university, his car started shaking on the highway. He stopped to check on the problem. While doing so, he found a hundred-dollar bill there in the middle of nowhere.

Next, we push toward deeper concepts by arguing that if we examine any significant event carefully, we would find many unusual occurrences and patterns that may seem like coincidences. Again, we ask students to think of examples for this. The student who found a hundred-dollar bill mentioned that the shaking of the car was a signal for him to stop because he needed the money badly. As a more universal case, we usually present examples such as the following, discussed earlier. Think about September 11 (9/11), for instance. The number 911 is used for emergencies. The twin towers looked like the numeral 11. So perhaps all the things that happened had something to do with the number eleven. Let us look at a few of them. First, $9 + 1 + 1 = 11$. The first flight to hit the twin towers was Flight 11 with 92 people on board—$9 + 2 = 11$. September 11 is the $254^{th}$ day of the year, and $2 + 5 + 4 = 11$ (also $365 - 254 = 111$). There are eleven letters each in *New York City*, *Afghanistan*, *the Pentagon*, and *George W. Bush*. Also, New York was the eleventh state admitted to the union, 119 ($1 + 1 + 9 = 11$) is the area code for both Iraq and Iran, and Flight 77, which crashed in Pennsylvania, had sixty-five people on board; $6 + 5 = 11$. Finally, recall the March 11 (2004) attack in Spain. There were exactly 911 days between it and the September 11 (2001) attack. These are all interesting facts, but taken together, do they mean anything? At this point we let students express their views about patterns of this type and their relations to the coincidences.

After the preliminary discussions, we continue by posing the question, Are coincidences as unlikely or as surprising as we think? We ask students to think about this example. People who win the lottery often attribute their winning to either their amazing luck or some special system they used in choosing a lottery number. Yet someone was bound to win, and it was merely luck that a particular person held the winning entry. We could conclude that many events classified as coincidences are bound to happen, even though the particular form of, let us say, a coincidence, is unpredictable. We then ask students to tell us what they think about the question and the example. This topic usually creates a lot of discussion among students.

We end this part by referring to a question about Evelyn Marie Adams, who won the New Jersey Lottery twice, in 1985 and 1986. Newspapers widely reported that this event had a probability of one in seventeen trillion. We ask students to think about the following statement: Given enough tries, the most outrageous things are virtually certain to happen (the law of large numbers). After discussing this, we return to the supposed one-in-seventeen-trillion double lottery winning and argue that this figure is the right answer to the wrong question, which is, What is the probability that a *preselected* person who buys just *two* tickets for separate lotteries will win on both?

The more relevant question is, What is the probability that *some* person, among the many millions who buy lottery tickets (most buying multiple tickets), will win twice in a lifetime? It has been calculated that such a double winning is likely to occur once in seven years, with the likelihood approaching certainty for longer periods.

Next, we turn to an example used in the questionnaire. One strange historical coincidence concerns presidents of the United States. Three of the first five presidents of the United States died on the same day of the year. That date was none other than the Fourth of July. Of all the dates to die on, that must surely be the most significant to any American. This might, of course, be part of the explanation for why the coincidences happened. You can imagine the early presidents being really keen to hang on until the anniversary of the country's independence, a date that meant so much to them, and giving up the ghost as soon as they knew they had reached it. This is apparently what happened to Thomas Jefferson, the third president. John Adams, the second president, actually died a few hours after Jefferson. We ask students to express their views about this example and ask if they think we have a strong reason to believe that this was a coincidence. It is interesting to note that this event surprises many students even more than the September 11 example.

Sometimes, we continue with an example from the world of sports, such as the Pro Football Hall of Fame. What is the probability of having two Hall of Famers from the same high school? Do you think this is a rare event? Here are some examples: Al Davis and Sid Luckman, George Halas and Leo Nomellini, Mel Renfro and Arnie Weinmeister, Elroy Hirsch and Jim Otto, Hugh McElhenny and Bill Walsh, and Bobby Layne and Doak Walker.

We then ask what they think about the examples discussed so far and whether they think these are really examples of coincidences. We also ask if they still think that coincidences are events with a very low probability of occurrence (rare events). The majority say yes. So, we continue with the next question. We ask if they know anything about poker. If not, we explain the basics and continue with an example of a hand of poker. We point out that the chance of getting a royal flush is very low (1 in 650,000). Thus, if we were to get a royal flush, we would be very surprised. But the chance of any hand in poker is very low, we point out. Here is the problem: we do not notice when we get all the others, but we notice when we get a royal flush. We ask if they can show that this is the case. We ask them to try it as homework. We usually go over it and the birthday problem described below at some stage during the course.

We usually point out that some of the arguments we are using may seem counterintuitive. We explain that they stem from the fact that on one hand, the world is so large that any event is likely to happen, and on the other hand, it is so small that it makes occurrences of unlikely events so surprising that one may classify them as coincidences. One relatively simple example of this is the birthday problem. Students have already responded to the question about this problem. We usually refer to some of the responses and the following facts. There are 365 days in a year, so we need to assemble 366 people in a room to guarantee at least one birthday match. But how many people do we need in a room to guarantee a 50 percent chance of at least one birthday match? We ask students to guess a number. Usually, their answers vary a great deal. We let them discuss or defend their guess. We then point out that, to most people's surprise, the answer is twenty-three. Next we talk about additional facts about birthday matches that often surprise them. Here are some examples: with only forty-one people, the chance of at least one common birthday is more than 90 percent. With eighty-eight people, the chance of at least three common birthdays is more than 50 percent. After covering the laws of probability, we show how these are calculated.

If students show interest, we then continue as follows. If we want a 50 percent chance of finding two people born within one day of each other, we need only four-teen people, and if we are looking for birthdays a week apart, the magic number is seven. Incidentally, if we are looking for an even chance of finding someone having a specific person's exact birthday, we need 253 people. We then ask why, despite num-bers like these, people are constantly surprised when they meet a stranger with whom they share a birth date, a hometown, or a middle name. Again, we let students discuss this. Next, we change the question and put it in the following format. Why do you think most people are amazed by the overlap of this type and yet conveniently ignore the countless things they do not have in common with others? At this point, we ask students to discuss this further and try to find other examples of this type and, if they like, present them to the class.

To emphasize the point, we next present the following simple example involving probability. We ask students to calculate the probability that two randomly selected people will have birthdays on, for example, May 25 and October 13. We usually choose two students in the class and use their birthdays. The answer they should find or sug-gest (after we have provided hints) is $(1/365)^2$. We then change the dates to, say, June 9 and June 9 (again we choose someone's birthday in the class). Though unsure, they eventually produce the same answer. Then, we remind them that in both cases the probability is less than 1 in 133,000. We ask them if they consider this a small probabil-ity. Most students answer yes. Next, we ask which of these two events they find more surprising. All of them, of course, refer to the latter. This reveals that, although the two events are equally likely, the latter creates a great deal of surprise and therefore may be classified as a coincidence. We then ask students if they can think of other examples of this kind and, more importantly if they are convinced that the two main components of a coincidence are probability and the degree of surprise.

We end the class by looking at a couple of classical number patterns. Several of our students consider these coincidences. Some find them more surprising than some of the coincidences presented earlier. We usually remind students that noticing coincidences has played an important role in scientific discoveries. Some believe the ability to see obscure connections (those most people miss) is among the more important abilities a scientist can have. A good example of this comes from stories about Isaac Newton and his discoveries.

## References

Noubary, Reza, and Behzad Noubary. "Coincidences: A Motivating Theme for an Introductory Probability Course." *Proceedings of the Annual Meeting of the Decision Sciences Institute* (November 2008): 1601–1606. www.decisionscience.org.

Wynn, Dylan. *The History of Coincidences.* West Conshohocken, PA: Infinity, 2003.

# Beautiful Number Patterns

*Number patterns can elude even the brightest minds.*

Numbers are fascinating because they have some unusual properties. These properties bring some new "life" to the subject and make us take note of their beauty. In "The Beauty in Numbers" author Alfred S. Posamentier considers the following as some charmers of mathematics that depend on the surprising nature of its number system. Here, not many words are needed to demonstrate the charm, for it is obvious at first sight.

$1 \cdot 1 = 1$

$11 \cdot 11 = 121$

$111 \cdot 111 = 12321$

$1111 \cdot 1111 = 1234321$

$11111 \cdot 11111 = 123454321$

$111111 \cdot 111111 = 12345654321$

$1111111 \cdot 1111111 = 1234567654321$

$11111111 \cdot 11111111 = 123456787654321$

$111111111 \cdot 111111111 = 12345678987654321$

$0 \cdot 9 + 1 = 1$

$1 \cdot 9 + 2 = 11$

$12 \cdot 9 + 3 = 111$

$123 \cdot 9 + 4 = 1,111$

$1,234 \cdot 9 + 5 = 11,111$

$12,345 \cdot 9 + 6 = 111,111$

$123,456 \cdot 9 + 7 = 1,111,111$

$1,234,567 \cdot 9 + 8 = 11,111,111$

$12,345,678 \cdot 9 + 9 = 111,111,111$

$1 \cdot 8 = 8$

$11 \cdot 88 = 968$

$111 \cdot 888 = 98568$

$1111 \cdot 8888 = 9874568$

$11111 \cdot 88888 = 987634568$

$111111 \cdot 888888 = 98765234568$

$1111111 \cdot 8888888 = 9876541234568$

$11111111 \cdot 88888888 = 987654301234568$

$111111111 \cdot 88888888 = 98765431901234568$

$1111111111 \cdot 8888888888 = 987654321791234568$

$9 \cdot 9 = 81$

$99 \cdot 99 = 9,801$

$999 \cdot 999 = 998,001$

$9,999 \cdot 9,999 = 99,980,001$

$99,999 \cdot 99,999 = 9,999,800,001$

$999,999 \cdot 999,999 = 999,998,000,001$

$9,999,999 \cdot 9,999,999 = 99,999,980,000,001$

$999,999 \cdot 1 = 0,999,999$

$999,999 \cdot 2 = 1,999,998$

$999,999 \cdot 3 = 2,999,997$

$999,999 \cdot 4 = 3,999,996$

$999,999 \cdot 5 = 4,999,995$

$999,999 \cdot 6 = 5,999,994$

$999,999 \cdot 7 = 6,999,993$

$999,999 \cdot 8 = 7,999,992$

$999,999 \cdot 9 = 8,999,991$

$999,999 \cdot 10 = 9,999,990$

$9 \cdot 9 + 7 = 88$

$98 \cdot 9 + 6 = 888$

$987 \cdot 9 + 5 = 8888$

$9876 \cdot 9 + 4 = 88888$

$98765 \cdot 9 + 3 = 888888$

$987654 \cdot 9 + 2 = 8888888$

$9876543 \cdot 9 + 1 = 88888888$

$98765432 \cdot 9 + 0 = 888888888$

Posamentier says the famous mathematician Carl Friedrich Gauss (1777–1855) had superior arithmetic abilities to see relationships and patterns that eluded even the brightest minds. Posamentier thinks that the following are additional charmers of mathematics that depend on the surprising nature of its number system.

$1 \cdot 8 + 1 = 9$

$12 \cdot 8 + 2 = 98$

$123 \cdot 8 + 3 = 987$

$1,234 \cdot 8 + 4 = 9,876$

$12,345 \cdot 8 + 5 = 98,765$

$123,456 \cdot 8 + 6 = 987,654$

$1,234,567 \cdot 8 + 7 = 9,876,543$

$12,345,678 \cdot 8 + 8 = 98,765,432$

$123,456,789 \cdot 8 + 9 = 987,654,321$

$123456789 \cdot 9 = 111,111,111$

$123456789 \cdot 18 = 222,222,222$

$123456789 \cdot 27 = 333,333,333$

$123456789 \cdot 36 = 444,444,444$

$123456789 \cdot 45 = 555,555,555$

$123456789 \cdot 54 = 666,666,666$

$123456789 \cdot 63 = 777,777,777$

$123456789 \cdot 72 = 888,888,888$

$12345679 \cdot 81 = 999,999,999$

## References

Posamentier, Alfred S. "The Beauty in Numbers."
http://docplayer.net/26335538-1-the-beauty-in-numbers.html.

# Valid Mathematical Modeling

*There is more to mathematical modeling than just putting makeup on the data.*

Much remains to be learned about the construction of useful models in mathematics, because they ought to be useful not only to mathematicians but also to practitioners. This emphasizes the need to develop models applicable to a wide variety of disciplines together with the means of incorporating the rules of a particular field of application. Such models should also be understandable to their users with basic mathematical knowledge in their own jargon.

As an example, let me use my area of research: earthquake modeling. Many earth scientists think that in a great deal of mathematical modeling in this field, the emphasis has been on mathematics with little or no attempt to tie together the mathematical concepts with geological facts. They view this approach of modeling essentially as a mathematical exercise with a bit of geological justification. We may refer to this as geo-mathematics. In contrast, consider a situation in which a geological problem is investigated with mathematical tools but the mathematics is considered of purely secondary interest. The objective is to derive geological models that are testable, not to develop elegant mathematics (though both may occur). We may refer to this as mathematical geology. The point is that if one attempts to construct models with some basis in geological facts, there is a good chance that their analysis will lead to results that are both mathematically tractable and physically meaningful. Moreover, the validity of such models can be verified with methods other than goodness of fit. Often a by-product of such an approach is a model with the least number of parameters. Finally, the same can be said about bio-mathematics and mathematical biology.

In general, one finds two different possible attitudes toward applying mathematics and probability to areas such as biology, ecology, or (my own personal interest) seismology. In one of these, modeling is carried out solely based on goodness of fit. Curve fitting using regression and time series modeling are the best candidates for those who like this approach. In the second approach, the existing deterministic models developed by experts in a chosen discipline are either analyzed further or an extension is made to them by considering, for example, time-dependent solutions and spatial patterns, or by adding random variation. The latter is of more interest because of lack of knowledge, or uncertainties. Here the critical problem is to incorporate random variation into an established deterministic formulation in a way that is geologically meaningful and yet mathematically tractable.

In a simple language, mathematical modeling refers to the processes of seeking patterns or relationships between variables and presenting or expressing them using symbolic language. Models are but approximations of certain aspects of complex reality. A good model should lend itself to validation beyond a goodness of fit and should be acceptable to experts in the field. In short, we have to judge it not in terms of right or wrong, but in terms of insight and use.

# Why Japanese and Chinese People Cannot Tolerate Alcohol

*Well, that is what I have heard.*

According to data presented in the *Global Status Report on Alcohol and Health* by the World Health Organization, there are far fewer alcoholics in Japan and China than there are in many European countries. A reason for this may be their marked inability to tolerate alcohol. Scientists from the Institute of Human Genetics at the University of Hamburg have discovered that this manifestation is of genetic origin, because of an enzyme defect.

Alcohol (ethanol or ethyl alcohol), although a semi-luxury beverage, is also a drug that acts on the central nervous system to affect the essential psychomotor functions and has a long history in every cultural circle. Intemperate indulgence had always been regarded either as a bad habit or a sin, and the realization that alcoholism is a disease came only at the turn of the 21st century. Today alcoholism is one of the world's greatest health problems. Apart from environmental, sociocultural, and psychological influences, recent epidemiological studies have provided clear evidence of a genetically conditioned predisposition toward alcoholism. However, it is extremely difficult to draw the line between genetic influences on one hand, and social, cultural, and environmental factors such as religious upbringing, the price and availability of alcohol, and family drinking habits on the other. The dramatic rise in alcoholism and its associated diseases in the postwar period (after WWII), especially in Europe, is clearly attributable to an increase in per-capita consumption. This goes hand in hand with alcohol abuse, physical and mental dependence, and social and family problems, although severe addiction has been observed in only a small part of the population and to varying degrees of intensity in different cultural circles.

The question arises about whether alcoholics' personalities might differ from the majority of the population's even before the onset of the disease, whether we can talk about alcoholism as abnormal behavior, or whether alcoholics' biogenetic structure might be the underlying cause of their abnormal drinking habits, i.e., the development of their addiction.

There can be no doubt that the metabolism of alcohol is subject to a number of different influences that trigger individual variations in behavior patterns or toxic reactions after alcohol has been consumed. Articles such as "Genetic Research: Who Is at Risk for Alcoholism?" have addressed the role of genetics in alcoholism. The study cited in this particular article, conducted on families, twins, and adoptive relationships, revealed that genetic influence plays a major role in alcoholism. In 1999, the proportion of women among the 2 or 3 percent of the German population who were alcoholics (a total of some 1 to 2 million people) was only 10 percent. Today they represent some 30 percent, a rise that has brought a concomitant increase in the incidence of fetal alcohol syndrome, which has become the most common deformity of uniform genesis observed among newborn babies.

In the course of their studies on the problem of alcoholism, scientists in Hamburg have discovered an enzyme defect to be the underlying genetic cause of alcohol intolerance. It had long been known that a majority of Koreans were unable to tolerate alcohol compared with people of European ancestry, although the reason for this was attributable to neither state decrees nor strict morality. In other words, for many people of Mongoloid origin, consuming even small quantities of alcohol brings on flushing accompanied by reddening of the face, an accelerated pulse rate, and abdominal pain.

## References

Foroud, Tatiana, Howard J. Edenberg, and John C. Crabbe. "Genetic Research: Who Is at Risk for Alcoholism?" *Alcohol Research and Health* 33, no. 1 (January 2010): 64–75. https://pubs.niaaa.nih.gov/publications/arh40/64-75.pdf.

Goedde, H. W., H. G. Benkmann, L. Kriese, P. Bogdanski, D. P. Agarwal, D. Ruofu, C. Liangzhong, C. Meiying, Y. Yida, X. Jiujin, L. Shizhe, and W. Yongfa. "Aldehyde Dehydrogenase Isozyme Deficiency and Alcohol Sensitivity in Four Different Chinese Populations." Institute of Human Genetics, University of Hamburg. *Human Heredity* 34, no. 3 (1984). https://www.karger.com/Article/Pdf/153459.

World Health Organization. *Global Status Report on Alcohol and Health.* https://www.who.int/substance_abuse/publications/global_alcohol_report/msbgsruprofiles.pdf.

# Teenage Pregnancy

*Who is responsible for this problem?*

Teenage pregnancy is caused by lack of advice, awareness, family, and access to reproductive health education and services. Lack of knowledge about consequences as well as sexual violence can cast expectations on girls to become young mothers. Around the world, many young girls are forced into marriage because of religious or familial beliefs. Child marriage is a key factor in teenage pregnancies, especially on the continents of Africa and South America. The World Health Organization provides many statistics regarding adolescent pregnancy. They say that around 16 million girls between the ages of fifteen and nineteen give birth in developing regions and an additional 2.5 million girls fifteen years old or younger give birth each year. Of girls between the ages of fifteen and nineteen, 90 percent of births occur within marriage, which may be associated with the pressure to marry some girls face in some parts of the world. In the United States, our number of teen pregnancies is about 3 percent, according to statistics from the Office of Adolescent Health. Although this seems like a high percentage, it is significantly smaller than that of Africa.

In certain parts of Africa, most women do not have access to the resources they need to learn about giving birth and becoming a mother. Some places in Africa have higher levels of poverty and unemployment than others. These areas typically have more teen pregnancies. According to the United Nations Population Fund 2013, Sub-Saharan Africa had the highest amount of prevalence for teen pregnancy in the world.

The number of teenage pregnancies has decreased over the years with technology and other resources that have become available, yet in developing countries it might take longer for the number to drop significantly.

All over the world, teenage girls are getting pregnant between the ages of thirteen and nineteen, although they often think it will never happen to them. Teenage pregnancy is serious. It affects both young men and young women, but young men do not have to go through the same things that young women do. Teenagers may have to drop out of high school or college because of pregnancy. Pregnancy at a young age affects not only a teenager's appearance and personal life, but also the ability to get an education.

According to the Centers for Disease Control and Prevention, in age groups fifteen to nineteen, 22.3 per thousand women got pregnant in 2015, a drop of 8 percent from 2014. Since 2016, teenage pregnancy rates have been dropping. *Time* magazine reported that in that year, rates of teenage pregnancy hit a low of 9 percent globally.

According to the website Abort73, which uses data from the Guttmacher Institute and the Centers for Disease Control, nine other countries have higher rates of reported abortions than the United States: Bulgaria, Cuba, Estonia, Georgia, Kazakhstan, Romania, Russia, Sweden, and Ukraine. In North America, abortion is legal, with some limitations. In Latin America abortion is legal in every country except El Salvador. According to the Guttmacher Institute (2018), "during 2010–2014, an estimated 56 million induced abortions occurred each year worldwide. This number represents an increase from 50 million annually during 1990–1994, mainly because of population growth." Abortion rates have grown globally mainly because of population growth; women in developing countries have a greater chance of having an abortion. The safety of abortions has improved worldwide, and laws are becoming less restrictive. According to the Guttmacher Institute's 2018 report, "between 2000 and 2017, 33 countries expanded the circumstances under which abortion is legally permitted." Many countries allow women to have abortions according to their reasoning, health, and age. Some countries have a higher rate of abortion while also having a lower national income.

## Summary

Abortions are legal in most countries around the world, albeit with restrictions. Globally, abortion rates have increased, although they have decreased in the United States. Unmarried women are more likely to get an abortion, but their main reason is simply not being ready to have a child.

# References

Abort73.com. "U.S. Abortion Statistics," 2009. http://abort73.com/abortion_facts/us_abortion_statistics/.

Centers for Disease Control and Prevention. "About Teen Pregnancy." https://www.cdc.gov/teenpregnancy/about/index.htm.

Guttmacher Institute "Induced Abortion Worldwide." Fact Sheet, March 2018. https://www.guttmacher.org/fact-sheet/induced-abortion-worldwide.

Office of Adolescent Health. "Trends in Teen Pregnancy and Childbearing." https://www.hhs.gov/ash/oah/adolescent-development/reproductive-health-and-teen-pregnancy/teen-pregnancy-and-childbearing/trends/index.html.

Samuelson, Kate. "Teen Birth Rates in the U.S. Hit a Record Low." *Time*, July 3, 2017. http://time.com/4843652/teen-birth-rates-record-low/.

United Nations Population Fund. "Motherhood in Childhood: Facing the Challenge of Adolescent Pregnancy." New York: United Nations Population Fund, 2013.

World Health Organization. "Adolescent Pregnancy." http://www.who.int/news-room/fact-sheets/detail/adolescent-pregnancy.

# Abortion

*An Ongoing Debate.*

Abortion is the ending of a pregnancy before the fetus is capable of survival outside the uterus. Abortions are performed for numerous reasons, including fetal abnormalities, rape and incest, and as a choice reflective of the life and health of the mother or baby. People with opinions about abortion can be divided into two main camps: those who believe in abortion rights and those who are against abortion. The abortion-rights movement advocates for the legalization and acceptance of abortion, whereas the anti-abortion movement opposes abortion and often, euthanasia. Those who are against abortion oppose not only women who decide to get abortions, but those involved in the procedure, including certified midwives, nurse practitioners, nurses, and physician assistants.

Women seek abortions for reasons such as rape, their inability to support a baby, and health problems. Most women who are unmarried or who are young think abortion is the right answer to their problem. In the United States, the three main reasons woman get an abortion are not being ready for a child, not being able to afford to take care of a child, and being finished with having children. Abortion rates in the United States are decreasing each year. According to Abort73 there were approximately 914,000 abortions in the United States in 2015 and an estimated 926,240 in 2014—down from 1.06 million in 2011, 1.21 million abortions in 2008, 1.2 million in 2005, 1.29 million in 2002, 1.31 million in 2000, and 1.36 million in 1996. Abortions typically take place during the first trimester but can occur until the woman is twenty-eight weeks pregnant. Abortions are legal in the United States, with some restrictions, most of which deal with protecting the woman's health and safety. The United States does not have the highest percentage of reported abortions in the world.

According to Abort73, "In 2014, the highest percentage of pregnancies were aborted in the District of Columbia (38%), New York (33%), and New Jersey (30%). The lowest percentage of pregnancies were aborted in Utah (5%), South Dakota

(4%), and Wyoming (<2%)." Why is there such a range between abortion numbers in different states? According to the article "State Implementation of Supreme Court Decisions: Abortion Rates Since Roe v. Wade" by Susan B. Hansen, this is because the likelihood of obtaining an abortion in practice varies enormously from one state to another. The increasing concentration of abortion services in large metropolitan areas in conjunction with varying state political cultures that fund abortions for poor women and impose restrictions on a woman's abortion decision result in unequal access to abortion and a wide range in abortion rates (Hansen 1980).

Here are more statistics. According to the study by the Guttmacher Institute, Pennsylvania studies show that as of 2014, 60 percent of women having abortions were in their twenties, 59 percent had one or more children, 75 percent were economically disadvantaged, and 62 percent reported a religious affiliation. In most states, only physicians may perform abortions. It seems that what is happening requires further education and attention to why there is such a range of abortion numbers in different states.

## A Short Discussion

Abortion has sparked some lengthy discussions. Some consider abortion wrong and believe that a woman is morally obligated to carry the baby to term. Some even call abortion murder and believe that a fetus has a right to use the woman's body.

Some people say that if a woman doesn't want the baby, why did she become pregnant in the first place? All sorts of birth control methods would have prevented the baby from existing. It was not the baby's choice to be conceived in the first place. It was the mother's choice. So why is the baby punished for that? This of course may not apply to the 1.5 percent of all abortions that are a result of rape.

## References

Guttmacher Institute. "State Facts About Abortion: Pennsylvania." Fact Sheet, 2018. https://www.guttmacher.org/fact-sheet/state-facts-about-abortion-pennsylvania.

Hansen, Susan B. "State Implementation of Supreme Court Decisions: Abortion Rates Since Roe v. Wade." https://www.jstor.org/stable/2130465?seq=1#metadata_info_tab_contents.

"U.S. Abortion Statistics." Abort73.com, 2009. https://abort73.com/abortion_facts/us_abortion_statistics/.

# Poems

*Family: The Best Source of Happiness.*

## Fiftieth Anniversary

I wrote the following poem for the fiftieth wedding anniversary of a relative:

These days staying together fifty years is really rare;
Calling your marriage an exception is certainly fair.

You showed us how to make a long-lasting team;
Rain or shine, you kept the promise and the dream.

After all these years, your feelings shine as gold;
You cherished each other to love and to hold.

Half a century has passed since you began as one.
Did any love get lost along the way? Surely none.

Working together, you made your life happy and fun.
Is there any better partnership than yours? Bar none.

We always looked up to you both since the beginning;
We appreciate the love you have been spreading.

X great children, y lovely grandchildren are fruits of love for sure;
Fifty years, 18,250 days, 438,000 hours, and we wish you many more.

Kids outgrow their toys and material things, rich or poor,
But they always cherish your love and care that is for sure.

## Love of Child and Grandchild

You came to my life one beautiful sunny day;
You changed everything, it's certainly fair to say.

It was a miracle happening to the family, including me,
A dream I witnessed and could clearly see.

Days passed watching you play, grow, change, and learn;
First smile, first tooth, first step, and things that are supposed to be.

Now you are stronger, smarter, kinder, a loving individual who cares;
You are all I wished for and everything else you could possibly be.

That beautiful baby did not die, but changed; that is easy to see.
A mature gentleman with knowledge and a wonderful life history.

What the future holds for us, nobody knows, not even you and me;
Let us be grateful for all the joy experienced, not as you and I, but as we.

Now a grandfather, all is coming back to me, a beautiful feeling; hope you agree.
Smile, cry, wonder, dream, and all beauty of life beyond self, beyond me.

I now see that life is all about family, kindness, and loving; that is the key.
All these joys can be found and experienced only in a family tree.

CPSIA information can be obtained
at www.ICGtesting.com
Printed in the USA
BVHW011154250819
556740BV00009B/485/P

9 781480 880337